Bringing Heaven to Earth Because He Has Returned

Bringing Heaven to Earth Because He Has Returned

Robert A. Jones

Writers Club Press
New York Lincoln Shanghai

Bringing Heaven to Earth Because He Has Returned

All Rights Reserved © 2002 by Robert Alvin Jones

No part of this book may be reproduced or transmitted in any form or by any means, graphic, electronic, or mechanical, including photocopying, recording, taping, or by any information storage retrieval system, without the permission in writing from the publisher.

Writers Club Press
an imprint of iUniverse, Inc.

For information address:
iUniverse
2021 Pine Lake Road, Suite 100
Lincoln, NE 68512
www.iuniverse.com

All Scripture quotations, unless otherwise indicated, are taken from the New King James Version. Copyright © 1982 by Thomas Nelson, Inc. Used by permission. All rights reserved.

Special thanks to my friends, Christina Matijasic for the cover design, and Eric Wintersteller who prepared the graphics for printing.

ISBN: 0-595-24829-2

Printed in the United States of America

Dedicated to my dear wife, Pat
A faithful partner in the kingdom journey

Contents

List of Illustrations ix

List of Tables xi

Introduction 1

CHAPTER 1   RETHINKING THE TIME OF THE
            SECOND COMING 11

CHAPTER 2   SEVEN SURE SIGNS THAT JESUS HAS
            RETURNED 23

CHAPTER 3   TRACKING PAUL'S MINISTRY AND
            GOD'S PLAN 35

CHAPTER 4   TRACKING PAUL'S THOUGHTS ON
            THE SECOND COMING 45

CHAPTER 5   PERFECTING IN THE NEW
            TESTAMENT 55

CHAPTER 6   THE REAL ENEMY 75

CHAPTER 7   THE CHRONOLOGY OF DANIEL'S
            SEVENTIETH WEEK 87

CHAPTER 8   THE PERIOD OF THE SEVEN
            TRUMPETS 101

CHAPTER 9   FOUR SIGNIFICANT DAYS OF
            ATONEMENT 107

CHAPTER 10 DANIEL'S SEVENTIETH WEEK AS IT
            HAPPENED 127

CHAPTER 11	GOD HAS AN EXCITING MYSTERY TO REVEAL	163
CHAPTER 12	DISCOVERING GOD'S ETERNAL JUBILEE	173
CHAPTER 13	FROM BETROTHAL TO MARRIAGE	183
CHAPTER 14	BUILDING THE NEW TEMPLE	195
CHAPTER 15	GRACE AND ACCOUNTABILITY	205
CHAPTER 16	OVERCOMING THROUGH THE MIGHTY WARRIOR	215
CHAPTER 17	THE LAST FRONTIER	225
CHAPTER 18	THE VIEW FROM THE MOUNTAIN	237
APPENDIX	FIGURING JULIAN DATES FROM JEWISH LUNAR CALENDAR	253
Notes		257
Bibliography		263
About the Author		265

List of Illustrations

Figure 1 Time Interval between Seventh Trumpet and Parousia 53

Figure 2 First Beast of Revelation Thirteen 80

Figure 3 Relation between the Two Beasts of Revelation Thirteen 82

Figure 4 Period of Authority of Beast plus Seventy-Five Days 92

Figure 5 Daniel's Seventieth Week 94

Figure 6 Historical Events Related to Last Three Trumpets 103

Figure 7 Hypothesis for Time Framework of the Seven Trumpets 104

Figure 8 The Years of Four Significant Days of Atonement 114

Figure 9 Time Interval between Seventh Trumpet and Parousia 169

List of Tables

Table 1 Three Annual Jewish Festivals *109*
Table 2 Relating Jewish Dates to Julian Equivalents *256*

Introduction

The writing of this book goes back to the time when I began the authentic disciple walk during a fifty-day period beginning early in December 1964 and ending the latter part of January 1965. The assassination of John F. Kennedy in November 1963 stirred me deeply to want to invest my life for the cause of good in the face of such evil that I thought could never happen in our country. I was already serving as a young pastor but was convicted I was spiritually lacking to be able to lead my people aright. Our denomination, then the Evangelical United Brethren Church before the merger with the Methodist Church, challenged its people beginning in 1964 with a quadrennial emphasis: "Jesus Christ Renews His Church." That timely emphasis following right after Kennedy's assassination challenged me to earnestly seek the Lord, turning from whatever sin He revealed.

This time of spiritual renewal climaxed in 1964-65 during this fifty-day period. The Lord cleansed me afresh from sin and released His Holy Spirit in my heart. The Bible came alive at this time. I can still remember reading John 1:1 when this happened. This text refers to Jesus as the Word, as God, and as the One through whom all things were created. Intellectually, I believed Christian teaching about the Trinity affirming that Jesus was part of the Godhead. It was as if my spiritual eyes were now opened to see Jesus in a new light. I saw that this One, born miraculously as that baby at Bethlehem when the Word became flesh, was also back there at the beginning when all things were created. In fact, it was all created through Him. That blew my mind, and I can still remember sitting there in a kind of stunned silence. From that moment on, I was drawn to look to Jesus for the truth since He was God living on earth, and to the Bible as the book where I could learn about what this unique God-man did and taught. During my days in seminary, I was mainly interested in the intellectual journey and spent more time reading books about the Bible than the Bible itself. That changed after this encounter with Christ. From that moment on, the desire to follow Jesus drew me to the Bible convinced I would discover there the light I needed to guide myself and those I served along the New Testament journey and thereby do my part for God's kingdom in this world.

I began at that time to read the New Testament from the beginning, drinking in the words as if reading them for the first time. I read the Bible through as a boy, and studied it in the intervening years. Something was different now. It was as if I saw myself sitting at the feet of Jesus taking in His every word. I soon came upon Matthew 16:28 where Jesus tells His hearers that He would return during their lifetime. Those words captured my attention. Seeing myself back there with those first disciples, it was clear to me that Jesus was saying that He would return during their lifetime. I had been taught that the first followers of Jesus believed the Second Coming would happen during their lifetime, but were mistaken. This explanation now faded in light of my new understanding about Jesus. He was truth and witnessed to the truth and would not have misled His disciples or anybody else. He was clearly telling them that some of them would be alive at the time of His Second Coming.

I did not know how to deal with this new thought. This was certainly not the world I expected after the Second Coming. I had some vague idea that Jesus would make everything right at His Return and there would finally be peace. This new word from Scripture was diametrically opposed to all my thoughts in this regard and threatened an entire area of thinking shaped over the years by church tradition. Not knowing what to do with this new light, I put it on the "backburner" of my mind. As I continued through the New Testament, I kept coming upon other verses witnessing to the same expectation that the Second Coming would occur during their lifetime. In fact, all the writers shared this conviction and they reported Jesus Himself as teaching it.

Sometime back in 1965, I made the decision that I would believe the New Testament witness over against the tradition of the church that had conditioned my thinking. I did not understand how this could be the world in which the Second Coming occurred, but I accepted it because God's word was clear to me at this point. At the time, I knew of nobody else who believed this and would discover how strongly some Christians can react upon learning what I believed the Scripture taught. Nevertheless, convinced that this was the clear witness of God's word, I began the process to reshape my thinking about the Second Coming believing that it occurred at the conclusion of the apostolic generation. I did not know where this would lead me. I remember the Holy Spirit witnessing that what I was going through was something like what Abraham went through when God called him to go into a far country, not knowing where he went.

This book did not come about by reading scholars who were still looking for the Second Coming to happen. I now looked for the fulfillment of the prophecies during the first century. It was an exciting study to read those historical records and discover how the prophecies were fulfilled back then. As I patiently waited rather than force conclusions, the pieces have come together over the years to form the prophetic picture of the Return of Jesus as He was glorified in His people and rendered judgment upon the powers of darkness.

As I kept going to the New Testament to understand how the prophecies were fulfilled, I discovered that the apostles talked with their people very little about trying to understand the fulfillment of the prophecies in historical events. They focused on helping the people grow to spiritual maturity so they would be ready to be united with Jesus when He returned. Paul taught his people that they were betrothed to Christ when they repented and believed in Jesus. He would return later when He would reveal Himself as their Bridegroom. The apostles prepared their people spiritually by teaching and helping them to apply God's word in cooperation with the sanctifying work of the Holy Spirit. This growing and maturing in the faithful prepared those betrothed to Christ for the revelation of their Lord as the Divine Bridegroom and knowing Him in the most intimate of relationships possible on this earth.

I thus found myself being led upon two journeys inseparably bound to one another. On the one hand, I continued to look back into the historical records of that day in order to understand how the prophecies were fulfilled. On the other hand, I began to search the New Testament to discover how the apostles prepared their generation for the Return of Christ. This led me to make careful word studies in the Greek regarding key words associated with the experiential dimension of the Second Coming. This helped me to understand the spiritual journey and its climax into which the apostles guided those first Christians. This research came to show Paul's second-coming expectations in his earlier epistles such as 1 and 2 Thessalonians, 1 and 2 Corinthians, and Romans were actually being realized in the Body of Christ as reflected in Paul's later letters. I am thinking especially of Ephesians and Colossians where he talks about how God has revealed a mystery to the apostles concealed from all previous generations. This book will examine this mystery that occurred at the seventh trumpet.

I also found that beyond the Bible, the devotional classics were of great value. *Abide in Christ* by Andrew Murray impacted me the most, but the Lord also led me to other classics such as *The Practice of the Presence of God* by Brother Lawrence; *The Imitation of Christ* by Thomas a Kempis; *Testament of Devotion* by Thomas Kelley; and *Game with Minutes* by Frank Laubach. These writers all witnessed to this personal walk with Jesus and helped me to understand more about the intimacy that Jesus wants with His betrothed. I also began to keep a journal in those early years to help me retain what God was teaching me in my spiritual journey. I found that I was like Israel of old, prone to readily forget the lessons God was teaching me as I lived my days in this world so filled with distractions and temptations.

Jesus and the apostles are gone leaving their testimony in the New Testament. God has preserved this witness as our basic text, and given the Holy Spirit to be the Counselor instructing us in such matters. The only way to cut through all the confusion about this hidden topic is to focus on God's word in the New Testament and to ask the Holy Spirit to give us understanding. The mystery unveiled during the days of the Second Coming can only be brought to light in this way. We must learn and believe God's promises and let His word shape our lives. I believe God is working once again to unveil this mystery to the Body of Christ in this generation.

The distinction will be made in this book between the cosmic and the experiential dimensions of the Second Coming. The former consists of those one-time events, such as God taking His power and beginning to reign (Rev. 11:15-17), rewarding His people and punishing the powers of evil (Rev. 11:18), and terminating the Old Covenant (Heb. 8:13). These one-time events resulted in restructuring the spiritual universe in which we now live and establishing the New Covenant as the sole God-initiated agreement for any person to relate to God. In addition to this cosmic dimension, the first Christians made exciting discoveries in their faith and experience through the revelation of Jesus Christ. This experiential aspect of the Second Coming is of an ongoing nature and open to us today.

In 1995, I published the first book *He Has Returned*. This book dealt primarily with the cosmic dimension presenting the scriptural and historical evidence that provides the basis for venturing into this new approach to the Second Coming. Both Scripture and history support the conviction that Jesus returned during the lifetime of the apostles. I was asked to share this with a group of ministers shortly after the book came out, and afterwards, a friend asked me the following question. "Bob, what you are trying to elicit from us is the intellectual decision that the Second Coming occurred during the first century?" It dawned on me that this was correct. I deliberately avoided in that first book discussing the experiential dimension because I was not ready to write about it. I had not dealt with what this practically means in the life of each Christian and the Body of Christ. It struck me that I was not ready to pursue this ministry. Pastors are not going to "rock the boat" with a new idea, especially one about which many people have such strong convictions, unless they see the implications of what this means for today.

It became clear that a new book was needed dealing with the experiential dimension of the Second Coming as well as the cosmic dimension. It was important to clarify what it means to live in a world where Jesus has returned. More time would be needed for such a book. God had more work to do within me. He also needed to give more light. This second book would have to make clear what those first Christians experienced when Jesus returned as well as the pathway leading to this climax. This would inspire the necessary faith to enable one to get out of the boat of tradition when once rocked and believe the Second Coming happened during the first century as Scripture teaches. *Bringing Heaven to Earth because He Has Returned* seeks to clarify the discoveries made by the apostolic generation and present the historical evidence to show the second-coming prophecies were fulfilled in the historical events of that day.

The creation of this book has been basically sandwiched between two national tragedies in our country. It began sometime after Kennedy's assassination in 1963 and was nearing completion when terrorists shocked our country by venting their hatred in cowardly acts killing many innocent people in 2001. Some Christians see this as proof positive that the terrible days of the Second Coming are upon us. Those who know the Bible are aware how terrible those days were forecasted to be. Evil powers portrayed by a beast are given authority "to make war with the saints and to overcome them" (Rev. 13:7). That in fact happened at the conclusion of the apostolic generation as many first-century Christians suffered martyrdom.

This book lifts up a note of hope, victory, and the necessary cooperation spelled out in the New Testament, but so often ignored by Christians. When you accept the New Testament witness that Jesus returned at the conclusion of the apostolic generation, you look at the present moment in a different light. You do not see each crisis as a sign that the last days are here, but continual wake-up calls to go to the Scripture and finally get it straight regarding the cooperation God requires and the authority He has given to us to exercise. Under the terms of the New Covenant whereby we are not only forgiven but receive the Holy Spirit and spiritual gifts, God has provided everything we need to overcome sin, death, and the powers of darkness because we live in a world where Jesus has returned. He will not put this world together without our cooperation. He stands ready to supply all we need *when we are ready to fully cooperate by following through with our repentance and by doing God's will with all our hearts as He has clarified in Scripture.*

While I do not believe that there is any 1,260-day period ahead when powers of evil will be given authority over the peoples of this earth to wreak havoc in this world, I do believe there are days of suffering and stress ahead. It seems to take such things to wake us up. I do believe Jesus reigns right now, and everything is in place to put our lives and this world together. It requires faithful disciples who are learning the commands of Jesus that determine what they believe and how they live. "If anyone desires to come after Me, let him deny himself, and take up his cross, and follow Me" (Matt. 16:24). This gives us a clue regarding the all out commitment Jesus expected from His followers. I believe exciting days lie ahead in the midst of whatever suffering through which we must pass. Victory will emerge for those who walk as faithful disciples with Jesus our Risen and Reigning Lord. May His Name be praised forever!

When I finished *He Has Returned* in 1995, I thought I was alone in this approach to the Second Coming. Sometime after that, I discovered on the Internet that there were others who believed that the Second Coming happened at the conclusion of the apostolic generation. This viewpoint has come to be called the "preterist" position that means "fulfilled" in regard to the second-coming prophecies. It was good to learn that I was not alone. The development of this book, however, took a different line. Pastoral concerns from the very first led me to look not only to the biblical and historical evidence that Jesus returned but also beyond this to the spiritual journey and its climax reflected in the later writings of the New Testament.

As mentioned before, I found that as Paul prepared the first Christians for the Second Coming, he said very little about how prophecy was being fulfilled in the historical events of their day. He was concerned about how to prepare the faithful so they were spiritually ready to receive the revelation of Jesus Christ when He returned. It is through the ministry of Paul as we trace the development in his thought through his writings that we understand the way to maturity and the climax experienced by those first Christians. Pursuing this experiential dimension of the Second Coming definitely influenced my understanding about how the prophecies were fulfilled during the events of that day. While Paul helps us understand what those first Christians experienced during Jesus' Return, it is primarily through the revelation given to John and Daniel that we understand the fulfillment of second-coming prophecies in the historical events of the first century. This book is the result of this twofold journey looking into these two intertwined aspects of the Second Coming that began for me in 1965.

I am more convinced than ever that "the ball is in our ball park." We err in waiting for events that will never happen because they already occurred. We need to awaken to all that God has already accomplished through the Incarnation and Return of Jesus Christ. Here we shall discover all we need to conquer sin, death, and the powers of darkness as we cooperate with the One who right now reigns over all things and works to "make all things new." What an exciting vision the New Testament holds before all who belong to Jesus. If terrorists can be motivated to invest their lives for destruction through hatred and killing of innocent people, how much more ought Christians to be deeply motivated to invest their all in the cause of the kingdom of God as revealed through Jesus. He brought love, healing, and reconciliation to a world of hurting lives and broken relationships. He reigns right now and has a part of the action for each of His followers who are willing to be His hands, feet, and lips as He works to accomplish the biblical vision of peace upon our earth. This climax will occur in the future as we learn to submit to the authority of the reigning King who right now is orchestrating His plan to bring heaven to this earth.

1

RETHINKING THE TIME OF THE SECOND COMING

Where do you begin when dealing with a topic that runs counter to tradition passed down through the centuries in the church? I was led to begin where it all began for me, in the pages of the New Testament. The newly released Holy Spirit created in me years ago a hunger to learn about God's word from the writers of the New Testament, and especially from the lips of Jesus. I would soon be forced to face some verses I had basically ignored because I accepted theories explaining away the obvious meaning. With my renewed desire to learn what Christ taught, I was soon confronted with Jesus telling His followers that He would return for them. I could no longer simply dismiss the words. I would eventually find that all the New Testament writers believed that the Second Coming would occur during their generation.

Paul wrote to the Corinthians. "Behold, I tell you a mystery; we shall not all sleep, but we shall all be changed…at the last trumpet" (1 Cor.15:51-52). "We shall not all sleep" means that some in Paul's generation would still be alive on earth "at the last trumpet" when Jesus returned. James wrote: "Establish your hearts, for the coming of the Lord is at hand" (James 5:8). Peter wrote: "But the end of all things is at hand" (1 Pet. 4:7). John wrote: "Little children, it is the last hour; and as you have heard that the Antichrist is coming, even now many antichrists have come, by which we know that it is the last hour" (1 John 2:18). After noting the behavior of people walking according to ungodly lusts, Jude writes how the apostles warned about such people "in the last time" (Jude 18). Jude believed the presence of these people showed they were in the last days. The writer of Hebrews joins the chorus. "For yet a little while, and He who is coming will come and will not tarry" (Heb. 10:37).

The writers of the Gospels share this conviction as we shall see in this book, and witness that it originated with Jesus. His followers did not report something different from what their Lord taught. Jesus Himself said He would return during the lifetime of His first followers. "Assuredly, I say to you, there are some standing here who shall not taste death till they see the Son of Man coming in His kingdom" (Matt. 16:28). "Some standing here who shall not taste death" means they will still be alive when the "Son of Man" comes "in His kingdom" which was part of the Second Coming. Paul similarly reported, "We shall not all sleep" when the trumpet will sound. Some will still be alive. The witness of the New Testament writers and of Jesus Himself is unanimous: He would return for His first followers during their lifetime.

Because we have approached such texts with the presupposition that Jesus has not returned, interpreters have tried to find some meaning other than the obvious, often requiring considerable mental gymnastics. Let us use Matthew 16:28 as an example and first look at the context of this saying. The disciples have finally come to recognize that Jesus is the Messiah through Peter's confession at Caesarea Philippi (Matt. 16:13-20). From that moment on, Jesus begins to tell His disciples that He would have to suffer and die at Jerusalem and then be raised on the third day (Matt. 16:21-23). Peter objected to Jesus' gloomy prediction, and Jesus laid it on the line to His first followers.

> Then Jesus said to his disciples, "If anyone desires to come after Me, let him deny himself, and take up his cross, and follow me. For whoever desires to save his life will lose it, and whoever loses his life for My sake will find it. For what is a man profited if he gains the whole world, and loses his own soul? Or what will a man give in exchange for his soul? For the Son of Man will come in the glory of His Father with His angels, and then He will reward each

according to his works. Assuredly I say to you, there are some standing here who shall not taste death till they see the Son of Man coming in His kingdom." (Matt. 16:24-28)

Jesus tells them plainly what it will cost them to follow Him through to the end. They will have to lose their lives through the denial of self and the bearing of a cross. He lets them know that the sacrifice will be worth it. They will be rewarded when He returns "in the glory of His Father" and "in His kingdom." Jesus goes further. Some of them will still be alive when that takes place. "Assuredly I say to you, there are some standing here who shall not taste death till they see the Son of Man coming in His kingdom." Jesus is clearly speaking about the Second Coming when His followers will be rewarded for their faithfulness in the midst of the suffering and persecution that lies before them.

Laboring under this presupposition that Jesus has not returned, persons have sought other explanations than the obvious. If one approaches this text from the perspective that the Second Coming did not happen, then "the Son of Man coming in His kingdom" must refer to some other event during the lifetime of Jesus' hearers. Some of these "forced" interpretations regarding when the Son of Man would come in His kingdom have included the Mount of Transfiguration, the Resurrection, and Pentecost.[1] None of these events that occurred during the lifetime of Jesus' hearers could possibly be correct. Jesus did not come in His kingdom nor reward the faithful on the Mount of Transfiguration, at Easter, or at Pentecost.

Let us look at each of these suggestions. The Mount of Transfiguration could not be the time when the kingdom of God would come. Jesus was transfigured according to Matthew 17:1 six days after Matthew 16:24-28. Jesus says that only "some" will still be alive when the Son of Man comes in His kingdom. If He were thinking of an event that would occur a week later, He would not have said that "some" would still be alive when most likely "all" of them would still be alive. As we shall soon see, the kingdom still had not come at Easter or Pentecost, hence it could not have occurred at the earlier time of the Mount of Transfiguration.

Before looking at the suggestions regarding the Resurrection or Pentecost as the time Jesus came in His kingdom, let us refresh our memory as to why the expectations for the coming of the kingdom or its restoration to Israel were running especially high at this time around Holy Week. The disciples now knew that Jesus was the long-awaited Messiah, though confused as to why He must die. Word spread quickly about the amazing miracle of raising Lazarus from the dead, and John tells us this was a major factor why the large crowd came out on Palm Sunday to greet Jesus (John12:17-18). This response among the populace was of sufficient magnitude to cause the Jewish leaders to say that the whole world was going after Him (John 12:19). The people were looking for the Messiah who would restore the kingdom to His chosen people. Many undoubtedly wondered whether this miracle-worker could be that person.

Because of this, Jesus told a parable in Luke 19:11-27 just before entering Jerusalem on Palm Sunday because "they thought the kingdom of God would appear immediately" (Luke 19:11). Jesus corrects this mistaken opinion and prepares them for His imminent death by telling them a story about a nobleman who goes to a far country to be appointed king or receive a kingdom. After being endowed with such authority, he returns to see how his servants did with what he invested in them so he may reward the faithful. Jesus speaks about His imminent Crucifixion, Resurrection, and Ascension when He would leave this earth and go to the far country of heaven. He would invest in His followers by giving them the Holy Spirit and spiritual gifts with which to serve. He would then return at a later time to reward the faithful. This would begin at the seventh trumpet according to Revelation 11:15 at which time Jesus receives the kingdom. Some of His hearers would still be alive for that climactic event that would take place in a little over thirty years. Jesus thus corrects the mistaken opinion that the kingdom was about to come during Holy Week. His parable indicates that this will occur at the Second Coming.

Easter is further eliminated as the disciples ask Jesus after Easter and about ten days before Pentecost the following question. "Lord, will You at this time restore the kingdom to Israel?" (Acts 1:6). Jesus' response shows that it had not yet come at Easter nor was it to come at Pentecost. If the kingdom were about to come at Pentecost and be restored to the people, Jesus would have responded to their query something to the effect. "O yes, the long-awaited day is almost here, and in just a few days after I return to heaven, I will pour out the Holy Spirit and the kingdom will come." Note Jesus' response. "It is not for you to know the times or seasons which the Father has put in His own authority" (Acts 1:7). He proceeds to tell them that they will shortly receive the Holy Spirit. After Jesus ascends to heaven, angels tell the disciples that they will see Jesus return as they have just seen Him taken up from them. That date, known only by the Father, will be the time when Jesus will return with the kingdom and restore it to His people.

The people did not understand the nature in which His kingdom would come. It would not be tied to a particular nation on this earth as it had to Israel during the days of the Old Covenant. This kingdom would come to the faithful among the people from any nation, Jew or Gentile, who responded to the New Covenant. Repentance from sin and turning to obey God opened the way to enter into this New Covenant. Such are the kind of people God has looked for from the very first. He would give His Holy Spirit to them and the faithful who continued the walk would appropriate the sanctifying work of the Spirit to form the Christlike nature within. Such would receive the kingdom when Jesus returned. We shall see that the later epistles in fact witness to this happening in the lives of the faithful on this earth from among the nations.

The destruction of Jerusalem has been another suggestion regarding what Jesus meant by the Son of Man coming in His kingdom. Jerusalem was destroyed in A.D. 70 during the lifetime of some of Jesus' hearers. The context of Matthew 16:28 shows Jesus is not talking about such judgment that was part of the second-coming events and came upon the Jewish people during those last days for rejecting the Messiah and the New Covenant. Jesus speaks about the rewards and the kingdom that will come at His Return to His faithful followers who have denied themselves, taken up their crosses, and followed their Lord faithfully to the end. This interpretation would have us believe that Jesus promised those first Jewish followers that if they remained faithful, they would be rewarded by the destruction of their beloved city. I don't think so. Jerusalem would indeed be destroyed during the Second Coming as part of God's judgment during those last days. Jesus in Matthew 16:28 speaks about the reward that will come to the faithful remnant when the Son of Man comes in His kingdom, and some of Jesus' hearers would still be alive.

Interpreters are forced into such explanations when they begin with the premise that it cannot possibly mean what it says. I ask, "Why not?" Why can't we take Jesus at His word? Why can't Jesus simply mean that some of the people hearing Him speak just prior to the Mount of Transfiguration would still be alive when He, the Son of Man, would return in His kingdom and His Father's glory with the angels? At least, this is what He says, and I think it is time for us to examine anew all those verses that said Jesus would return for His first followers. It is time to believe Jesus and the witness of the apostles over centuries of post-apostolic tradition passed down through the church.

Montanus in the late second century A.D. believed Jesus would return during his lifetime. Such unrealized expectations have continued through the centuries. I remember sitting in my grade school classroom watching the clock approach the predicted end of the world. Some persons in a nearby state sold their belongings and went to a hill expecting to meet their returning Lord. Persons since then are for the most part wiser and refuse to set a date, but continue to say that His coming is very soon because of all the signs pointing to this. The apostles also believed the signs pointed to His Return for their generation, and their writings became Scripture.

As stated in the Introduction, I thought I was alone in this understanding when I first came to believe Jesus returned for His first followers. Since 1995, I have discovered others who believe the Second Coming happened during the apostolic generation, though differing in understanding about how the prophecies were fulfilled. It has been encouraging to see how the numbers are growing. One study Bible recently included the preterist view when listing the different approaches to understanding the Second Coming. I believe the numbers will multiply in the future as second-coming expectations continue to go unfulfilled. I believe more and more Christians will go back to the New Testament and examine more carefully what it has said all along about the time of the Second Coming.

It is important to distinguish between the cosmic and the experiential dimension of the Second Coming. The former consists of those one-time events, such as God taking His power and beginning to reign (Rev. 11:15-17), rewarding His people and punishing the powers of evil (Rev. 11:18), and terminating the Old Covenant (Heb. 8:13). These one-time events resulted in restructuring the spiritual universe in which we live. In addition to this cosmic dimension, the first Christians made exciting discoveries in their faith and experience through the revelation of Jesus Christ. This experiential aspect of the Second Coming is ongoing in nature and open to all followers of Christ since His Second Coming.

The latter or experiential dimension began after the seventh trumpet and was appropriated among the faithful in the days following before Jesus removed them from the earth. This is when He revealed Himself, His kingdom, and manifested His glory in them fulfilling what the New Testament calls a mystery. Revelation 10:7 reports: "But in the days of the sounding of the seventh angel, when he is about to sound, the mystery of God would be finished, as He declared to His servants the prophets." Paul first witnesses to this future mystery associated with the Second Coming in 1 Corinthians 15:51-52. "Behold, I tell you a mystery: We shall not all sleep, but we shall all be changed—in a moment, in the twinkling of an eye, at the last trumpet." Paul proceeds to tell us in the next sentence that when the trumpet sounds, "The dead will be raised incorruptible, and we shall be changed." Paul first witnesses to the reality of this in Ephesians and Colossians as he tells how "the mystery of Christ," hidden from all previous generations, has been revealed to the apostles (Eph. 3:4-6). As we shall see in chapter 4, "Tracking Paul's Thoughts on the Second Coming," Ephesians and Colossians fulfill Paul's earlier second-coming expectations. They are being realized as part of a mystery, and Paul is seeking to help the faithful appropriate this light. We shall examine this "mystery" related to the experiential dimension of the Second Coming in this book.

I have heard it said by people when they first hear of this approach to the Second Coming, "What is there to look forward to if He has already returned?" There is indeed much to look forward to in a world where Jesus has already returned. The challenge before us is to appropriate the same discoveries the apostolic generation made related to the mystery of Christ, as well as work with the reigning King to accomplish His great plan to bring heaven to this earth. While there will be great spiritual warfare in which we must overcome to claim the victory, it will be nothing like what those first Christians had to go through when the powers of darkness were delegated authority for 1,260 days even to kill the saints. So terrible were those days that God shortened them for the sake of the elect, as we shall see in this book.

The Bible tells us about two kinds of life present on earth. There is human life passed on from Adam to all human beings. This life corrupted by sin has left a trail of hatred, broken relationships, violence, murder, fornication, adultery, greed, theft, etc. Jesus introduced a second kind of life to this earth consisting of holy character expressing itself in righteous acts and loving deeds. "The first man was of the earth, made of dust; the second Man is the Lord from heaven" (1 Cor. 15:47). "And as we have borne the image of the man of dust, so shall we bear the image of the heavenly Man" (1 Cor. 15:49). Every believer is "predestined to be conformed to the image of His Son" (Rom. 8:29).

Jesus was this "heavenly Man." When would they bear that Christlike nature or the "image of the heavenly Man?" It would happen at the last trumpet during the Second Coming. The sanctifying work of the indwelling Holy Spirit would climax with the formation of the Christlike or Divine nature within the faithful. When one believes the witness of the New Testament that Jesus has returned, one implication is that we also may be completed in this life. It happened during the apostolic generation.

The world desperately needs such persons who are pressing on to this goal as they work in concert with the indwelling Holy Spirit. We have become a global community requiring that we learn to live together in peace. Scientific advances are bringing within human grasp the power to do things with enormous consequences. We need persons progressing through the sanctification process whereby the Holy Spirit transforms us from within into the likeness of Christ that we may bear the likeness of the man from heaven while still on earth. Such persons can be entrusted with the important decisions that will be needed in the future in all fields of endeavor. They will not be motivated by personal gain but to honor and glorify the living God. Only the Body of Christ can lead the way in this marvelous revolution. God never planned for peace to come at once upon the earth. Peace can only come after Jesus begins to reign and when we have Christlike people emerging on this earth. The New Testament reveals that this way is "straight and narrow" and those who walk it die out to sin enabling the Holy Spirit to complete His sanctifying work. There is no lack in God's resources to pull it off. It is also possible when you live in a world where He has returned.

I believe the time is right. There are now more persons than at any time since the apostolic generation making the disciple journey as spelled out in the apostolic witness in the New Testament. It is spreading around the world as pastors and people are going back to the Scripture. Just as the invention of the printing press aided the Reformation in making the Bible accessible to Christ's followers, so now the Internet, books, and videos have made it possible to communicate the Christian faith much more rapidly throughout this earth. The numbers of disciples will continue to grow with all the means of communication at hand enabling God to more readily communicate His word. Where does this disciple journey end? Is there a climax on earth before leaving the body at death to go to heaven? With more people, lay and clergy, searching, studying, and living by the Bible, it is already beginning to emerge that the apostles discovered some amazing things during those days of Jesus' Return as He manifested His glory in His faithful prior to taking them off the earth. They tell us about this in their latter writings.

In summary, this book discusses two matters practically ignored by the church since the apostolic generation when the faithful were removed. It will challenge each reader to rethink his or her position regarding the time of the Second Coming. It will also place before the reader the challenge that God not only intends to change you into the likeness of Christ, but also is able to do it while you still live on earth. We shall investigate the New Testament writings to seek to clarify the discoveries made by the apostolic generation during those last days in such chapters as "Perfecting in the New Testament," "God Has an Exciting Mystery to Reveal," "Discovering God's Eternal Jubilee," "From Betrothal to Marriage." I believe God wants to move His people beyond all the speculation about the cosmic dimension of the Second Coming that has already happened to discover the ongoing experiential dimension waiting to be appropriated by all who go on to maturity in Christ. The same discoveries await us today and the emergence of such Christlike persons constitute the building blocks for peace upon the earth and bringing heaven to our planet. All of this is true when one accepts the New Testament witness that Jesus returned for His first followers as He taught and they believed.

Let me ask you a question? Why would God have provided for the New Covenant, the forgiveness of sin, the gift of the Holy Spirit, the imparting of spiritual gifts to build up the Body of Christ, and not finish the job? It is down here on earth that He needs Christlike people. The New Testament witnesses that God did finish the job fulfilling the promises made to the Jewish people, and opening the doors to share this great salvation with the Gentiles. He did this during the days when Jesus returned as He said He would, and to which His first followers bear witness.

Let me ask the reader another question. Do you believe that those who have died in the faith have been raised from the dead and gone to be with the Lord? That is not the case if Jesus has not returned. Those who have died in the faith join a large throng of disembodied spirits who still wait for the trumpet. Not until then are the dead raised. So some of you may actually already embrace beliefs that are only true if the Second Coming has occurred.

I realize what a quantum leap in Christian thinking this represents. Do not make it until you are convinced that the Bible clearly teaches this. Only then will you be able to confidently disentangle yourself from the traditional view and stand against the spiritual attacks of the powers of darkness. However, I believe you will see in the Scripture that every New Testament writer comes from the perspective that Jesus will return during the apostolic generation. We shall look in the next chapter at seven signs pointing to the Return of Jesus for the apostles and the first Christians. No other generation could ever see the fulfillment of these biblical signs pointing to the Lord's Return. We shall also see how Paul's later writings fulfill earlier second-coming expectations. Such data is the basis for believing Jesus returned back then.

It is time to let the Bible say what it says about the time of the Second Coming, no longer dismissing those verses as mistaken perceptions or making the words mean something other than they obviously say. Isaiah 55:9 probably applies to the Second Coming as much as any other area of theological thinking. "For as the heavens are higher than the earth, so are My ways higher than your ways, and My thoughts than your thoughts." I realize how mind-boggling it seems at first when accepting the biblical witness in this regard, because this is certainly not the world I envisioned after the triumphant Return of Jesus Christ. *My venture shared in this book began when I let the witness of the word determine my thinking, rather than my thinking determine the witness of the word.*

2

SEVEN SURE SIGNS THAT JESUS HAS RETURNED

People point to current events as signs indicating Jesus is about to return during their day. When the European Common Market reached ten nations some years ago, there were persons who interpreted this as a sign pointing to the fulfillment of the ten horns on the beast in Revelation 13, hence the approach of the last days. Some make similar claims by tracking current developments in Israel or targeting different persons as the antichrist. I want to draw your attention to seven major signs that were indicators of the last days according to the Bible. God alerted His people through the wisdom given to the prophets. He wanted them to know when those climactic days would be upon them. As we shall see, some of these signs included the coming of "Elijah the prophet" as the forerunner to the Messiah, the coming of the Messiah Himself, along with the pouring out of the Holy Spirit. The continual burnt offering at the temple in Jerusalem would end and the temple and city would be destroyed during the last days. All these signs happened during the apostolic generation marking them as the generation when Jesus would return.

ELIJAH THE PROPHET

The last book of the Old Testament points to one of the signs showing when the generation to experience the last things had arrived. "Behold, I will send you Elijah the prophet before the coming of the great and dreadful day of the Lord" (Mal. 4:5). Whenever this person, "Elijah the prophet," emerged on the stage of history, his presence and ministry would point to the approaching climactic events associated with the Day of the Lord and the Second Coming. This sign went undetected by everyone except for Jesus Christ. John the Baptist was this "Elijah the prophet." On one occasion, Jesus told His hearers about the new day dawning with the ministry of John the Baptist. "For all the prophets and the law prophesied until John" (Matt. 11:13). Jesus continued in the next verse: "And if you are willing to receive it, he is Elijah who is to come" (Matt. 11:14). Jesus clearly identified John the Baptist as the Elijah foretold for the last days.

Even John the Baptist did not know that he was this key figure in biblical prophecy. When priests and levites came from Jerusalem at the beginning of his ministry to question John about himself, they asked, "Are you Elijah?" (John 1:21). They knew the prophecy. They wanted to know if John the Baptist was this long-awaited person associated with the coming of the Messiah and the Day of the Lord. John answered them by saying that he was not this person indicating even he did not understand the full significance of his ministry in the providence of God. John told his questioners that he understood his ministry in terms of Isaiah 40:1-3 as the voice crying in the wilderness to prepare the way of the Lord. Jesus did understand the fuller significance of John's ministry in biblical prophecy. The law and the prophets had already given way to the ministry of Elijah the prophet who would be followed by the ministry of the Messiah and the making of the New Covenant. The emergence of Elijah in the ministry of John the Baptist indicated according to Scripture that the "great and dreadful day of the Lord" was drawing near that would bring reward and punishment. That day was part of the Second Coming and came upon the Jewish people during the decade of the sixties with the three-and-one-half-year siege of their land by the Roman armies. This ended with the destruction of Jerusalem and the temple in A.D. 70. The ministry of John the Baptist pointed to the approaching "great and dreadful day of the Lord."

POURING OUT THE HOLY SPIRIT

The prophet Joel spoke about another sign foretelling the approach of the last days. Let us look at these words as Peter quotes the prophecy.

> And it shall come to pass in the last days, says God, that I will pour out My Spirit on all flesh; your sons and your daughters shall prophesy, your young men shall see visions, your old men shall dream dreams. And on My menservants and on My maidservants I will pour out My Spirit in those days; and they shall prophesy. I will show wonders in heaven above and signs in the earth beneath: blood and fire and vapor of smoke. The sun shall be turned into darkness, and the moon into blood, before the coming of the great and notable day of the Lord. And it shall come to pass that whoever calls on the name of the Lord shall be saved. (Acts 2:17-21)

Centuries before Christ, the prophet Joel spoke about things that would happen prior to the Day of the Lord. Persons sometimes quote these words and apply it to their generation inferring that the Second Coming is drawing near. They overlook Peter's use of this passage. He says Pentecost fulfilled Joel's prophecy back then and thereby indicated that the last days were drawing near for their generation.

Acts 2:1-12 tells us about Pentecost. In the previous chapter, Jesus instructed His disciples to remain at Jerusalem until He ascended to heaven and poured out the Holy Spirit. "But you shall receive power when the Holy Spirit has come upon you; and you shall be witnesses to Me in Jerusalem, and in all Judea and Samaria, and to the end of the earth" (Acts 1:8). Jesus returned to the Father and poured out the Holy Spirit as He promised. Accompanied with speaking in tongues, some Jews jumped to the conclusion that the followers of Jesus were drunk. Then Peter stood up with the Eleven and addressed the crowd.

> "Men of Judea and all who dwell in Jerusalem, let this be known to you, and heed my words. For these are not drunk, as you suppose, since it is only the third hour of the day. But this is what was spoken by the prophet Joel." (Acts 2:14-16)

Notice that Peter inseparably links together "the last days" with the event of Pentecost because of this prophecy. God had said through the prophet Joel that in the last days, He would pour out His Spirit. His first followers had just experienced that according to Peter who was there and describes what happened on Pentecost in Acts 2:1-4. They were filled with the Holy Spirit accompanied by speaking in other tongues, a rushing mighty wind from heaven, and tongues of fire that rested upon each of them. Peter tells the crowd that this strange event fulfilled what the prophet Joel had foretold would occur "in the last days." This would be the prelude to their sons and daughters prophesying, young men seeing visions, and old men dreaming dreams. The New Testament reflects such visions and dreams inspired by the Holy Spirit. They would also see wonders in the heaven and signs on earth as the last days drew nearer. Peter announced the Good News that "whoever calls on the name of the Lord shall be saved." While there have been fresh outpourings of the Holy Spirit since then, there is only one Pentecost fulfilling Joel's "last-days" prophecy. Peter's generation witnessed yet another sign pointing to the approach of the last days back then, excluding all future generations as the time for the Second Coming.

THE MINISTRY OF THE MESSIAH

The first coming of the Messiah also indicated that the last days were at hand. When the Lord of heaven finally came to earth as the Jewish Messiah, He validated the first sign of the last days regarding the coming of Elijah who was to prepare the way for the Lord. He also brought about the second sign by pouring out the Holy Spirit that also indicated the last days were at hand. Without the arrival of the Jewish Messiah, the first two signs would have never occurred. This unique God-man for whom the Jews were waiting fulfilled these signs through His ministry.

John believed he was preparing the way for the momentous event when the Lord of heaven would appear as the long-awaited Jewish

Messiah. "Behold! The Lamb of God who takes away the sin of the world!" (John 1:29) John realized how unworthy he was in the presence of Jesus, destined to be the Savior from sin and the One who would pour out the Holy Spirit.

> "I indeed baptize you with water unto repentance, but He who is coming after me is mightier than I, whose sandals I am not worthy to carry. He will baptize you with the Holy Spirit and fire." (Matt. 3:11)

Jesus lived up to everything John foretold. After His ministry of truth and healing, Jesus took away sin by His death and then after rising from the dead poured out the Holy Spirit.

Jesus was the Jewish Messiah and the Lord of heaven who had come to earth. He knew who He was and fully understood the significance of His mission. On one occasion, He turned the tables on his questioners by asking them about the Christ or Messiah. "Whose Son is He?" (Matt. 22:42) They replied that the Messiah is David's son. Quoting Psalm 110:1 where David calls the Messiah "Lord," Jesus then stumped his antagonists. "If David then calls Him 'Lord,' how is He his Son?" (Matt. 22:45) The answer to that question would have helped them to understand the identity of Jesus. There is only one way that David's Lord could also be his son or descendant. It would require a miracle of incarnation where the Lord whom David worshiped entered this world born in the line of David to a woman. This is the miracle of Christmas when the Lord became a helpless infant born to the Virgin Mary by the Holy Spirit. His entrance into this world would occur between two early signs indicating that the last days were at hand for that generation. When Jesus began His ministry, He would validate the first sign of the last days and then after His Crucifixion and Resurrection, He would bring about the second sign at Pentecost.

The first sign regarding the last days was related to the person and work of John the Baptist who understood his ministry as the fulfillment of Isaiah 40:3, "The voice of one crying in the wilderness:

Prepare the way of the Lord." John identified himself as the one to fulfill this ministry (John 1:23) when he called the people to repent of sin and turn to the ways of righteousness because the kingdom of heaven was at hand. If Jesus never came, John's claim to be preparing the way for the Lord would have been false. Jesus validated John's ministry through His own ministry. He stepped onto the stage of history and accomplished those mighty acts witnessing to the power of the kingdom of God foretold by the prophets regarding the Jewish Messiah. John prepared the way for this and Jesus' ministry confirmed it. The Elijah who was to come prior to the last days had indeed come. The Messiah for whom John prepared the way had come. To those who had ears to hear, this was a wake up call that the long-awaited fulfillment of the prophecies was at hand.

Joel 2:28 also said that the Spirit would be poured out as another sign that the last days were drawing near. We have seen Peter's testimony as recorded in the Acts of the Apostles indicating this took place at Pentecost fulfilling Joel's prophecy. That occurred as a result of the ministry of the Messiah. In fact, Jesus was the One who sent the Holy Spirit. "It is to your advantage that I go away; for if I do not go away the Helper [Holy Spirit] will not come to you; but if I depart, I will send Him to you" (John 16:7). In sending the Spirit at Pentecost, Jesus was fulfilling His promise to His disciples and at the same time triggering another sign foretold in the Old Testament prophecies that the last days were at hand. Hence, the ministry of the Lord of heaven, the Jewish Messiah, this unique God-man, again confirmed that the last days were drawing near for that generation.

GOSPEL PREACHED THROUGHOUT THE WORLD

In Matthew 24, Jesus taught about something that would be accomplished just before the end during the apostolic generation. All persons on earth would have the opportunity to hear the Good News that He came to announce. "And this gospel of the kingdom will be preached in all the world as a witness to all the nations, and then the end will come" (Matt. 24:14). After His Crucifixion and Resurrection, Jesus told His disciples He would ascend to heaven and pour out the Holy Spirit empowering His followers to witness "in Jerusalem, and in all Judea and Samaria, and to the end of the earth" (Acts 1:8). He told the apostles they would take the gospel throughout the world. While others assisted in the spread of the gospel, God chose Paul as His primary spokesman for the gospel to the Gentiles, and Peter served that function to the Jewish world. Paul reflects this in Galatians 2:7 where he writes, "They saw that the gospel for the uncircumcised had been committed to me, as the gospel for the circumcised was to Peter."

Writing near the end of his ministry, Paul makes an amazing statement in Colossians 1:23 that the gospel "was preached to every creature under heaven." I have no idea how Paul understands this to have been accomplished. This text has opened the door for all kinds of interpretation to explain that Paul meant something other than what he said. When you believe the biblical witness that the Second Coming occurred during the apostolic generation, then it is not difficult to believe the witness of Paul at this point. At the time he wrote Colossians, God's spokesman to the Gentiles says "every creature under heaven" has heard the gospel fulfilling another condition after which Jesus said the end would come.

People today seek to evangelize the whole world believing when that has been completed, Jesus will return in accord with His promise. We want to continue to take the gospel to all people, but need to remember that this was accomplished during the apostolic generation according to Paul. When the apostle witnesses to this fulfillment in Colossians, he reveals yet another sign that was realized indicating that Jesus' Return was near for Paul and his people.

PERSECUTION OF CHRISTIANS

Jesus foretold persecution for His followers when He returned. In Mark 13, Matthew 24, and Luke 21, Jesus describes the events associated with the Second Coming. Persecution awaited His followers during the last days.

> But before all these things [the second-coming events], they will lay their hands on you and persecute you, delivering you to the synagogues and prisons, and you will be brought before kings and rulers for My name's sake. (Luke 21:12)

The Lord revealed similar things to His first followers in the Revelation given to John. The powers of darkness would be given authority during the last days "to make war with the saints and to overcome them" (Rev. 13:7).

This broke out against the first Christians at the end of the apostolic generation during the reign of the Roman Emperor Nero toward the end of A.D. 64. Tacitus describes the torturous deaths to which the first Christians were subjected. It is also interesting to observe that the numerical value of Nero Caesar written in Hebrew totals 666, the number of the name of a person who would be the instrument of great evil during those last days[2] (Rev. 13:18). Each character in the Hebrew alphabet has a numerical value. One of the ways to write Nero Caesar in Hebrew is the following: נרון קסר. Assigning the corresponding numerical value to the Hebrew characters spelling Nero Caesar yields the following: נ (50), ר (200), ו (6), נ (50), ק (100), ס (60), ר (200). Simple math produces a sum amounting to the prophetic number of 666. Nero proved to be such a person as he instituted the persecution of the first Christians. What Jesus said would occur for His followers when He returned did in fact happen at the conclusion of their generation. Jesus was speaking to His disciples back then, not some far off generation, preparing His first followers for the persecution they would pass through during the last days. He did not want them to be caught off guard, but to be fully ready for the trials that lay ahead. It happened just as He said.

CONTINUAL BURNT OFFERING ENDS

The prophet Daniel gives precise time intervals for second-coming events that help us to understand the chronology for those final events. We read about one of these in Daniel 12:11. "And from the time that the daily sacrifice is taken away, and the abomination of desolation is set up, there shall be one thousand two hundred and ninety days." Josephus who lived during that time tells us that the daily sacrifice ended on *Tammuz* 17, A.D. 70.[3] Some refer to the period during Antiochus Epiphanes when the continual burnt offering was discontinued as the fulfillment of this prophecy. What happened under Antiochus in the Second Century, B.C. was only a temporary disruption of the continual burnt offering. It resumed a few years later, and then continued until the year A.D. 70 when Roman armies destroyed Jerusalem and the temple. It has never been offered again since that time. This was the end of the continual burnt offering and the fulfillment of Daniel 12:11 which occurred during the last days.

Sacrifices had been an integral part of the Old Covenant enabling the living God to dwell in the midst of His people. Not only did the sacrifices end during those last days, the New Testament tells that the Old Covenant was about to end, having been replaced by the New Covenant. Just after referring to the New Covenant, Hebrews 8:13 says that God has made the Old Covenant obsolete. "Now what is becoming obsolete and growing old is ready to vanish away." It did just exactly that during those last days. The endless parade of sacrificial animals necessary under the Old Covenant gave way once and for all to the superior sacrifice of the Lamb of God, our Savior Jesus Christ, when Roman armies destroyed the temple and the City of Jerusalem in A.D. 70. Since then there has been no temple, no Old Covenant, nor any need for any kind of sacrifices. The ending of the continual burnt offering at the temple points to yet another sign fulfilled during the apostolic generation making it clear that the second-coming events were taking place.

Some people talk about building another temple there in Jerusalem and resuming the priestly sacrifices to prepare for the Second Coming. Such a building would now have no status before God. What made those temples in Jerusalem special was the Old Covenant and the priestly ministries ordained by God that provided for the atonement of sin so God could relate to a sinful people. That covenant no longer exists. Such priestly ministries utilizing animal blood in a rebuilt temple would have absolutely no effect at this time in history as God operates under the terms of the New Covenant based on the ultimate sacrifice of the sinless Lamb of God and the priestly ministry in heaven by our Lord Jesus Christ.

DESTRUCTION OF THE TEMPLE

The most readily observable sign pointing to the time of the Return of the Lord was the destruction of the temple at Jerusalem. The living God bound Himself to the Israelites through the terms of the Old Covenant. His eyes were upon the prayers offered in this temple and received the worship of his people under the ministry of the duly appointed priesthood. God had instructed Moses on how to build first the portable tabernacle and later the temple that housed the Ark of the Covenant in the Most Holy Place. For one thousand years from the time of Solomon to those last days, three different temples occupied this site. During the last days when Jesus returned, the temple along with the city would be destroyed and the Old Covenant would come to an end. This was foretold in Revelation 11:2 as part of the second-coming events where John tells us that "they will tread the holy city under foot for forty-two months" (Rev. 11:2). Josephus tells about this history and we shall look at much of that in this book. It began in A.D. 67 and concluded in A.D. 70 in accordance with the prophecy.

During the last week in Jesus' life, He sat with His disciples on the Mount of Olives looking over toward the temple. He told them "not one stone shall be left here upon another; that shall not be thrown down" (Matt. 24:2). They wanted to know when this disaster would happen. Remember, Jesus was speaking to His disciples and not to future generations. His Jewish followers back then were the ones who would be impacted by the destruction of the beloved temple. This was the center of their life and worship for centuries as the covenantal people of God. Jesus responds to their question regarding when this will happen by telling them about many things associated with the Second Coming of Jesus Christ. These were the terrible days prophesied about the final judgment upon Israel for rejecting the mercy of their God offered through the Messiah and the New Covenant. The temple and the beloved city would be destroyed at this time.

Jesus says there will be "wars and rumors of wars" (Matt. 24:6) along with famines and earthquakes (Matt. 24:7). His followers will be hated and killed (Matt. 24:9). They will see Daniel's "abomination of desolation" (Matt. 24:15) "in the holy place" (Matt. 24:15) referring to the corruption of the worship of God to take place at the temple in Jerusalem. This will lead to the destruction of the temple and the city. Jesus then concluded His discourse with a remarkable statement. "Assuredly I say to you, this generation will by no means pass away till all these things are fulfilled" (Matt. 24:34). "All these things" were the events of the Second Coming and Jesus clearly said they would happen back then, and the most visible was the destruction of the temple and Jerusalem occurring in A.D. 70 following the great corruption of the worship of God at the temple. Those first disciples were left with no doubt that they were the ones who would pass through those days when all the things spoken by the prophets would be fulfilled. Jesus was preparing them for all the suffering and persecution they would experience in the years ahead so they would not be caught off guard. He would return for His faithful in the midst of all the tribulation of those days and take them to their eternal reward.

All seven of these indicators pointing to when the Second Coming would occur took place during the apostolic generation. Let us summarize these signs fulfilled back then. First, Elijah the prophet emerged through the ministry of John the Baptist portending the "great and dreadful day of the Lord." Second, the Holy Spirit was poured out at Pentecost, an event that was to occur "in the last days." Third, the Lord of heaven came as the Jewish Messiah fulfilling the first two signs through His ministry. Fourth, the gospel was preached throughout the world following which Jesus said, "then the end will come." Fifth, Nero, the numerical value of whose name is 666, initiated the persecution of Christians foretold by Jesus to happen during the days of the Second Coming. Sixth, the continual burnt offering came to an end as prophesied to occur in those last days. Seventh, Gentiles destroyed the temple and Jerusalem just as Jesus predicted would happen when He returned.

The Bible said all these things would occur during the generation to experience the last days. All seven of these signs or indicators regarding the Second Coming took place during the apostolic generation. No other generation will ever qualify for the fulfillment of all seven signs. Christians will seek to take the gospel throughout the world, continue to undergo persecutions around the world, and Jerusalem may undergo some major wars with its neighbors. There will, however, never be another "Elijah who is to come," there will never be another Messiah to live in human form on this earth, there will never be another Pentecost fulfilling Joel 2:28, and there will never be another temple employing animal sacrifices that will have any status before God. The Bible leaves no doubt regarding its perspective when Jesus returned: *during the lifetime of the apostolic generation.*

3

TRACKING PAUL'S MINISTRY AND GOD'S PLAN

God set forth through the apostle Paul His plan for saving the world. It began with the Good News of the Jewish Messiah. God made a New Covenant through the Messiah open to both Jews and Gentiles who turn from sin to follow Christ and trust in the mercy offered through Him. From the first, Paul taught his converts the importance of maturing in the walk with Christ in order to be ready for His Return. Some wonderful things would happen at that time, a kind of climax and conclusion to their faith and experience. This maturing included not only turning from sin and embracing the ways of righteousness, but also serving Christ in ministry as a part of His plan for each individual follower. Paul likened the church to a body, calling it the Body of Christ. As the members served the needs of others according to their ministries guided by Christ the head, the Body of Christ would grow and the Holy Spirit would join the believers together with bonds of love.

Paul did not teach his people that once they responded to Jesus as Savior and Lord they were now "saved" and just had to sit back or hold on until Jesus returned. Paul taught the converts they had become recipients of God's grace, the Holy Spirit, and spiritual gifts with which to serve. They were to press on guided by God's word inspired by the Holy Spirit through the apostles as they prepared for the climax to their journey at the Second Coming. The awareness that Jesus would return for them, not some distant generation, inspired those first believers to follow through in preparation to meet Christ. God, who is always true to His word, did not disappoint them. We need to learn and master the same preparation for Jesus' Return. We need to understand what they experienced when Jesus returned so we can appropriate the same victory.

Paul's ministry does not begin until the decade of the forties, so let's first go back one decade earlier, to Jesus and the apostles, which is the foundation Paul builds upon. The decade of the thirties begins with what the Jewish people awaited but few recognized—the ministry of the Jewish Messiah, Jesus of Nazareth. After His life, death, Resurrection, and Ascension, we know little about the apostolic generation during the decade of the thirties. We do know the first converts through the New Covenant and its provision for the forgiveness of sin received the Holy Spirit conceiving new life within and empowering them for following and serving Christ. According to Acts 2:42, our spiritual ancestors devoted themselves to the mastery of four disciplines: *the apostles' teaching, the breaking of bread, fellowship, and prayer.* These helped them to continue to turn from the sin to be shunned and the righteousness and servanthood to be embraced. They learned the lifestyle of a disciple through the first disciples of Jesus. They approach the future with a definite purpose. They prepare for the Return of their Lord when they must do final battle with the powers of darkness. Training like Olympic runners, except in regard to spiritual matters, they discipline themselves in these four ways in order to run their spiritual race to the end when they will be evaluated by their Lord and hopefully receive the crown of glory. They have not been saved just to sit back idly. They look to the Lord and His word so they can walk faithfully in the new way of the dawning kingdom. The Holy Spirit teaches them these things through the ministry of the apostles and they practice their faith regularly through witnessing and serving.

Next we come to the decade of the forties. Paul, converted shortly after Jesus concludes His earthly ministry, still lives in his hometown of Tarsus as he learns more about Jesus through the ministry of the Holy Spirit. God takes Paul up into the "third heaven" (2 Cor. 12:2) in the early forties to prepare him for his coming missionary work to the Gentiles. Sometime after the midpoint of the forties, Barnabas brings Paul to Antioch for a year. The church there sends Paul out on his first and second missionary journeys around the end of this decade. There is no revelation yet of the King of glory. He waits until more come to Him from among the Gentiles, and His present followers continue to mature.

We then come to the decade of the fifties. Paul writes 1 and 2 Thessalonians at the beginning of this decade. The Thessalonian correspondence shows Paul teaching his converts from the first to prepare for the Second Coming of Jesus Christ. He refers to the Thessalonians as those who "turned to God from idols to serve the living and true God, and to wait for His Son from heaven" (1 Thess. 1:9-10). The expectation heightens when Paul writes 1 Corinthians around A.D. 55. He tells his people how they should be "eagerly waiting for the revelation of our Lord Jesus Christ" (1 Cor. 1:7). Paul concludes this letter in 1 Corinthians 16:22 with the Aramaic word *maranatha* meaning, "O Lord, come!"

Something significant occurs during the mid-fifties as reflected in 1 and 2 Corinthians and Romans. The Spirit begins to witness about a mystery associated with Christ's anticipated Return. "Behold, I tell you a mystery: We shall not all sleep, but we shall all be changed—in a moment, in the twinkling of an eye, at the last trumpet" (1 Cor. 15:51-52). Paul proceeds in the next sentence to say that "the dead will be raised incorruptible, and we shall be changed." We see that the Spirit is beginning to reveal to them a mystery to be completed during the Second Coming when they "shall be changed."

The Spirit prepares them for the climax to take place during the approaching Return of Christ. Not only were believers crucified with

Christ in baptism, but they also begin to share a kind of resurrection life. Romans 6:4 witnesses to this: "Just as Christ was raised from the dead by the glory of the Father, even so we also should walk in newness of life." Writing in the mid-fifties shortly after the Corinthian correspondence, Paul concludes the Letter to the Romans as follows. "Now to Him who is able to establish you according to my gospel and the preaching of Jesus Christ, according to the revelation of the mystery which was kept secret since the world began, but now has been made manifest, and by the prophetic Scriptures has been made known to all nations, according to the commandment of the everlasting God, for obedience to the faith—to God, alone wise, be glory through Jesus Christ forever. Amen" (Rom. 16:25-27). The revelation of the mystery of Christ to occur at the last trumpet has been shown to Paul and will be realized when Jesus returns to complete His life within His people.

During this period in the mid-fifties, I believe Paul witnesses to a kind of Divine foretaste of the approaching mystery and the anticipated completion or sharing in the glory of God. He writes in 2 Corinthians 4:6: "For it is the God who commanded light to shine out of darkness who has shone in our hearts to give the light of the knowledge of the glory of God in the face of Christ." I believe this shining "in our hearts" to give the "light of the knowledge of the glory of God" was a foretaste of the coming glory, encouraging them to face what suffering they must pass through in the days ahead.

The Holy Spirit leads Paul to build the Body of Christ by helping people discover their spiritual gifts and engage in the corresponding ministries. We read about this in 1 Corinthians and Romans as Paul makes it clear that each believer has at least one gift. The Body of Christ needs each member functioning just as a normal healthy body needs each part to function properly. Paul teaches about the love of Christ bonding the members to one another. God prepares these first believers through the Holy Spirit to be the temple where the Lord manifests His glory during the Second Coming.

Paul leads his converts into the new ways of the approaching kingdom of God. In the Corinthian correspondence, we see the apostle guiding people "called to be saints" (1 Cor. 1:2) along the way of righteousness. Corinthian Christians encountered all kinds of evils. They struggle against the old nature within and engage in spiritual warfare against the powers of evil in the world. Paul warns the Corinthians: "The unrighteous will not inherit the kingdom of God" (1 Cor. 6:9). Paul then details the unrighteous behavior that can disqualify them. "Neither fornicators, nor idolaters, nor adulterers, nor homosexuals, nor sodomites, nor thieves, nor covetous, nor drunkards, nor revilers, nor extortioners will inherit the kingdom of God" (1 Cor. 6:9-10). Paul prepares his people as Jesus taught: "Seek first the kingdom of God and His righteousness" (Matt. 6:33) and "enter by the narrow gate" (Matt. 7:13). They follow through with their repentance turning from what God reveals to be sin and walking in the ways revealed through His word.

Pride threatened to divide the church at Corinth. Some boasted about their identification with particular Christian leaders. Paul urges them to aim at love that he beautifully describes in 1 Corinthians 13. More important than speaking in tongues, than having the gift of prophecy and knowledge and understanding all mysteries, more important than mountain-moving faith and giving our bodies to be burned, love unites God's people. It wards off spiritual attacks by the enemy who tries to create discord in God's family and weaken believers through criticism and gossip. Like a skilled master builder, Paul prepares the Body of Christ for its returning Lord, guiding them away from anything impeding their spiritual progress.

Paul also teaches the importance of discipline in the thought life. He tells the Corinthians: "I fear, lest somehow, as the serpent deceived Eve by his craftiness, so your minds may be corrupted from the simplicity that is in Christ" (2 Cor. 11:3). In the previous chapter while speaking about spiritual warfare, he says that it is important to bring "every thought into captivity to the obedience of Christ" (2 Cor. 10:5). Paul relates the importance of such disciplined thought life in Romans written shortly after 2 Corinthians: "Do not be conformed to this world, but be transformed by the renewing of your mind" (Rom. 12:2). Truth in the thought life, like oil necessary to keep a lamp burning, prepares the faithful in Paul's generation to meet their returning Lord.

The Holy Spirit draws Paul to the Old Testament prophecies during this time in the mid-fifties when God gives him a foretaste of the coming glory. This helps him understand what lies ahead so Paul may prepare the saints for the dawning mystery. He searches the Old Testament to clarify what God is about to do in the last days when Jesus, the Jewish Messiah, returns to be glorified in His waiting people. Paul quotes from 134 different Old Testament texts in his epistles, according to H. Wayne House in his *Chronological and Background Charts of the New Testament*.[4] The Epistle to the Romans contains 56 of the 134 Old Testament texts. Taken together with the Corinthian correspondence, these three letters contain 81 of the 134. This total is based upon the assumption that Paul wrote Hebrews that contains 34 such Old Testament texts. During this time when God granted a foretaste of His glory, the Holy Spirit takes Paul to God's revealed word in the Old Testament so the apostle may understand the mystery to be fulfilled during the last days when Christ returns to manifest His glory in the faithful.

God removes Paul from general circulation for the next six or seven years spanning the period A.D. 57-63. The apostle is imprisoned for two-year periods first in Caesaria and then in Rome. These confinements along with travels to and from the prisons give Paul time to assimilate the writings of the Old Testament preparatory to his final three-and-one-half years of witness. Many times we try to hasten progress in the spiritual life. God knows that real spiritual growth requires time. Paul needs time to get things straight in his mind and heart so he can prepare people for Christ's Second Coming. He does not fight against God's ways, but accepts the imprisonments and puts the time to good use. When he emerges from these confinements at

Caesarea in the late fifties and Rome in the early sixties, and after possibly going on to evangelize in Spain as he indicates in Romans 15:24, Paul is ready for his final period of witnessing, beginning in A.D. 63.

The stage is now set for the last part of God's plan, the revelation of Jesus Christ and the completion of His life in His waiting people joined together as members of His Body. This will occur at the seventh trumpet as their faith and experience comes to a climax. We shall examine in this book Paul's witness to this in Ephesians and Colossians as he talks about how a mystery hidden from all previous generations has been fulfilled. Knowledge of the Scripture and its precious promises support the necessary faith to overcome the assault of the powers of darkness and appropriate the mystery. Paul and Peter lead the first believers through this spiritual warfare into the completion of Christian faith and experience as Jesus returns to be glorified in His waiting and prepared people.

Let us make one final observation regarding this pathway of discipleship that leads to maturity and prepares for the appearing of Jesus and His glory in the lives of His people as God's mystery is fulfilled. God looks carefully at the development in our hearts, just as He told Samuel on one occasion: "Man looks at the outward appearance, but the Lord looks at the heart" (1 Sam. 16:7). He looks for the fully surrendered heart, repentant of all sin, and yielded to the will of the Lord as disciple and servant. Sex, money, and power represent three areas where we are vulnerable, and must learn from Scripture the holy attitudes and righteous actions in these areas God intends for His people. There will be no revelation of Jesus Christ in the heart that refuses to recognize and repent of sin. God looks for surrendered hearts dying to sin and yielding to the Lord as disciple and servant. Jesus taught in the Sermon on the Mount. "Blessed are the pure in heart, for they shall see God" (Matt. 5:8).

No division remains in the pure heart. It no longer limps along between the word of God and the desires of the flesh and the world. Pure hearts love God and align themselves with His word through

Scripture as they turn from sin or anything else that dishonors the living Lord. That beatitude reaches its fulfillment during the second-coming days when God reveals His Son and glory to the pure heart. Paul beautifully witnesses to such a heart in his own life through Philippians as he stands at the threshold of being raised up into heavenly places during the days of the appearing of Jesus Christ. Listen to what the Holy Spirit has done in the heart of this man.

> But what things were gain to me, these I have counted as loss for Christ. But indeed I also count all things loss for the excellence of the knowledge of Christ Jesus my Lord, for whom I have suffered the loss of all things, and count them as rubbish, that I may gain Christ and be found in him. (Phil. 3:7-9)

These words witness to a heart ready to be united with Christ and dwell in the Divine Presence. Paul testifies about a life seeking neither fame nor fortune but only living for God out of a love-filled heart. Paul has learned the ways of a servant, in which His Divine Lord walked before him. Though Jesus was God on the earth, He humbly took the form of a servant, and called His people to follow in those footsteps. Those who faithfully followed their Lord made exciting discoveries as He returned. In like manner, the Holy Spirit is preparing the faithful today to appropriate the mystery revealed to and fulfilled within the faithful during those last days.

Through the ministry of the apostle Paul, God revealed His strategy to repopulate this earth with Christlike people. He sent His Son, the Jewish Messiah, who instituted a New Covenant of grace providing a second chance for us on this earth. God offered forgiveness for our sin, the gift of the Holy Spirit to create new life, and spiritual gifts with which to serve. All who entered into this New Covenant through repentance and faith became part of a new group on this earth called the Body of Christ. We may think of this as a "spiritual factory" originally designed to take the raw material of sinners and produce the finished product of Christlike people. The New Testament tells us how the apostles built this Body of Christ to accomplish God's plan. It was fully dependent upon God's power released through the Holy Spirit working in the lives of the members of the Body of Christ and their ministries. The Scripture reveals God's strategy to repopulate this earth with the kind of people who will someday bring peace to this earth.

4

TRACKING PAUL'S THOUGHTS ON THE SECOND COMING

Paul was God's spokesman to the Gentiles. In this chapter, we shall look at his writings and trace the development in his understanding about what would happen during the days of the Second Coming. God revealed the truth to Paul over the years of his ministry until he was finally ready to lead his people into the victory awaiting them when Jesus returned. Confusion will ensue if we fail to understand this development in his thinking. His earlier writings consist of the Thessalonian correspondence written in the early fifties followed by the Corinthian letters and Romans written in the mid-fifties. The Thessalonian correspondence reports Paul's earliest understanding about the Second Coming of Christ. Let us look at the most detailed passage.

> But I do not want you to be ignorant, brethren, concerning those who have fallen asleep, lest you sorrow as others who have no hope. For if we believe that Jesus died and rose again, even so God will bring with Him those who sleep in Jesus. For this we say to you by the word of the Lord, that we who are alive and remain until the coming [*Parousia*] of the Lord will by no means precede those who are asleep. For the Lord Himself will descend from heaven with a shout, with the voice of an archangel, and with the trumpet of God. And the dead in Christ will rise first. Then we who are alive and remain shall be caught up together with them in the clouds to

meet the Lord in the air. And thus we shall always be with the Lord. (1 Thess. 4:13-17)

The coming or *Parousia* is the time when Paul anticipates that the faithful will be taken from the earth. "We who are alive and remain [until the *Parousia*] shall be caught up together with them in the clouds to meet the Lord in the air" (1 Thess. 4:17). Paul continues in the same verse to say that from that moment on, they will always be with the Lord. He also believes that the dead in Christ will have already been raised at an earlier time when the trumpet of God sounds. "For this we say to you by the word of the Lord, that we who are alive and remain…will by no means precede those who are asleep" (1 Thess. 4:15). "The dead in Christ will rise first" accompanied "with the voice of an archangel, and with the trumpet of God" (1 Thess. 4:16). Paul says nothing about the length of time between the "trumpet of God" when the dead are raised and the later event of the *Parousia* when they are joined by those caught up from the earth. When we come to the chapters dealing with chronology, we shall see that the period of time was approximately three years.

Paul also believes at this early time in his ministry that the sanctification process will reach its climax at the *Parousia* as God will "establish your hearts blameless in holiness before our God and Father at the coming [*Parousia*] of our Lord Jesus Christ with all His saints" (1 Thess. 3:13). "All His saints" refers to those who would be previously resurrected from the dead at the trumpet. Paul appears to understand at the beginning of his ministry that this perfecting or completing would occur for the faithful on earth at the *Parousia* when Christ would return to remove them from the earth, raising them to their glorified body and taking them to be forever with Himself. The important thing to observe about Paul's understanding at this early time in his ministry is this. The trumpet when the dead are raised *occurs prior to the Parousia*. This latter event is when Jesus comes to remove the faithful and take them to heaven to be forever with their Lord. He will come at the *Parousia* with those previously raised from the dead at the earlier event of the trumpet.

We saw in the last chapter that Paul begins to look more intently into the Old Testament during the time in the mid-fifties when he writes 1 Corinthians, 2 Corinthians, and Romans. These letters contain 81 out of 134 Old Testament texts in Paul's letters, with a high of 56 in Romans. It is precisely during this period that God begins to reveal something more to Paul about the time of the trumpet prior to the *Parousia*. In 1 Corinthians 15:51-52, he speaks about a mystery to occur at this time when the dead would be raised, only now, those on earth will also undergo a change.

> And as we have borne the image of the man of dust, we shall also bear the image of the heavenly Man. Now this I say, brethren, that flesh and blood cannot inherit the kingdom of God; nor does corruption inherit incorruption. Behold, I tell you a mystery: We shall not all sleep, but we shall all be changed—in a moment, in the twinkling of an eye, at the last trumpet. For the trumpet will sound, and the dead will be raised incorruptible, and we shall be changed. (1 Cor. 15:49-52)

Paul stated earlier in 1 Thessalonians 4:16 that the dead would be raised at "the trumpet of God." "The last trumpet" in 1 Corinthians 15:52 is the same trumpet because the dead are also raised at this time. What is new for Paul, however, in this Corinthian passage is the occurrence of a mystery at this trumpet involving the saints while they are still on earth prior to the *Parousia*. At the very same moment when the dead are raised, those on earth will also be changed. "We shall not all sleep" (1 Cor. 15:51) again indicates Jesus would return for this climactic event at the trumpet while some of the Corinthians were still alive on earth.

When we look at the context, the change occurring for those on earth at the same moment that the dead are raised is the completion within of "the image of the heavenly Man" (1 Cor. 15:49) or the

Christlike nature, or the climax of the sanctification process. The dead in their resurrection would have received "the image of the heavenly Man" and the glorified body. At the very same moment, those on earth while still in their physical bodies received that same completed life perfected in the dead as they were raised. The Epistle to the Hebrews affirms this truth that the Old Testament faithful who died through the years and were commended for their faith did not receive what had been promised. This was because God "provided something better for us [the faithful of the apostolic generation], that they should not be made perfect apart from us" (Heb. 11:40). The faithful dead of the Old Testament and the faithful of the apostolic generation were perfected at the same time. That climactic moment occurred "in the twinkling of an eye, at the last trumpet" (1 Cor. 15:52).

Paul clearly was preparing the Corinthians and Romans for this climax. He exhorts the Corinthians along with himself to "cleanse ourselves from all filthiness of the flesh and spirit, perfecting holiness in the fear of God" (2 Cor. 7:1). He encourages the Romans to submit themselves "as slaves of righteousness for holiness" (Rom. 6:19) knowing that the end result will be "everlasting life" (Rom. 6:22) or God's own life of holiness, the kind of life present in Christ.

Paul writes Philippians just before the seventh trumpet. "The Lord is at hand" (Phil. 4:5) reflects Paul's belief that Jesus' Return is near. Paul's heart also clearly reflects one who has matured through the sanctifying work of the Holy Spirit. "But indeed I also count all things loss for the excellence of the knowledge of Christ Jesus my Lord, for whom I have suffered the loss of all things" (Phil. 3:8). Paul reflects a heart where dwells the kind of love for God that the Creator of the universe yearns for and deserves.

Paul tells us in Philippians what he expects to happen at the imminent Return of Christ. It has not yet happened, but he is determined to do all in his power to cooperate with the Holy Spirit to enable it to happen. "Not that I have already attained, or am already perfected; but I press on, that I may lay hold of that for which Christ Jesus has also laid hold of me" (Phil. 3:12). The completion of the sanctification process that Paul attributed to the *Parousia* in 1 Thessalonians 3:13 is now seen to occur at the earlier time of the trumpet along with a spiritual resurrection.

When Paul talks about resurrection power, he clearly speaks about something to happen in this life, rather than in the next life where the promise of resurrection power ensures victory over death with a new body. "Not that I have already attained" would be superfluous were he speaking of being raised to the resurrection body in the next life. Paul speaks in Philippians 3:10 about an experience involving resurrection power while still on this earth but not yet attained at the time of writing to the Philippians. It is interesting to observe that in Philippians 3:11 when Paul says that he hopes to attain this resurrection from the dead, he uses the word *exanastasis*. He usually employs *anastasis* for resurrection, and the use here of *exanastasis* where the prefix *ex* means "out of" or "from within" may be his effort to distinguish this spiritual resurrection as different from the resurrection when the faithful receive a new body. In any event, he clearly anticipates experiencing resurrection power while living on this earth.

In like manner when he says that he has not yet "been made perfect," he expects this to happen in this life, or such words would again be superfluous if it was to happen when Christ removed His faithful from the earth. He understands that he has been "taken hold of" by Christ to the end that God might not only form the Christlike nature within him but also raise Him in heavenly places by resurrection power. Paul determines to let nothing rob him of this climax to Christian faith and experience. He expresses his resolve in Philippians 3:13-14: "One thing I do, forgetting those things which are behind and reaching forward to those things which are ahead, I press toward the goal for the prize of the upward call of God in Christ Jesus."

I want to add a paragraph here about the matter of perfection. We often hear that this is utterly impossible in this life, and to even think about it lays impossible demands upon believers. If we view perfection as a human accomplishment, that is true. The Scripture never says that human beings can perfect themselves, and for anyone to ever attempt to do so is absolutely futile. In fact, one thing we must learn is utter dependence upon God, for nothing of the flesh or human effort will avail to perfect ourselves. The Bible witnesses, however, that God working in the lives of cooperative disciples through the provision of the New Covenant is fully able. We know that is true, for with our God all things are possible, and He earnestly desires to accomplish this. Such people will worship and serve Him taking care to see that He gets the glory. All He needs is our cooperation as spelled out in the New Testament to do what He has said He will do.

The seventh trumpet sounds shortly after Paul writes Philippians. His expectations associated with the trumpet are being realized as part of a mystery when we come to his Letters of Ephesians and Colossians. The mystery anticipated in 1 Corinthians 15:51-52 has now occurred. First, the Holy Spirit is forming the Christlike nature within responsive believers. Paul writes in Colossians. "To them God willed to make known what are the riches of the glory of this mystery among the Gentiles: which is Christ in you, the hope of glory" (Col. 1:27). Paul continues in the next verse witnessing to this conclusion of Christian faith and experience in the forming of Christ within the believers to whom Paul ministered. "Him we preach, warning every man and teaching every man in all wisdom, that we may present every man perfect in Christ Jesus" (Col. 1:28).

Paul tells us in Ephesians 4:13 that the end result of building the Body of Christ on this earth is for the members of Christ to mature, coming to "the measure of the stature of the fullness of Christ." Notice carefully Paul's words. God destined believers while still on earth not for part of the nature of Christ, but "the measure of the stature of the fullness of Christ." Paul earlier taught that those God "foreknew, He also predestined to be conformed to the image of His Son" (Rom. 8:29). From the very first when the sanctification process began, God had in mind to form Christ within the disciples of Jesus. His intention was to create Christlike people on this earth. During those last days, the living God enabled faithful disciples through the apostolic ministry to attain "the whole measure of the fullness of Christ" or bear "the image of the heavenly Man" while still on earth. Paul writes similarly to the Galatians as he tells about agonizing over them like a woman in birth pains "until Christ is formed in you" (Gal. 4:19).

Ephesians and Colossians also show that the second expectation of being raised with Christ in heavenly places has occurred in the saints while still on earth. Note that this is not a position given to the believers at their conversion, but something revealed during the days of the seventh trumpet to those who had responded as faithful disciples and grown to maturity climaxing with the formation of the Christlike nature within. Paul had been a Christian for years when he wrote Philippians, yet he still desires to know the "power of His resurrection." Paul had not yet attained this resurrection power at the time of writing Philippians. Something new, however, has happened by the time he wrote Ephesians and Colossians. Paul tells us in Ephesians 2:6 that God "raised us up together, and made us sit together in the heavenly places in Christ Jesus." God has now manifested resurrection power in Paul by raising him to heavenly places.

Paul prays for the Ephesians that God may reveal to them "the exceeding greatness of His power" (Eph. 1:19) which is the same power "He worked in Christ when He raised Him from the dead and seated Him at His right hand in the heavenly places" (Eph. 1:20). While Paul is still living on this earth, resurrection power accomplishes the mystery of raising him and the faithful of that generation to sit with Christ in heaven, enabling them to enjoy every spiritual blessing in the heavenly places. Paul says the same thing in Colossians 3:1 as he speaks about those who were raised with Christ. Resurrection power has brought them to victory over the powers of darkness. Paul's earlier desire reflected in Philippians 3:10 to "know…the power of His resurrection" has now occurred. Paul writes truly amazing things in Ephesians and Colossians that are part of a mystery revealed during those last days.

Paul's use of the preposition "*sun*" translated "with" likewise reflects the impact of resurrection power raising him to be "with" the Lord of heaven. Prior to Ephesians and Colossians, whenever Paul uses "*sun*" in regard to Christ, it refers to the next life. At his conversion, God placed Paul "in Christ," but he will not be "with Christ" until he is raised to heaven. In his earliest letter, Paul states "we shall always be with [*sun*] the Lord" (1 Thess. 4:17) after he and the faithful are taken from the earth at the *Parousia* to join those first raised from the dead. In the midst of the imprisonment from which he writes Philippians, Paul says he prefers to depart, or leave this earth, and be "with [*sun*] Christ" (Phil. 1:23). Paul is already "in Christ," and will be "with [*sun*] Christ" when Jesus removes him to heaven.

After the mystery revealed to the apostolic generation during the days of the seventh trumpet and reflected in Ephesians and Colossians, Paul is now "with Christ" while still on earth as a result of resurrection power. God "raised us up together [*sunegeiro*]" and "made us sit together [*sunkathidzo*] in the heavenly places in Christ Jesus" (Eph. 2:6). Since they have been raised (*sunegeiro*) with Christ, Paul admonishes the Colossians to "seek those things which are above" (Col. 3:1) and to "set your mind on things above" (Col. 3:2). Paul gives the reason for this lofty pursuit in Colossians 3:3. "For you died, and your life is hidden with [*sun*] Christ in God" (Col. 3:3). Paul and the faithful experienced the climax of Christian faith and experience possible while still on the earth. They have already died to the old nature. As part of this great mystery, they have been spiritually raised to be with Christ while still on earth.

Paul came to understand that there were two stages to the resurrection for those on earth, one associated with the trumpet and the other with the *Parousia*. During the time of the trumpet, the faithful would be raised spiritually and then at the *Parousia*, they would be taken from the earth and receive the glorified body. Figure 1 illustrates this significant period in history.

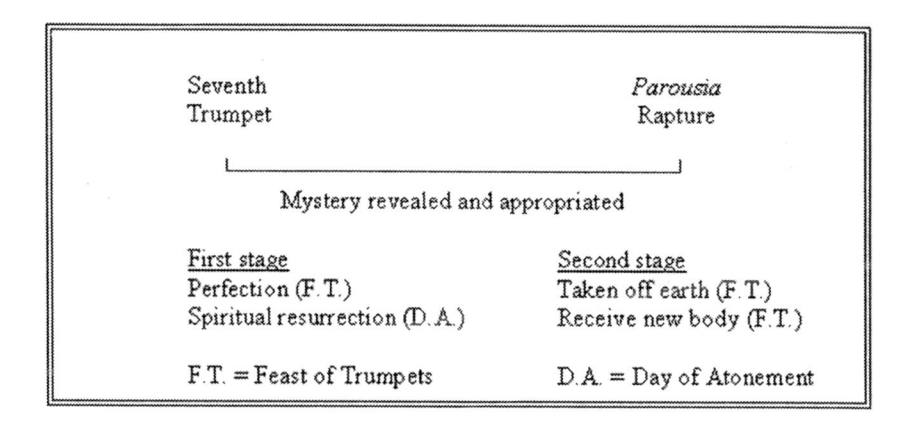

```
         Seventh                         Parousia
         Trumpet                         Rapture
                 |_____|
                  Mystery revealed and appropriated

         First stage                    Second stage
         Perfection (F.T.)              Taken off earth (F.T.)
         Spiritual resurrection (D.A.)  Receive new body (F.T.)

         F.T. = Feast of Trumpets       D.A. = Day of Atonement
```

Figure 1 Time Interval between Seventh Trumpet and Parousia

The Book of Revelation likewise shows that the resurrection took place in two separate stages for those on earth. The *Parousia* when Jesus returns with the clouds to remove His people from the earth occurs in Revelation 14:14-16. Jesus likened to a reaper comes upon a cloud and gathers the ripe harvest of the saints. Here they receive the glorified body. The seventh trumpet, however, sounds earlier in Revelation 11:15 followed by God's great mystery that we shall further discuss in chapter 11 when the faithful on earth underwent a spiritual resurrection. These two separate events are described as great signs in Revelation 12:1 and Revelation 15:1. They deal with these two stages of the resurrection whereby the saints on earth come into the reward or inheritance promised to them. We need to take care to distinguish between these two stages of the resurrection in order to understand the Book of Revelation and Paul's theology about the Second Coming.

Understanding that the Second Coming happened at the conclusion of the apostolic generation helps in dating Paul's later letters. The Book of Acts enables us to date his earlier letters as it covers Paul's ministry and travels from the late forties to his first imprisonment at Rome ending around A.D. 62. He wrote to the Thessalonians in the early fifties and to the Romans and the Corinthians in the mid-fifties. When we see that the seventh trumpet occurred back then and understand what happened in the lives of the faithful while still on earth, we can separate Paul's later letters into pre-seventh trumpet and post-seventh trumpet categories. First Timothy, Titus, and Philippians fall into the first category. Ephesians, Colossians, Hebrews, 2 Timothy, and Galatians are part of the latter category. We shall see why this is so when we come to chapter 10, "Daniel's Seventieth Week As It Happened." Here we shall look at Paul's letters in terms of their theological content as well as other information that will help in dating these letters during this climactic period that occurred from A.D. 63 to A.D. 70.

While the New Testament does not report who wrote the Epistle to the Hebrews, the early church historian Eusebius tells us that Clement asserts that Paul wrote the letter in the Hebrew language and Luke later translated it into the Greek.[5] I don't know any person more qualified. Paul was a highly intellectual Jew having a mind for such insight and the Spirit prepared his heart to witness to such light so that God received the glory and not Paul. The Epistle to the Philippians reveals how the sanctifying work of the Holy Spirit through the years prepared the heart of this keen-minded intellectual to love Christ and thus be able to faithfully handle the fullness of the truth entrusted to His care. Paul was also the primary spokesman to the Gentiles, and the truth of this new faith coming out of Jewish roots would need to be made clear from the first. I believe the witness of Clement was accurate in reporting that Paul wrote the Epistle to the Hebrews in that language and Luke later translated it into the Greek.

5

PERFECTING IN THE NEW TESTAMENT

Nobody can be perfect. Most Christian thinking reflects that position without looking more closely. This statement is true if we think of Christians being perfected as a result of some super-human effort. It is true that persons cannot make themselves perfect. It is absolutely impossible. The Bible however witnesses to things that though impossible for people are nonetheless possible for God. The New Testament tells us some amazing things. In addition to the witness that the Second Coming happened about two thousand years ago, it also tells us that persons were perfected during those last days. This did not result from human effort but the power of God working by the activity of the Holy Spirit through the sanctification process in fully cooperating lives. We need to learn what this practically means for our lives.

Let us move beyond traditional thinking on this matter, and look carefully at what God tells us in Scripture. We shall examine the Greek verb, *teleioo*, translated "to perfect" meaning to bring something through to its intended completion or desired end. Regarding the Christian life, we are talking about the perfecting of the Christlike nature in the faithful. "One cannot be perfected in this life" is the common belief. We can understand this, especially as we look at the world about us and as we look within our own souls. Yet, if we believe the Bible to be God's revelation of His word, we must forever return to that basic source to see if our thinking is correct. Let us look at how Paul uses the word *teleioo* meaning "to perfect." He uses it first in Philippians anticipating such perfecting as a future occurrence, but still during his lifetime. He then uses it nine times in Hebrews as he expounds on the subject after it has happened. Perfected persons have emerged by the time that Hebrews was written.

PAUL'S PASSION FOR PERFECTION

The first use of *teleioo* in the New Testament is by Paul in Philippians written just before the trumpet. The Holy Spirit has worked deeply in Paul's heart. He earnestly looks forward to being perfected and experiencing resurrection power. Let us listen to his testimony.

> But indeed I also count all things loss for the excellence of the knowledge of Christ Jesus my Lord, for whom I have suffered the loss of all things, and count them as rubbish, that I may gain Christ and be found in Him…that I may know Him and the power of His resurrection…Not that I have already attained, or am already perfected; but I press on, that I may lay hold of that for which Christ Jesus has also laid hold of me. (Phil. 3:8-12)

Paul's words show what he envisioned would occur at the last trumpet. "The Lord is at hand" (Phil. 4:5) expresses the imminence of Jesus' Return. Paul wants to know the power of the Resurrection and to be perfected. The pathway is to be "conformed to his death" (Phil. 3:10). This does not mean that we are all to be crucified, as was Jesus. It means that we are to die completely to the old nature so the Holy Spirit may complete the Christlike nature within that is totally submitted to God's will in all our circumstances. This sets us apart as servants whose existence is defined by our love for God and our inner drive to serve and obey our Master in heaven. "Not My will, but Yours, be done" is written on the hearts of those who are becoming like Christ in His death. Paul has not yet attained such perfection or the power of the Resurrection. He is close and expresses his unshakable resolve in this regard with the words in Philippians 3:13: "One thing I do."

> Not that I have already attained, or am already perfected; but I press on, that I may lay hold of that for which Christ Jesus has also laid hold of me. Brethren, I do not count myself to have apprehended; but one thing I do, forgetting those things which are behind and reaching forward to those things which are ahead, I press toward the goal for the prize of the upward call of God in Christ Jesus. (Phil. 3:12-14)

While Paul writes Philippians before the seventh trumpet, he writes Hebrews in the following year after that trumpet as the light continues to shine regarding what they are passing through. His expectations are being realized regarding perfection and entrance into the Divine Presence in heaven. When writing to Gentiles who did not have the understanding of the Old Testament, Paul talks about resurrection power raising them to heaven where God resides. To the Hebrews who understand the Old Covenant sacrificial system and priestly ministry, Paul can go into more depth about what has made this victory possible. Paul says that Jesus, as a far superior High Priest taking His own precious blood before the throne in heaven, has secured everlasting Atonement for sin, provided for perfection, and opened the way for us on this earth into the very Divine Presence dwelling in the heavenly tabernacle.

JESUS PERFECTED THROUGH SUFFERING

Paul first uses *teleioo* in Hebrews with regard to Jesus. In fact, three times he refers to how Jesus was perfected through suffering. Because our faith asserts that Jesus was God in the flesh, it may surprise the reader that the New Testament tells us that Jesus was perfected. Let us look at these three uses.

> For it was fitting for Him, for whom are all things and by whom are all things, in bringing many sons to glory, to make the author of their salvation perfect through sufferings. (Heb. 2:10)

> Though He was a Son, yet He learned obedience by the things which He suffered. And, having been perfected, He became the author of eternal salvation to all who obey Him. (Heb. 5:8-9)
>
> For the law appoints as high priests men who have weakness, but the word of the oath, which came after the law, appoints the Son who has been perfected forever. (Heb. 7:28)

What does it mean for Jesus to be made perfect? Christians believe that Jesus was a unique person combining in Himself our human nature through His mother Mary along with the Divine nature through His heavenly Father. Christian faith affirms the biblical witness that it was not Joseph, but God, the first member of the Trinity, who fathered Jesus.

The New Testament tells us about this unique life in Jesus. John does likewise when he says: "The word became flesh" (John 1:14). This mystery defies explanation regarding what it meant for Jesus to combine in Himself our human nature and the Divine nature. When Paul says in Hebrews that Jesus was perfected, it indicates that the flesh or His human side opened up the possibility for sin and disobedience to which we all fell. Paul also suggests this when he says that Jesus Himself was "tempted" and therefore understands and "is able to aid those who are tempted" (Heb. 2:18). Paul further witnesses to this internal struggle for Jesus when he writes that during the "days of His flesh," Jesus "offered up prayers and supplications with vehement cries and tears to Him who was able to save Him from death, and was heard because of His godly fear" (Heb. 5:7). Such a struggle represented by these words would hardly be present if overcoming temptation to sin was an automatic thing for Jesus. Fortunately for us, He met every temptation victoriously. His final and greatest test of obedience and suffering came at the Cross. During the night before in the Garden of Gethsemane, He asked His Father if it was possible to avoid the terrible suffering ahead in the Crucifixion, yet remaining fully submissive to the Father's will. "Not my will, but Yours, be done" (Luke 22:42). Hebrews tells us that

Jesus was perfected through His suffering climaxing at the Cross. The perfecting of the combined Divine-human nature within Jesus resulted in a new Christlike nature for us on this earth that could also be victorious over sin.

Jesus could have summoned angels to rescue Him from the Cross and destroy His enemies. He remained faithful to the Father's will. His heart was clearly fixed at the point of obeying God to the very end. Even in the limitations of a human body where this unique God-man wrestled with the possibility of sin because of His human side, Jesus was victorious. He resisted every temptation by Satan to disobey the Father and fall to sin. Through the pathway of suffering climaxing in His finest hour at the Cross, He was perfected and offered Himself as a perfect sacrifice for the sin of the world. Through His death, He provided not only for cleansing from sin but also a new nature for us on this earth that could overcome sin. Paul properly refers to Jesus as the second Adam because of this new life perfected within Him as He lived in a human body in this world. The moment we respond to Jesus trusting in the cleansing from sin He won at the Cross, we also receive the Holy Spirit within who begins from that very moment to produce through the sanctification process this same kind of life perfected in Jesus.

OLD COVENANT POWERLESS TO PERFECT

Three of the uses in Hebrews of *teleioo* let us know that the provisions of the Old Covenant were powerless to perfect God's people.

> For on the one hand, there is an annulling of the former commandment because of its weakness and unprofitableness, for the law made nothing perfect; on the other hand, there is the bringing in of a better hope, through which we draw near to God. (Heb. 7:18-19)

> It was symbolic for the present time in which both gifts and sacrifices are offered which cannot make him who performed the service perfect in regard to conscience. (Heb. 9:9)

> For the law, having a shadow of the good things to come, and not the very image of the things, can never with these same sacrifices, which they offer continually year by year, make those who approach perfect. (Heb. 10:1)

We shall shortly see that the blood shed by the sinless Son of God in His final act of obedience has the power through the New Covenant to perfect this same kind of life in those who respond. Hebrews points to the limitations of the Old Covenant. The law was weak and useless in regard to perfection. The blood of animals was not able to perfect the worshiper or his conscience. Perfection was absolutely impossible under the provisions of the Old Covenant.

God never abandoned His original desire to have people who would love, serve, and worship Him. He told the prophets about His plan to make a New Covenant. "I will put My laws in their mind and write them on their hearts" (Heb. 8:10 quoting Jer. 31:33). This kind of life was perfected in Jesus, and the New Covenant provided the basis for this same life to be perfected in the faithful. God would thereby put His laws on the minds of His people and write them on their hearts. "Not my will, but Yours, be done" would distinguish these hearts from all other human beings, hearts wanting and now able to fully obey God. He could unite Himself with such people and achieve the intimate union He desired from the first. "I will be their God, and they shall be My people" (Heb. 8:10). During those last days when Hebrews was written, the writer tells us that the Old Covenant with all its weakness had become obsolete and "what is becoming obsolete and growing old is ready to vanish away" (Heb. 8:13). The Old Covenant came to an end during those second-coming days with the ending of the continual burnt offering and the destruction of the temple and the City of Jerusalem. The New Covenant remains as God's final agreement with the people of this earth, Jew and Gentile, offering forgiveness and the provisions of His grace to change us into the kind of people He will admit to His heaven and Presence.

PERFECTING THROUGH JESUS

The study of this word *teleioo* in the New Testament is very instructive about the matter of perfection. It is the basis for our understanding of this topic. Three of the uses refer to Jesus being perfected through suffering climaxing at the Cross. Three of the uses refer to the absolute impotence of the Old Covenant, the law, and the blood of animals to perfect God's covenant people. The last three uses refer to the sufficiency of the blood of Jesus to perfect the saints through the New Covenant coming to completion at Jesus' Return. We also see that such perfecting was accomplished for the dead Old Testament faithful together with the faithful of the apostolic generation still living on earth, another witness that the Second Coming was in the process of occurring. This letter was written after the seventh trumpet but before the *Parousia* that is anticipated in "a little while" (Heb. 10:37).

> Let us look closely at these last three uses of *teleioo*.
>
> But this Man, after He had offered one sacrifice for sins forever, sat down at the right hand of God, from that time waiting till His enemies are made His footstool. For by one offering He has perfected forever those who are being sanctified. (Heb. 10:12-14)

Here is the witness to the perfecting power released in this world through the blood of His Cross. The word "forever" in Hebrews 10:12 and Hebrews 10:14 is a translation of the same Greek phrase "*eis to dienekes.*" It literally means "into perpetuity" referring to something that happens initially and continues to operate perpetually from that time on.

This three-word phrase is used four times in the New Testament, all in Hebrews. The first usage is in Hebrews 7:3 referring to the perpetual operation of the priesthood of Melchizedek. Hebrews 10:1 refers to the continual offering of sacrifices by the priests under the Old Covenant. In Hebrews 10:12 and 10:14, the words refer to the perpetual effects set into operation by the one sacrifice of the sinless Son of God at the

Cross. Hebrews 10:12 says the blood of Christ operates perpetually to deal with sin through cleansing and sanctifying. Hebrews 10:14 reports that the same blood operates perpetually to perfect the Christlike nature in those who are being sanctified. This perfecting that completes the sanctification process happened at the seventh trumpet.

There is so much in these verses. We are told that after Jesus set into perpetual operation this cleansing and sanctifying that provided the remedy for sin, He "sat down at the right hand of God from that time waiting till His enemies are made His footstool" (Heb. 10:12-13). We are told in the next verse the reason for this expectant waiting. His blood also has the power to perfect. How will the enemies of Jesus be made a footstool for His feet on this earth? When perfected people begin to emerge. They will live, as did Jesus on this earth, as servants of God with a single desire to obey their Lord and glorify Him. Such persons, now doing things God's way and no longer their own way, will be part of that great company of people who will claim this earth for the One to whom it rightfully belongs and under whose feet God will place the enemy.

The next use of "to perfect" in Hebrews tells how those great Old Testament heroes of the faith such as Enoch, Noah, Abraham, Moses, and David all had to wait for the fulfillment of the promises until the time of the last generation. That occurred during the apostolic generation that received the Incarnation and Return of the Messiah when He inaugurated the New Covenant and fulfilled the promises.

> And all these, having obtained a good testimony through faith, did not receive the promise, God having provided something better for us, that they should not be made perfect apart from us. Therefore we also, since we are surrounded by so great a cloud of witnesses, let us lay aside every weight, and the sin which so easily ensnares us, and let us run with endurance the race that is set before us. (Heb. 11:39-12:1)

This was exactly what Paul witnessed to in 1 Corinthians 15:51-52. We observed in the previous chapter that at the last trumpet, in the twinkling of an eye, when the dead were raised, the faithful on earth were also perfected or changed into the likeness of Christ. At the very same moment when Enoch, Noah, Abraham, Moses, David and all the other faithful during the Old Testament period came into the promises and were perfected, the faithful on earth were likewise perfected. Those first raised from the dead are that great cloud of witnesses cheering on from heaven those on earth to run the race faithfully to the end during those terrible, once-and-for-all-days of the Second Coming.

There was great rejoicing in heaven after the seventh trumpet. Paul reminds those on earth still going through great tribulation and suffering of this glorious reality. Division, strife, and corruption occupied the earthly Jerusalem and Mount Zion during those last days. In his Letter to the Hebrews, Paul directed the focus for those first faithful toward heaven where they would all gather at the *Parousia*, if not before through martyrdom.

> But you have come to Mount Zion and to the city of the living God, the heavenly Jerusalem, to an innumerable company of angels, to the general assembly and church of the firstborn who are registered in heaven, to God the Judge of all, to the spirits of just men made perfect, to Jesus the Mediator of the new covenant, and to the blood of sprinkling that speaks better things than that of Abel. (Heb. 12:22–24)

Paul says that Jesus was "the firstborn from the dead" (Col. 1:18). When Paul refers to "the church of the firstborn who are registered in heaven" in Hebrews 12:23, I believe he refers to the great cloud of witnesses of those Old Testament faithful who were raised from the dead at the trumpet. They have received the Christlike nature as well as the glorified body. "The spirits of just men made perfect" in the same verse refers to those faithful of the apostolic generation still confined to a body on this earth, but who have come through to the climax of the sanctification process with the forming or perfecting of Christ within. Such perfected lives clearly point to a time after the seventh trumpet.

LOOKING FOR PERFECTION TODAY

What do such perfect persons look like as they begin to emerge on this earth? Are they "spiritual freaks" who stand out? Do they never make mistakes or err in judgment? What does it mean to be perfected? Such persons, though standing out in some ways through selfless service and witness, will not call attention to themselves or seek glory and praise from other people. Their passion will be to glorify God and they will do this by obeying Him in all things and being His servants as they minister to the needs of others. They will unashamedly witness to Jesus Christ along with their good works so God receives the glory.

Jesus is our example of perfection. The New Testament calls Him the second Adam. The sanctification process and the final perfecting will complete within us the same nature that was perfected in Jesus. The life of the first Adam who fell to sin could be best characterized by the words: "I'll do it my way." The life of the second Adam perfected in Jesus is best described by His words: "Not my will, but Yours, be done." Yes, that can happen in our lives if we are willing to submit to God's authority. He can make us like Jesus in His desire to obey God in all things.

The basic problem regarding "perfecting" or being changed into the likeness of Christ comes from within. Our human nature wants no part of this and will fight it literally to the death. It will, in fact, require the death of that old nature, before God can perfect the new nature within us. The problem is not that we cannot be perfected. The problem is that we have old natures that do not want to live as citizens of heaven while on this earth. Our old nature is bent on pursuing pleasure and gratifying the desires of the flesh. It prefers to be thus served and entertained than taking the posture of a servant and living in submission to God's authority. We shall not be completed in Christ as long as we still cling to sin and the pursuit of personal pleasure. It requires full cooperation with the sanctifying process enabling the Holy Spirit to perfect the holy, righteous, and servant life that was perfected in Jesus. It can happen on this earth if we choose to fully cooperate as revealed in Scripture. He can pull it off. "Not my will, but Yours, be done" is the hallmark of such a life and stands in stark contrast to the old nature with its "I'll do it my way."

During those days when the sanctifying work of the Holy Spirit was nearing completion in Paul's life, he writes in Philippians about His understanding of Jesus' servanthood and humility and what that means for His followers.

> Let nothing be done through selfish ambition or conceit, but in lowliness of mind let each esteem others better than himself. Let each of you look out not only for his own interests, but also for the interests of others. Let this mind be in you which was also in Christ Jesus, who, being in the form of God...made Himself of no reputation, taking the form of a servant, and coming in the likeness of men. And being found in appearance as a man, He humbled Himself and became obedient to the point of death, even the death of the cross. (Phil. 2:3-8)

This is what perfected people will look like and we need them on this earth. They are servants who follow in the footsteps of their Lord who served before them. Though He was God, Jesus humbled Himself and took the form of a servant in obedience to His Father. His followers are His servants who live not by their own agenda or that of the world, but that of their Lord who reigns over all things "to make all things new." They march at His commands to meet needs about them so the reigning King may through the witness and good deeds of such servants touch the people in their part of the world.

Perfected people will not exalt themselves or project themselves as better than other people, for that is not the posture of the servant that is at the very heart of the Christlike nature. During His last evening on this earth, Jesus' disciples argued among themselves regarding "which of them should be considered the greatest" (Luke 22:24). Jesus then demonstrated this humble servanthood as He proceeded to wash their feet. "If I then, your Lord and Teacher, have washed your feet, you also ought to wash one another's feet" (John 13:14). Here was the Lord of heaven and earth bowing to wash the feet of His disciples on the night before He would die on the Cross for their sins. I am sure this lesson in humility and servanthood was indelibly written on the minds of those disciples who moments before took off on ego trips.

To be made like Christ means to become servants sensitive to the needs of others and ministering as God directs, however humbling the task. They will eagerly and joyfully serve in the ministries for which they have been gifted. They will be deeply committed to be the hands and feet of Christ in this world so the Master can again meet human need as He walks this earth through His people. Witness will accompany their good deeds so that God gets the glory. They will do something similar to what a Christian artist did one evening after singing an inspiring number. The audience responded with applause, and the artist at once looked upward and applauded turning the attention away from himself to God who inspired the number and gifted the artist to so beautifully sing it.

Paul also calls attention in Philippians 2:3-8 to another quality related to being a servant. Paul says "in lowliness of mind let each esteem others better than himself." How is it that somebody who has gone so far down the pathway toward perfection as reflected in Philippians says that we should in humility consider others as better than ourselves? I will tell you that many of the divisions in the Body of Christ and damaged relationships would improve overnight if members viewed other believers with such humility. I believe the reason Paul makes this statement is that the further down the road toward perfection persons travel, they become more aware of the depth of their own sin and its utter selfishness. One way we discover this as we grow in Christ is to get caught up in seeking the blessings ahead of the One who blesses. The revelation of such selfishness gets us back on target in seeking Jesus first and His will for our lives. Perfected people realize they are servants, and as paradoxical as it may seem, will have no difficulty in doing as Paul admonishes "in lowliness of mind let each esteem others better than himself." They are deeply aware of their old nature and how its sin has broken out in the past. The humility accompanying this awareness makes them a healing and unifying influence in the Body of Christ.

Perfected persons will not deliberately sin against their conscience and God will help keep them in this regard. It would be abhorrent for them to commit sin knowing how God hates sin and the terrible price He paid and all the suffering He endured to reconcile them to Himself. The conscience is their God-given guidance system to help them live in a world filled with sin, evil, and temptation. Paul says in 1 Timothy 1:18-20 that some persons are not holding on to a good conscience and are thereby making a shipwreck of their faith. In 1 Corinthians 8:9-13, Paul says it is a sin to violate the conscience. We do great harm to our spiritual lives when we violate our conscience. One of Paul's aims in his ministry is to get people to live with a "good conscience" (1 Tim. 1:5).

Paul says that the conscience can become seared meaning that it can be trained to think something is wrong that God has not declared to be wrong. Paul describes this in 1 Timothy 4:2-3 when he talks about persons who were forbidding people to marry and eat particular foods. If the conscience has been thus seared so as to think something is wrong that God has not declared so in Scripture, it needs to be retrained so that it aligns with God's will. This is why learning God's word through the Bible is important so that disciples of Jesus may walk confidently in the way God wants for His people, and to clarify where their conscience has been incorrectly trained. Perfected people will follow such an enlightened conscience as God's practical guidance system and He will help keep His faithful who have made clear their desire to thus walk.

The world will sometimes see them as enemies because Christians embrace biblical values that are often diametrically opposed to those of the world. Their witness to Christ may arouse opposition, but they will not cave in to pressure to compromise. You can disagree with them and mistreat them, but they will not seek vengeance. They will pray for their enemies and trust them into God's hands, knowing He is able to protect His people and deal with their enemies. The world will be a better place where they have lived because they have stood for truth. They will not lie no matter how convenient or expedient it might be. Their word will be their bond, and you can trust what they say.

Perfected people will love the world just like God. The New Testament has a special word, *agape*, for God's love. The Lord gave me a glimpse of that incredible *agape* love early in my ministry, in fact, during the two months when my heart was cleansed and the Spirit released. I was awakened from sleep by a phone call early Sunday morning around 2 A.M., the last day of a renewal event at our church. The Spirit opened my heart during those days to see that I had not loved the people I was serving as God wanted me to do as their pastor. I had been judgmental and critical. I confessed that to them, which also led several of them to open their hearts to me to confess things not right. I was ready at that time in my life for what God would show me that night regarding His special love. When I arrived, I saw, to say it kindly, one of the most "unlovely" persons I have ever met. Her hair was disheveled, clothes appeared to have been slept in, and the cat nearby cringed as she motioned with her hand for me to be seated. The room reeked with alcohol and smoke. Soon she would fill the air with foul language, anger, and resentment toward relatives, God, the church, and ministers.

All the while she was spewing out what had been eating away at her from within, I kept feeling this incredible compassion for this tortured person. Even though everything about her tended to repulse, this amazing and unexpected love flowed from within me to her. I knew it was not of me. I knew that was Christ in me revealing His great love for the world as I saw it in operation toward this person. After about forty-five minutes, she began to wind down. I looked her in the face, calling her by her first name, and said, "God loves you, and so do I." She could tell that I meant it. I shared a little more, prayed with her, and invited her to the service that morning, but she did not come. She returned a few days later to the nearby town from which she had come and wrote me a month later that she was going to try God and the church one more time. We moved a short time after this so I do not know how things worked out. I do know that early that Sunday morning, we both saw God's special love in operation, a love beyond human capability. I became convinced then that no matter how unlovable a person may be, there is none beyond the reach of His grace. In the intervening years, I have fallen far short of that love revealed that night. As we willingly reach out, Jesus stands ready to supply what we lack and touch the world about us with His love expressed in kind deeds and words. Through such actions, the Holy Spirit forms within us the love and character of Christ.

Paul stood at the threshold of being perfected when he wrote to the Philippians. He writes about another characteristic that will be seen in perfected persons. They will be content in whatever situation God may place them. They do not need material things or to be at the center of attention. The words of an old hymn reflect their hearts: "Where he leads me I will follow." In the words of another hymn, they will "brighten the corner" wherever God leads. Listen to Paul's witness in Philippians 4:12 as he brightened the jail cell where he was confined. In prison, he lacks material comforts and provision. In addition, some Christians were preaching Christ motivated by "envy and strife" (Phil. 1:15) trying to make Paul feel bad (Phil. 1:16) while he was confined there in prison. Reflecting a heart that has been molded to love God and serve Him, Paul rejoices from prison that the cause of Christ is advanced regardless of the motive. Paul does not need the world's things for fulfillment and is content in his situation because he accepts what has happened as from the Lord. He tells us the secret of his contentment in Philippians 4:13. "I can do all things through Christ who strengthens me." All of Paul's trials have aided the sanctification process to form

Christlike character within and make Him utterly dependent upon Christ. He is ready for the completion of the Christlike nature within and to be spiritually raised by resurrection power.

Paul witnesses in Ephesians and Colossians that Jesus returned bringing the faithful to completion and raising them spiritually to heavenly places. Hebrews 11:39-40 told that the perfecting would occur together for the dead Hebrew faithful from past generations and the faithful of the apostolic generation. The next chapter in Hebrews reports this perfecting has occurred as we read about the joyful assembly on the heavenly Mount Zion consisting of "an innumerable company of angels," "the church of the firstborn," and "the spirits of just men made perfect" (Heb. 12:22-23). The sanctification process had indeed come to completion as the existence of "just men made perfect" attests. The blood of Christ proved sufficient.

John Wesley believed in such perfecting very early in his ministry. Years later, he summarized his teaching in "A Plain Account of Christian Perfection." He tells what he means by "one that is perfect."[6] He has the mind of Christ and walks as Christ walked. He is holy and loves God with all his heart and serves Him with all his strength. He loves his neighbor and every man as himself. He does not commit sin. Wesley defines sin as "a voluntary transgression of a known law."[7] He also understands that such perfection does not exclude "involuntary transgressions which I apprehend to be naturally consequent on the ignorance and mistakes inseparable from mortality."[8] Because of this understanding, Wesley never used the phrase "sinless perfection." "I believe, a person filled with the love of God is still liable to these involuntary transgressions."[9] Wesley and all who follow the pathway marked out by the apostles are like pioneers exploring new spiritual frontiers opened when Jesus returned. We have much to learn.

There are two major hurdles for any individual to come to perfection in this life. The first is faith, believing not only that it is possible, but also that God can accomplish this through the provisions of the New Covenant. Some persons are talking today about perfection and being Christlike, yet say that it is impossible in this life. This may discourage many to seriously undertake such a goal when it is believed to be unattainable. The New Testament makes clear that the apostles believed it was attainable and their writings witness that it occurred.

The second hurdle is more difficult and at the heart of the matter. As we shared earlier, our human nature wants no part of this and will fight it to the death. We must all decide if we are going to surrender completely to God and become the kind of people He intended from the first, who would love Him and obey Him. All God needs is our surrendered wills that no longer want to do it our way but to do it God's way. We each make that choice in our hearts. Once we have made that decision, we really become the kind of clay that our Creator can mold and shape as He wills. Let no one think that the pathway is easy. There will be bumps and bruises along the journey. There is great comfort, however, in the faith that we belong to One whose love we can trust. His disciplines come from the heart of a loving Father who is preparing us to not only take our place in His heaven, but to maximize the blessing that we can be on this earth to the people that we touch. He is fashioning the kind of people He will bring into spiritual union with His Son.

The Old Covenant with its law and animal blood was powerless to perfect those related to God. The descendants of the first Adam were in hopeless bondage. Jesus came as the Jewish Messiah to win a far more important victory than that of deliverance from the Roman armies. He came to deliver us from the penalty and power of sin that left us in bondage to death and the powers of darkness. Jesus, the unique God-man, met every temptation and was perfected through His last trial at the Cross, as He bore the penalty for our sin. He became the Second Adam thereby introducing a new life possible for us on this earth. To all who respond to the gospel, repenting of their sin, the Holy Spirit comes into their lives and works from the first to change them into the likeness of Christ, finally perfecting within responsive lives the same life present in Jesus, the same life that fills all of heaven. This is the pathway to bring heaven to this earth.

I want to close with one final word. When we say God intends to change us into the likeness of Christ, it does not mean that we shall have infinite wisdom and knowledge so as to never err in judgment or make mistakes. It does not mean that we shall do everything that Jesus did. Though we may come to share the kind of life that was in Him and possess hearts fixed in their desire to obey God, we shall still be so much less than He was. His existence did not begin when He was born to Mary. The Bible says that He was back at the beginning and all things were created through Him (John 1:3). In His prior existence in heaven as part of the Godhead, He possessed wisdom, knowledge, power beyond what we can even imagine. You and I prior to our conversion have had a brief existence on this earth as sinful human beings. As a result of those earlier years, we carry around in our unconscious a whole background of darkness and death reflecting the scars of past sin and the deep ruts of fears and bad habits. While we may experience inner healing as we mature, and be endowed with spiritual gifts with which to serve, we shall still be so much less than Christ who was part of the Godhead. When we say that God can make us like Christ, we do not mean that we shall walk on water or raise the dead. We mean that we can have while still on this earth perfected Christlike natures described by the words of Jesus prior to His death: "Not my will, but Yours be done." Jesus will gift us to serve Him in that part of the world where we live. If it is ever necessary to walk on water or raise the dead, He will enable us to do that. Apart from such special things to advance His kingdom, to be made like Christ simply means we can share the life perfected in Him while we still live on this earth. It means we shall use the spiritual gifts He gives us with a single desire to glorify God and to obey His will in all things.

Yes, you and I can be made like Christ in that regard, if we choose to cooperate fully with the Holy Spirit, submitting to the Lord's disciplines and dying out to our old nature. Just before the *Parousia* occurs in Revelation 14:14-16, we hear the words: "Blessed are the dead who die in the Lord from now on" (Rev. 14:13). Such dying in the Lord occurred during those second-coming days, and the same blessings await our discovery. We can pass through death in the sanctifying process and the final perfecting and be raised to heavenly places while we still live in the body on this earth according to the apostolic witness in the New Testament. Amazing discoveries await those who appropriate the experiential dimension of the Second Coming.

6

THE REAL ENEMY

Before proceeding with the chronology of the Second Coming, I want to discuss the graphic figures used in the Book of Revelation to describe our real enemies in the spiritual realm. The Second Coming was not only a time for rewarding the faithful among God's people, but also rendering judgment upon the powers of darkness who had rebelled against the authority of God. This chapter will help the reader to perceive what this writer understands the Bible to mean by the different references to these spiritual foes.

I can still remember my mother saying to me. "Now, Robert, there is a devil." I was in college and caught up in the intellectual pursuits at a secular university. Mother was raised in the home of a minister of the Evangelical Church, and my father was a minister in the Evangelical Church. The Bible was an important part of my upbringing, but the world had clearly made its impact upon my young life. "We can explain such things in different ways because of the advances in knowledge and learning." Mother was not convinced by my response but wise enough to let the matter drop. When the Spirit was released in my heart during the encounter with God back in 1964-65, I was drawn to the Bible with a new desire to learn about God's word for my life. Jesus' instruction about the devil caught my attention right away. I soon discovered it was no longer a matter of intellectual debate, but a reality I would have to learn to deal with as a result of the spiritual journey upon which I had now embarked. I am still learning.

The Bible tells us that there is a life and death struggle going on in the spiritual world about us and it impacts our lives whether we know it or not. The Bible reveals that there are angelic beings and demonic powers that oppose God's people on this earth. Paul attests to the presence of spiritual powers of evil and the resultant warfare. "For we do not wrestle against flesh and blood, but against principalities, against powers, against the rulers of the darkness of this age, against spiritual hosts of wickedness in the heavenly places" (Eph. 6:12). These spiritual beings do all in their power to keep us away from the living God who created us and redeemed us in His Son, Jesus Christ. Once we have turned to God, then they will work to keep us from God's word where we learn how to please Him, and from reaching up to God in prayer and meditation where we receive guidance and strength. The powers of darkness know that they are in trouble when God's people learn all that He has made possible through the Incarnation and Return of Jesus Christ and how to appropriate through faith and obedience this victory over sin, death, and the powers of darkness.

The Book of Revelation uses vivid imagery to portray these powers of evil. They were about to receive their just punishment for centuries of opposing God's good plan. During those last days, they would also have their finest hour, as God would grant them authority to accomplish great destruction during those days when God was transitioning from the old age under the Old Covenant to a new day under the New Covenant. John describes a ten-horned and seven-headed beast combining the features of a lion, bear, and leopard. This beast would be given authority over a 1,260-day period during the days of the Second Coming to blaspheme God, His Name, and His dwelling, to war against and conquer the saints, and to have authority over all peoples of the earth (Rev. 13:5-7). John tells us about a dragon that tempted people to sin against God and then accused them before God for the very behavior inspired by the dragon. The dragon gives its authority to this ten-horned and seven-headed beast (Rev. 13:4) destined to accomplish great evil during those days of wrath. John then tells about another beast that rises out of the abyss or bottomless pit. The ten-horned and seven-headed beast will give all its authority to this beast from the abyss (Rev. 13:12; 17:12-13) and the latter will exercise this during those once-and-for-all days. Finally, John describes a harlot whose activity lured kings and peoples of the earth into illicit sexual activity. Those wonderful and yet terrible days of the Second Coming were the time for not only rewarding the faithful but also punishing the powers of darkness that chose to rebel against the authority of their Creator. After exercising their authority for great evil upon the inhabitants of the earth, they receive God's wrath and punishment during those climactic days of the Second Coming. We shall look at what the Revelation tells us about these spiritual powers of darkness.

THE DRAGON (Satan)

The first creature is a red dragon. Revelation 12:9 calls it "that serpent of old" whose activity led to the fall of man. This same verse identifies the serpent, hence the dragon, as "Satan" or "the devil." The first three chapters in Genesis tell us about Satan's intrusion into our lives on this earth. God had good plans for us. He wanted to live in intimate fellowship with His creatures. The beauty of their original habitat was evidence of His love and power. He provided for all they needed. Their part was to obey their Creator. God told Adam he could eat the fruit of every tree in the garden with one exception. He was not to eat of the tree of the knowledge of good and evil. God made clear what would happen to Adam if he chose to disobey. Death would overtake him. Satan enters the picture. First he cleverly goes after Eve who heard about the command second hand from Adam. The serpent convinces her that she will not die. Satan was a liar from the first. He then appeals to her desires to taste the fruit. Satan's lies and her own desires led her to disregard God's command and Adam did likewise. They ate and they died. We have all followed in their footsteps.

In this way, Satan gained authority over the inhabitants of the earth. Revelation 12:9-10 describes him as "the accuser of our brethren" and the one "who deceives the whole world." The Bible exposes Satan as an utterly morally bankrupt spiritual being. His lies resulted in our rebelling against God and leaving us in hopeless bondage to sin, death, and the powers of darkness. No human being would have ever been able to overcome such obstacles if God had not intervened. Jesus came on that mission from the Father to teach the way of God's kingdom, demonstrate its miracle-working power, and then reconcile us to God through the Cross. Satan's efforts to thwart God's plan by tempting the sinless Son of God failed. Jesus carried out the plan successfully that issued in the New Covenant providing for the forgiveness of sin and the Holy Spirit. Victory over sin, death, and the powers of darkness was completed during the days of His Return.

TEN-HORNED, SEVEN-HEADED BEAST (Roman Empire)

Revelation 13:1-10 portrays a beast "like a leopard, his feet were like the feet of a bear, and his mouth like the mouth of a lion" (Rev. 13:2). Centuries earlier, Daniel had a dream about four beasts representing four nations to whom God would give the kingdom after taking it from His people Israel. They would be subject to these nations, the first being Babylon that destroyed Jerusalem in 588 B.C. The first three beasts are portrayed as a lion, bear, and leopard in Daniel 7:1-6. Conservative scholars identify them as Babylon, Media-Persia, and Greece.[10] The last beast is described as terrible and greater than the first three beasts, but not portrayed as a particular animal or identified as a particular nation. During the days of this fourth beast, Daniel tells us "the saints of the Most High shall receive the kingdom, and possess the kingdom forever, even forever and ever" (Dan. 7:18). In other words, the second-coming events would occur during the time of this fourth nation. When John sees in Revelation 13:1-10 a beast that looked like a leopard with the feet of a bear and the mouth of a lion (Rev. 13:2), this undoubtedly pointed to the fourth nation in Daniel's dream that would be greater than the previous three. Combining the features of Daniel's first three beasts all in one separate creature indicates that this nation is greater than its three predecessors, as the whole is greater than any of its parts. Rome fits such a description. It is also the logical choice as it follows Babylon, Media-Persia, and Greece as the next major power.

The beast in Revelation 13:1-10 has ten horns and seven heads. Revelation 17:10 talks about these and says the seven heads are also seven kings. "Five have fallen, one is, and the other has not yet come." The remainder of the verse tells us about the length of the seventh king's reign. "And when he comes, he must continue for a short time." If we take Julius to be the first emperor, this description perfectly fits the first seven Caesars who ruled over the Roman Empire.[11] The first five were Julius, Augustus, Tiberius, Caligula, and Claudius. Nero was the king ruling when John received the Revelation. Galba was the seventh, and according to the prophecy, ruled only a short time, about seven months.

If there are seven earthly kings, what do these ten horns on the beast represent? Revelation 17:12 tells us that the ten horns are also kings. Let us examine the following possibility: the ten horns represent angelic beings entrusted with authority regarding the Roman Empire. These would complement the seven human kings and together would comprise the ruling authorities of the Roman Empire, exercising its God-given authority as the last of four Gentile nations to whom God's people were subject because of their persistent rebellion against God's authority. These were the real ruling powers operating in the Roman Empire using the Roman emperor at the time.

The Book of Daniel supports this understanding in its witness to such angelic authority. Daniel 12:1 refers to the angel Michael as "the great prince who stands watch" over your people. Revelation 12:7 tells about Michael and his angels warring against Satan and his angels and casting them from heaven. Daniel 10:13 tells about "the prince of the kingdom of Persia" who resisted an angel for twenty-one days, preventing him from coming to Daniel. Michael aids the embattled angel in this heavenly conflict. We see in these verses that God granted angels authority over nations. Daniel tells us that his fourth beast is a fourth nation that has ten horns (Dan. 7:7). If this identification of the ten horns is correct, then these seventeen beings, ten angelic and seven human, represented the ruling authorities of the Roman Empire during the first seven Caesars, portrayed as this beast in Revelation 13:1-10. History attests to the greatness of this nation as it ruled the known world of its day. Figure 2 portrays this concept.

```
                    10 Horns
                (Angelic Beings)
         ▲ ▲ ▲ ▲ ▲ ▲ ▲ ▲ ▲ ▲

                     Beast 1
                  Roman Empire
               (Revelation 13:1-10)

                    7 Heads
                   (Caesars)

              ◊ ◊ ◊ ◊ ◊ ◊ ◊
```

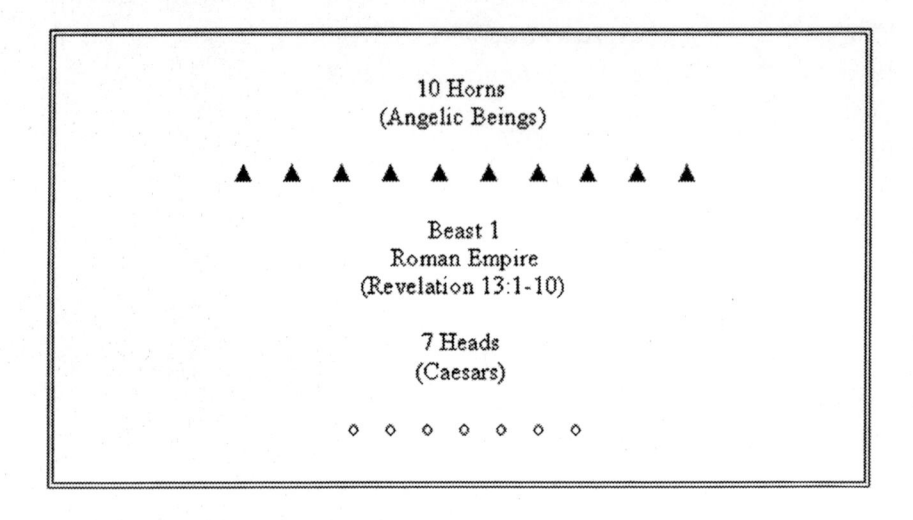

Figure 2 First Beast of Revelation Thirteen

John tells us in the Revelation that this beast will be given authority over a 1,260-day period for great destruction during the second-coming days. As referred to earlier in this chapter, Revelation 13:5-7 tells us that authority is given for the beast to blaspheme God, His Name, and His dwelling, to war against and conquer the saints, and to have authority over all peoples of the earth. This is beyond the authority given as the fourth nation of Daniel following in the line of Babylon, Media-Persia, and Greece. We shall see that such things did in fact happen at the conclusion of the apostolic generation during the years A.D. 66-70.

BEAST FROM ABYSS (*Apollyon*)

This beast emerges from the abyss at the fifth trumpet occasioning the first major woe. Revelation 9:11 calls him *Apollyon* or *Abaddon* which are the Greek and Hebrew words respectively for "destroyer." Revelation 17:8 describes him as the beast who "was, and is not, and will ascend out of the bottomless pit." "And is not" describes his period of confinement in the abyss removing him from any contact with this earth. For all practical purposes, he was non-existent with respect to this earth. We are not told what rebellion led to this banishment, but Jude and Genesis may provide a clue. "And the angels who did not keep their proper domain, but left their own habitation, He has reserved in everlasting chains under darkness for the judgment of the great day" (Jude 6). Genesis 6:1-2 may tell us about this rebellion against God's order of creation as "sons of God" left their domain as angels and chose to discover the delights of sexual love the Creator designed for human beings. Angels could take on human form. Two of the three men who appear to Abraham in Genesis 18 are identified as angels in Genesis 19:1. These angelic beings, led in the rebellion by *Apollyon*, may very well have been the ones confined to the abyss during the days of the flood because of their deliberate disregard and defiance of God's order in creation. The fifth trumpet sounded their imminent release and first major woe upon the earth.

Let me share up front my understanding about the unique relationship between this creature from the abyss and the Roman Emperor Nero. Then we shall look at the scriptural passages reflecting this. When *Apollyon* was released from the abyss, he went right for the most powerful figure in the world then, the Roman Emperor Nero. I believe he entered into and took possession of this central figure. Tacitus is probably reporting this very event when he tells us that prior to the burning of Rome in A.D. 64, Nero had entered a pagan temple to worship when a great trembling like seizures overtook him.[12] From this strategic position in the Roman emperor, *Apollyon* used all this power for destruction. Known for his depravity, a man who plotted the murder of his mother, Agrippina[13], Nero proved a suitable host for this creature from the abyss.

Revelation 13:18 identifies Nero as the human being involved in this diabolical relationship when the beast from the abyss is said to bear the human number of 666. As we saw in chapter 2, the numerical value of Nero Caesar written in Hebrew adds up to this precise total. Figure 3 portrays the relationship of *Apollyon* with Nero.

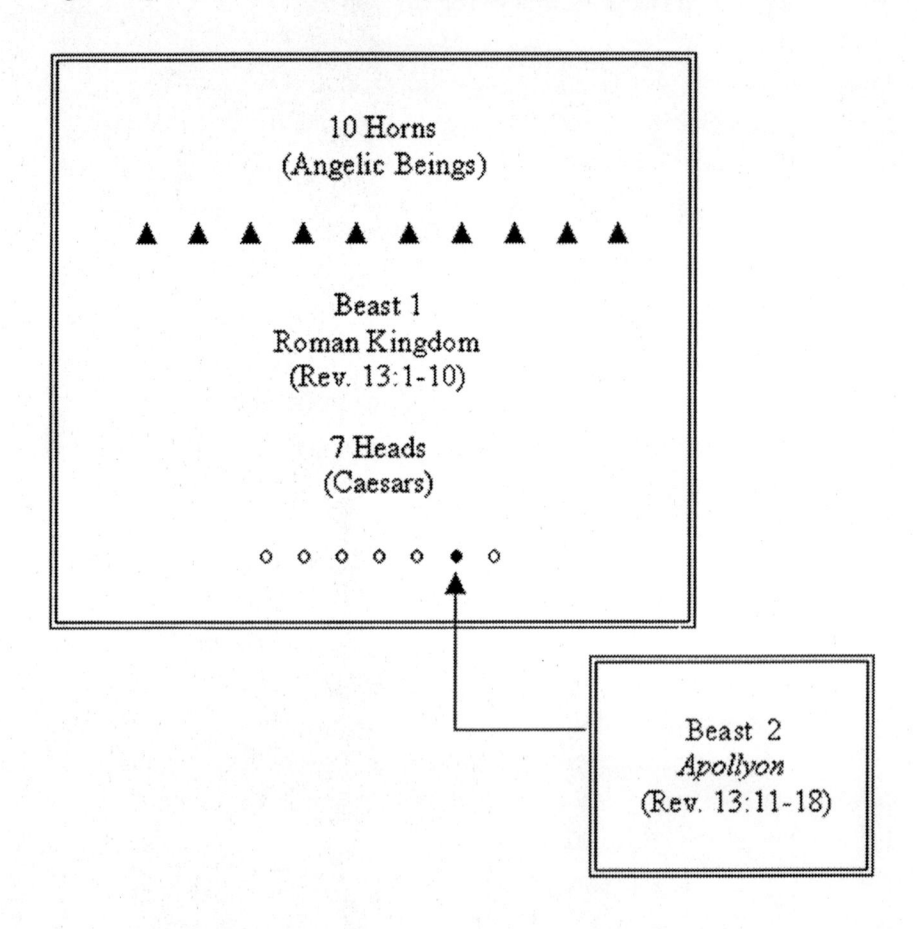

```
10 Horns
(Angelic Beings)

▲ ▲ ▲ ▲ ▲ ▲ ▲ ▲ ▲ ▲

Beast 1
Roman Kingdom
(Rev. 13:1-10)

7 Heads
(Caesars)

○ ○ ○ ○ ○ ● ○
```

Beast 2
Apollyon
(Rev. 13:11-18)

Figure 3 Relation between the Two Beasts of Revelation Thirteen

Revelation 17:11 refers to this creature from the abyss as an eighth king who belongs to the seven kings. This also witnesses to the unique relationship between *Apollyon* and one of the seven kings related to the beast portraying the Roman Empire. As a separate being, he is like an eighth king, but because he enters into Nero and takes possession of a king, it can be said that he belongs to the seven kings or Caesars. Daniel tells us that after the ten horns associated with the fourth beast or nation, another king arises who is different from the earlier ones (Dan. 7:24). "He shall speak pompous words against the Most High, shall persecute the saints of the Most High…for a time and times and half a time" (Dan. 7:25). I believe Daniel was prophesying about *Apollyon*.

Revelation 13:11-18 also describes *Apollyon* and his relationship with Nero. *Apollyon* persuades persons to make an image (*eikon*) for himself and the Roman Empire. I believe the Roman Emperor Nero was this image. Revelation 13:15 says *Apollyon* could give breath to the image of the beast, witnessing to this unique relationship between the two where Nero is used by *Apollyon* to advance his agenda for evil and harm. Colossians 1:15 refers to Jesus as the image (*eikon*) of the Father. Jesus was the one person on earth bearing His Father's nature and reflecting His life and ways. In somewhat similar manner, though not exactly the same, Nero was the image of *Apollyon* used to accomplish his evil purposes. There was an effort to deify Nero in A.D. 65,[14] probably inspired by *Apollyon* seeking to promote Nero as the image of the Roman Empire and of *Apollyon* himself. Without realizing it, Nero was being used in many different ways for purposes beyond his own understanding. Satan had given "his power and his throne and great authority" (Rev. 13:2) to the beast representing the Roman Empire. These ruling authorities of the Roman Empire then give all this authority to the beast from the abyss (Rev. 13:12). *Apollyon* through Nero used all this for great devastation during those last days of the old age.

Nero portrays what we would expect in a person possessed by this creature from the abyss. In addition to plotting the murder of his mother, Nero in a fit of temper kicked to death his pregnant wife Poppaea.[15] Historical records report about Nero and his sexual depravity immediately before the great fire at Rome in A.D. 64. The emperor provided banquets and entertainment using prostitutes and employing every vice imaginable. Tacitus describes one such event hosted by Tigellinus telling about all that took place at these occasions.[16] The burning of Rome occurs after this and popular opinion pointed to Nero as instigator of the fire so he could rebuild the city to his glory.[17] Nero blames the Christians and initiates their persecution.[18] Jesus while still on earth told His disciples that they would endure great persecution when He returned, and Nero initiated those days of suffering.

HARLOT (Babylon the Great)

A harlot portrays the fourth creature. Revelation 18:2 refers to her as "a habitation of demons, a prison for every foul spirit, and a cage for every unclean and hated bird." The harlot represents many evil spiritual creatures. She is the one "with whom the kings of the earth committed fornication, and the inhabitants of the earth were made drunk with the wine of her fornication" (Rev. 17:2). She is "drunk with the blood of the saints and with the blood of the martyrs of Jesus" (Rev. 17:6). These spiritual beings thrive upon enticing human beings into sexual sin and working toward the demise of God's people.

The Bible does not speak explicitly about the origin of such demonic powers that comprised the "harlot." They may have been the offspring of *Apollyon* and his hosts who joined themselves to women on earth and begot children who came to be called giants or Nephilim. We know that the souls of human beings went to *sheoul* at the time of the flood. *Apollyon* and his hosts were locked in the abyss. The souls of *Apollyon*'s descendants who perished at the flood would have been part human and part angel and for that reason perhaps not confined to *sheoul* or the abyss but left as disembodied spirits to roam the earth after the flood. Such an origin would account for their apparent sexual obsession and perversion.

These evil creatures located themselves about God's people on this earth in order to oppose God's work. We learn this from the different names she is given. She is called "Babylon the Great" in Revelation 17:5 while Revelation 11:8 refers to her as "the great city which spiritually is called Sodom and Egypt, where also our Lord was crucified." These verses report four of her locations in the past. The harlot situated herself at Sodom to oppose God's work during the days of Abraham. The harlot then moved to Egypt using that nation to enslave God's people and inflict all types of suffering and hardship upon the descendants of Abraham. She then moved to Babylon whence she takes her name, "Babylon the Great." In what may have been her crowning achievement, she led Israel and Judah to such covenant-breaking rebellion against God that He abandoned His people for a brief while (Is. 54:7-8). When the Messiah comes to the Jewish people, the harlot moves to Jerusalem, the place "where our Lord was crucified," again opposing the work of God. She was undoubtedly part of those evil spiritual powers behind the scene who crucify Jesus according to Paul in 1 Corinthians 2:8. Revelation 17:9 tells one further location for the harlot. "The seven heads [of the beast] are seven mountains on which the woman sits." Rome is built on seven hills. The harlot referred to as "the woman" here positions herself at the most strategic place on earth to oppose God's activity during the last days.

Revelation 13:10 admonishes its readers that these days call for patience and endurance and faith. Those first-century believers pass through tribulation contending with Satan, recently cast from heaven to earth, and struggling against *Apollyon*, recently released from the abyss. Satan gives his authority to the ruling powers of the Roman Empire (Rev. 13:2), and *Apollyon* exercises all of this for his own evil designs. The Revelation given to John prepares believers of that era to pass through the imminent terror. Chapter 13 opens their eyes to see the powers of evil unleashed in the world and operative through the existing power structure of the Roman Empire. Add to this the destructive and seductive ways of the harlot and we see why the Book of

Revelation was indeed a call to the saints for endurance and faith. It helped the Christians who passed through those terrible days to know that God was still in control and He would bring His faithful people successfully through those last days to their promised reward.

7

THE CHRONOLOGY OF DANIEL'S SEVENTIETH WEEK

I remember years ago having a dream where I was reading the front page of a newspaper. Near the bottom of the page was an inconspicuous article entitled: "The Second Coming has happened." It reported that Daniel provided important time intervals for understanding the chronology. That prompted me early in this venture to look at the Book of Daniel. Up to that time, I had not paid much attention to this Old Testament book that I would discover is the key to providing a chronological framework for the second-coming events.

Daniel tells about Seventy Weeks of Years in 9:24-27. This amazing prophecy links Hebrew history in the fifth century B.C. with an event occurring during the first coming of the Jewish Messiah, our Lord Jesus Christ. Sixty-nine weeks of years elapse between these two events, where each week of years represents seven years, amounting to 483 of what we might call prophetic years. This prophecy is fulfilled if we take Artaxerxes' decree in 444 B.C. to restore and rebuild Jerusalem during the time of Nehemiah and Jesus' appearance in the temple at Jerusalem on Palm Sunday in A.D. 33 as these events. The former begins the period of the first sixty-nine weeks, and then concludes with Jesus' appearance in the temple at Jerusalem on Palm Sunday. We shall look at this in the next paragraphs. Following a gap in time after the first sixty-nine weeks of years, the Second Coming occurs during the Seventieth Week or the last seven-year period.

Daniel and Revelation are sometimes called the apocalypses of the Bible. They both report the fulfillment of God's promises to His people through the prophetic word. As we look carefully at the description of time, it becomes clear that they are based upon what we might call a prophetic year consisting of 360 days where each year has twelve months consisting of thirty days each. God tells us in His word that powers of evil would be given authority during the last days to shatter "the power of the holy people" over a period of time consisting of "a time, times, and half a time" (Dan. 12:7, 7:25). The Hebrew word here for "times" is not the usual plural form but what is called the "dual number" thereby designating specifically "two times" or a total of three-and-one-half times in Daniel's unusual way of expressing this time interval. Revelation 13:5 describes this same period of time when powers of evil are given authority during the last days in a second way by referring to it as forty-two months. Revelation 12:6 and Revelation 12:14 report another way of expressing this interval of time in Daniel. The length of the woman's wilderness sojourn is described in the latter verse as "time, times and half a time" while the former describes this same interval of time as lasting 1,260 days. This tells us that Daniel's "time" consists of a 360-day year where the twelve months each have thirty days. The Bible employs these three ways of describing this three-and-one-half-year period: a time, times and half a time, forty-two months, and 1,260 days. Only with such a 360-day year can you account for 483 years between 444 B.C. and A.D. 33, the times of the two events fulfilling the prophecy. In terms of a 365-day year, you have around 477 years.

Daniel tells us about the terminal points for the first sixty-nine weeks of years or 483 prophetic years. "Know therefore and understand, that from the going forth of the command to restore and build Jerusalem until Messiah the Prince, there shall be seven weeks and sixty-two weeks." (Dan. 9:25). Artaxerxes' decree (Neh. 2:1-8) to restore and rebuild Jerusalem in 444 B.C. began this prophetic time period. Jesus knew Palm Sunday was that day climaxing Daniel's sixty-nine weeks of years. He was Messiah the Prince, Daniel's "Anointed One," and that was the long-awaited day for His "visitation" in Jerusalem and the temple as their King, the descendant of David and heir to his throne.

Jesus found a donkey upon which to ride fulfilling another sign to help people understand the significance of that day and its fulfillment of Old Testament prophecy. Zechariah had written "Behold, your King is coming to you; He is just and having salvation, lowly and riding on a donkey" (Zech. 9:9). Jesus came on that appointed day to Jerusalem and its temple. The crowds greeted Him on Palm Sunday singing His praises: "Blessed is the King who comes in the name of the Lord!" (Luke 19:38) Even the stones would have cried out in praise, if the people had been silent, for that was God's chosen King coming to Jerusalem that day, the One who would receive the kingdom and reign forever. Rather than rallying around God's chosen One, the Jewish leaders turned their Messiah over to be crucified before the end of the week, also foretold in the same prophecy where it says the "Messiah shall be cut off" (Dan. 9:26). Knowing the destruction that lay ahead for Jerusalem because it was not ready to receive its promised King on the day prophesied for His appearance, Jesus wept over the city because "you did not know the time of your visitation" (Luke 19:44).

Jesus' Palm Sunday appearance as God's Anointed One signaled the end of this sixty-nine weeks of years that began during the time of Nehemiah with the decree to restore and rebuild Jerusalem. Believing we still live in the time gap between Daniel's sixty-ninth and seventieth weeks, many conservative scholars still await the Seventieth Week of Daniel when the second-coming events will occur, a gap now amounting to nearly two thousand years. There was a time gap of about thirty years giving those of the apostolic generation time to mature and spread the gospel prior to Jesus' promised Return that occurs during Daniel's Seventieth Week at the conclusion of the apostolic generation. Let us proceed now to reconstruct Daniel's Seventieth Week and see that it did indeed occur at the conclusion of the apostolic generation. I cannot emphasize enough how much easier it is to understand when the prophecies were fulfilled and how the prophetic time intervals fit in history when you look back "after the fact." It becomes a matter of carefully examining the prophecies or time intervals and correlating them with the corresponding events that took place in the historical records.

Daniel only spoke about the three-and-one-half-year period of the authority of powers of evil that would occur during Daniel's Seventieth Week. In addition to this same period, John also tells us in the Revelation about another three-and-one-half-year period when two witnesses would be granted authority to prophesy and minister God's word so that the faithful could appropriate the promises made through the prophets. These two periods basically comprised the seven-year period of Daniel's Seventieth Week. Let us look at these two significant periods.

PERIOD OF AUTHORITY OF BEAST PLUS SEVENTY-FIVE DAYS

Daniel talked about how powers of evil would be given authority for a three-and-one-half-year period during the last days. They would be permitted to "speak pompous words against the Most High" and "persecute the saints of the Most High" who would be given into the hands of this power of evil (Dan. 7:25). The power of the holy people would be "completely shattered" (Dan. 12:7) during this period pointing to the ending of the Old Covenant that bound the living God to the Jewish people. John describes these powers of evil as a ten-horned and seven-headed beast identified in the previous chapter as the Roman Empire and its ruling authorities consisting of ten angelic beings and the Roman emperor on earth at the time. It had already been exercising God-given authority as Daniel's fourth nation. This 1,260-day period for desolation went beyond this. During the last days, it was permitted to blaspheme God, corrupt the worship at His temple, and persecute

His people (Rev. 13:6-7). Satan would grant all of his authority to this beast, and then *Apollyon* upon rising form the abyss would be permitted to use all of this for great desolation.

Daniel provides us additional information about this significant period. "And from the time that the daily sacrifice is taken away, and the abomination of desolation is set up, there shall be one thousand two hundred and ninety days" (Dan. 12:11). This interval of time can be related to history because the Jewish historian Josephus provides the precise date for the ending of the continual burnt offering. He lived through those last days at Jerusalem when the Roman armies besieged the city during the prophesied three-and-one-half-year period. Josephus tells us the continual burnt offering ended on *Tammuz* 17, A.D. 70, or July 13, A.D. 70.[19] The authority of the abomination that causes desolation would begin 1,290 days earlier on January 1, A.D. 67 according to Daniel 12:11. We know that this came first as his activity will lead to the corruption of the worship of God at the temple, the ending of the continual burnt offering, and finally the destruction of the temple by the Gentiles.

I believe the author of abominations and desolation at the temple in Jerusalem (Dan. 9:27) is John's "beast from the abyss" or *Apollyon*. According to Revelation 13:12, he exercises all the authority of the ten-horned and seven-headed beast representing the ruling authorities of the Roman Empire. Daniel 9:27 tells us "in the middle [half] of the week He shall bring an end to sacrifice and offering." The Hebrew word translated "middle" is better translated "half." This is the same Hebrew word used in 1 Kings 3:25 referring to Solomon's threat to divide a baby and give "half" to each of the women claiming to be the infant's mother. Daniel is simply saying that during the half of the Seventieth Week when authority is granted for great evil, this abominable desolating activity will bring about the end of the sacrifices at the temple in Jerusalem (Dan. 9:27). The continual burnt offering commanded by God under the Old Covenant, being only temporarily disrupted during the days of Antiochus Epiphanes, would end 1,290 days after the authority of the powers of darkness begins. The temple and the city would be destroyed and the Old Covenant would come to an end. The New Covenant would remain and be the basis for God relating to the inhabitants of the earth in the future, open to both Jew and Gentile.

Daniel 12:12 gives another time interval. "Blessed is he who waits, and comes to the one thousand three hundred and thirty-five days." I believe this may point to what was originally the grand climax for the faithful. The result of their waiting and enduring would be great blessing. There appears to be a logical progression in these dates presented in Daniel 12:11-12 beginning with the time when evil is granted authority for desolation during those last days. The other time intervals extend from this point. We know from Daniel and the Revelation that this authority for such evil will last forty-two months or 1,260 days. Daniel 12:11 tells us his activity brings the daily sacrifice to an end 1,290 days later. With the ending of the priestly activity that is always essential for God to relate to people in covenant, the destruction of the temple and the city followed shortly thereafter. Daniel 12:12 then tells us that blessed will be those who wait and come to the 1,335th day. This anticipatory waiting and the resultant blessing suggest that this date was originally the appointed time of the grand climax for God's people when His promises made through the prophets would be fulfilled. Figure 4 displays this information.

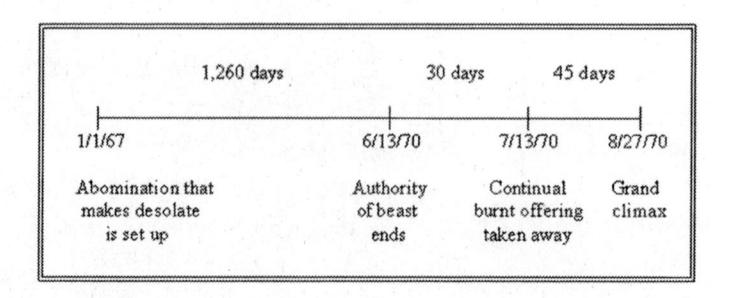

```
        1,260 days         30 days    45 days
   |-----------------------|----------|----------|
  1/1/67                 6/13/70    7/13/70    8/27/70

  Abomination that       Authority  Continual   Grand
  makes desolate         of beast   burnt offering climax
  is set up              ends       taken away
```

Figure 4 Period of Authority of Beast plus Seventy-Five Days

PERIOD OF TESTIMONY OF THE TWO WITNESSES

Revelation 11:3 speaks of another time interval as two persons prophesy and witness for 1,260 days, the same length of time allotted for the authority of the powers of darkness. Two people stand out in the New Testament record in this regard. They were Peter and Paul. God chose Paul as His spokesman for the gospel to the Gentiles, and Peter served that function to the Jewish world. Paul says this in Galatians 2:7 where he writes, "They saw that the gospel for the uncircumcised had been committed to me, as the gospel for the circumcised was to Peter." This final witness about Jesus' Return concludes their ministry on earth by preparing the saints to receive their reward during those last days. The writings of the two witnesses account for nearly two thirds of the New Testament. Paul and Peter together wrote sixteen letters (assuming Paul's authorship of Hebrews) and the Gospels of Luke and Mark probably find their inclusion because of their association with Paul and Peter. Their ministry also comprises most of the Acts of the Apostles. These two persons stand out clearly in the early church as the two witnesses for the Jewish Messiah during those last days of the old age. Revelation 11:3 tells us their period of testimony during the last days would continue for 1,260 days. This period preceded the Period of the Authority of the Beast who would be permitted to kill the witnesses after they finished their testimony according to Revelation 11:7.

DANIEL'S SEVENTIETH WEEK

Daniel's Seventieth Week consisted of seven 360-day years. This 2,520-day period when the prophecies were fulfilled, contained both the Period of the Testimony of the Two Witnesses and the Period of the Authority of the Beast with the former coming first. If we assume Daniel's Seventieth Week concluded on the 1,335th day of Daniel 12:12, and began with the 1,260-day Period of the Testimony of the Two Witnesses, then we must overlap the two 1,260-day periods by seventy-five days. This is because the grand climax of "the blessed" occurring on the 1,335th day came seventy-five days after the conclusion of the 1,260-day Period of the Authority of the Beast. Figure 5 portrays these facts.

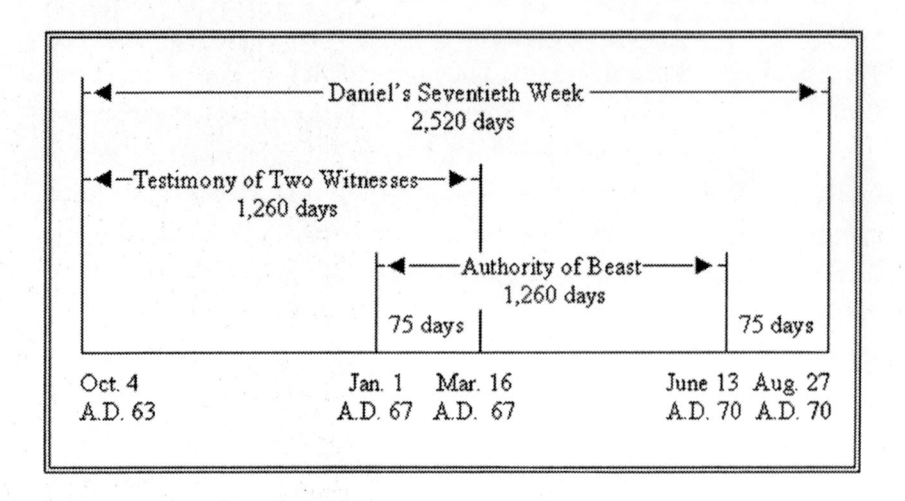

```
|◄─────────── Daniel's Seventieth Week ───────────►|
                    2,520 days

|◄──Testimony of Two Witnesses──►|
          1,260 days

                        |◄─────── Authority of Beast ───────►|
                                    1,260 days
                        | 75 days |                          | 75 days |

Oct. 4                  Jan. 1    Mar. 16              June 13    Aug. 27
A.D. 63                 A.D. 67   A.D. 67              A.D. 70    A.D. 70
```

Figure 5 Daniel's Seventieth Week

This overlap illustrated in figure 5 enables both 1,260-day periods and the additional seventy-five days leading to the original grand climax for "the blessed" to all be contained in the 2,520-day period of Daniel's Seventieth Week. We shall see in the remainder of this chapter and book that these assumptions are validated by what happened in history. This arrangement also places the beginning of Daniel's Seventieth Week on October 4, A.D. 63, the day after "the great day" concluding the celebration of the Feast of Booths in that year. As we shall soon see, this is an appropriate date in the providence of God to begin this climactic seven-year period when the second-coming events would occur.

REVIEWING THE CHRONOLOGY

Let us review this prophetic reconstruction of Daniel's Seventieth Week containing both 1,260-day Periods of the Testimony of the Two Witnesses and of the Authority of the Beast. Figure 5 summarizes this chronology resulting in five dates. The key date enabling us to relate this to a historical framework is a sixth date of July 13, A.D. 70 when the continual burnt offering ended. Josephus dates this *Tammuz 17, A.D. 70* that corresponds to July 13 as detailed in the Appendix. The following review will also show how this chronological framework fits with the historical events fulfilling the prophecies.

The first date is January 1, A.D. 67 when the beast's authority for desolation began. We arrive at this date as a result of Daniel 12:11 where the prophet writes: "And from the time that the daily sacrifice is taken away, and the abomination of desolation is set up, there shall be one thousand two hundred and ninety days" (Dan. 12:11). The activity of this power of evil results in ending the continual burnt offering along with other destruction witnessed to by Josephus who was there. Moving back in time 1,290 days from the key date of July 13, A.D. 70 when the continual burnt offering ended brings us to January 1, A.D. 67 when the beast's authority for great evil began. This is the very time when Nero commissioned Vespasian to begin the campaign against the Jews in Judea. The abominations also began at the temple this year.

The second date is June 13, A.D. 70 when the authority of the beast for desolation ended. Daniel 12:7 and 7:25 tells us this authority lasted for a "time, times, and half a time." We saw earlier in this chapter that this amounts to 1,260 days. Moving ahead this length of time from January 1, A.D. 67 brings us to June 13, A.D. 70, the time when the authority of the beast ended. We have seen and shall look further in this book at the evil accomplished by the powers of darkness in this regard as Jerusalem and the temple were turned over for destruction during those last days. Though the authority of the beast ended on June 13, the momentum of the evil already taking place carried over with the ending of the continual burnt offering thirty days later, and then the destruction of the temple and the city in the weeks ahead.

The third date is August 27, A.D. 70 for what we have called the original date for the grand climax. Just after telling us 1,290 days separate the end of the continual burnt offering and the beginning of the Period of the Authority of the Beast, Daniel writes: "Blessed is he who waits, and comes to the one thousand three hundred and thirty-five days" (Dan. 12:12). There appears to be a progression in these time intervals originating from the beginning of the Period of the Authority of the Beast. I believe this 1,335th day was the original grand climax for the saints. As we shall see later on in this book, that actual climax, the Day of the Lord, occurred earlier just as Jesus taught in Matthew 24:22 and Mark 13:20. God shortened those terrible days for the sake of the elect. In the original time framework according to Daniel, the grand climax was to be the 1,335th day and blessed were those attaining to it. Advancing forward 1,335 days from January 1, A.D. 67, the beginning point for the other two time intervals, brings us to August 27, A.D. 70, the original day for the grand climax and the conclusion of Daniel's Seventieth Week.

The fourth date is October 4, A.D. 63 when two significant prophetic periods began. Daniel's Seventy Weeks of Years resumed with the beginning of the Seventieth Week. Remember that Daniel's prophecies are based upon a prophetic year consisting of twelve months of thirty days each. Daniel's Seventieth Week consists of seven such years amounting to 2,520 days. Assuming that Daniel's Seventieth Week ends with the 1,335th day of the original grand climax or Day of the Lord, we then move back 2,520 days from August 27, A.D. 70. This brings us to October 4, A.D. 63. It is interesting to note that October 4, A.D. 63 is the day after the great day of the Feast of Booths held during *Tishri*, the seventh Jewish month. This would be an appropriate day in the plan of God to begin Daniel's Seventieth Week. The Feast of Booths celebrated the harvest season toward the end of the year. The Second Coming would occur during Daniel's

Seventieth Week at the conclusion of the apostolic generation culminating in a harvest of the saints when they would come into the Divine inheritance.

This fourth date of October 4, A.D. 63 also marked the beginning of the Period of the Testimony of the Two Witnesses. This is based on the assumption that this period started at the beginning of Daniel's Seventieth Week and was followed by the authority of the beast who would be permitted to kill the two witnesses. Peter and Paul would begin their final period of testimony to prepare the saints for the great spiritual harvest when Jesus would be revealed and manifest His glory in the faithful. John would have just received his vision during *Tishri* A.D. 63 that we shall discuss later in this book.

The fifth date is March 16, A.D. 67 when the testimony of the two witnesses ended. Just as the Period of the Authority of the Beast would last for 1,260 days, so likewise would the "Period of the Testimony of the Two Witnesses." Going forward in time from October 4, A.D. 63 we come to March 16, A.D. 67. With the beast's authority beginning on January 1, A.D. 67, we see these two periods overlap by seventy-five days. As shared earlier, this was because the original grand climax occurred seventy-five days after the Period of the Authority of the Beast. In this way, the ending of the continual burnt offering and the original grand climax are included in Daniel's Seventieth Week as prescribed by Daniel's time intervals. Again, history bears witness to the accuracy of this time line. As we shall see later on in this book, historical records date the martyrdom of Peter and Paul in A.D. 67 prior to Nero's death in A.D. 68. They would have completed their testimony on March 16, A.D. 67 and have been martyred sometime after that.

Daniel 8:14 presents one more time interval consisting of 2,300 days during which a power of evil will be loosed in the world to carry on his destruction. It is not necessary for determining the chronological framework of Daniel's Seventieth Week, yet it provides helpful information that we will discuss briefly. The activity of this evil power will result in the end of the daily sacrifices, the rebellion that causes desolation, and the surrender of the sanctuary and of the host that will be trampled underfoot (Dan. 8:13). Daniel 12:11 refers to this creature as the abomination that makes desolate and is undoubtedly *Apollyon* of Revelation 9:1-11. If we assume that August 27, the last day of Daniel's Seventieth Week, also concluded this 2,300-day time interval and that it began with Apollyon's release from the abyss, then moving back 2,300 days brings us to May 11, A.D. 64. History verifies the accuracy of this assumption. The persecution of the Christians would begin the latter part of A.D. 64. Then abominations at the temple in Jerusalem with the desecration of the worship of God, the ending of the continual burnt offering, and the destruction of the temple would all occur in this time period. The activity attributed to this power of evil occurred during this 2,300-day time interval from May 11, A.D. 64 through August 27, A.D. 70.

We shall bring this all together in the chapter entitled, "Daniel's Seventieth Week As It Happened." There we shall see that the exact time intervals provided by the prophet Daniel furnish us with an accurate chronological framework to understand the events of the Second Coming and interpret the historical events that occurred in history from A.D. 63 through A.D. 70. We are greatly helped in dating many of the New Testament writings when we know the time for the final three-and-one-half-year period of Peter and Paul's testimony, the time for the three-and-one-half-year period for the powers of evil to accomplish great destruction, and the date of the seventh trumpet. We are also helped by the internal evidence from the letters such as theological content, current events, references to seasons of the year, locales where Paul is staying, has been, or is going. I believe the reader will see that the New Testament writings in addition to saying that Jesus would return also witness that He did return in this climactic period when Old Testament prophecies came to fulfillment as the faithful received the inheritance.

Daniel reports in 2:21 that God was changing the times and the seasons. Israel had broken covenant with their Lord, and God was changing the way in which He would do business with this earth in the future. The Old Covenant limited to the Jewish people would give way in the future to the New Covenant that would be open to Jews and Gentiles. The lunar calendar operating among the Jewish people during the days of the Old Covenant would give way to a new solar calendar introduced by the Roman Emperor Julius. God would institute a new prophetic calendar consisting, as we have seen, of 360 days thereby simplifying the understanding of the prophecies about what God would be doing as He planned for these future changes.

New seasons would emerge centering around the Jewish Messiah. Christians under the New Covenant came to celebrate the birth of the Messiah, the unique God-man, through the Advent season and Christmas. Centuries later, the calendar would recognize Jesus' birth by separating all of history into those years before Christ and those years of our Lord. The Passover and Feast of Unleavened Bread would give way to Good Friday and Easter celebrating the death and Resurrection of the Messiah. The Feast of Weeks would give way to Pentecost celebrating the Messiah's pouring out of the Holy Spirit to all who enter into the New Covenant. It remains to be seen as the Body of Christ awakens to what it means to live in a world where Jesus has returned whether some new celebrations may arise related to those events associated with the third festival season for the Jewish people. What for Daniel was a future vision regarding the changes of times and seasons that God was instituting is for us an exciting reality where God has provided for victory over sin, death, and the powers of darkness.

During the years of transition from the Old Covenant to the New Covenant, God took the kingdom away from Israel and gave it to four nations in the years ahead: Babylon, Media-Persia, Greece, and Rome. God used Babylon to carry out judgment upon Israel for years of breaking the covenant. The Babylonians destroyed the temple and the city and carried the people away into captivity. God used the kings of Media-Persia to return the people to their homeland, rebuild their temple, and restore the City of Jerusalem. God used the Greeks to introduce the most precise language of the day and perhaps in all of history. With the spread of Greek culture through the conquests of Alexander the Great, the Greek language came to be used throughout the world. Despite Rome's conquest of the world, the Latin language had not replaced the Greek language during the New Testament period. As a result, the important writings of the New Testament would be in Greek optimizing through the translation process the transmission of the original meaning intended by the writers to all succeeding generations. Then God would use the Roman Empire with its military might and pride in law and justice to provide the best conditions possible back then to withstand the onslaught of the powers of darkness and their lawless ways as the first Christians would take the gospel out into the pagan world prior to the Return of Jesus. We read in the Acts of the Apostles time and again about how Paul was spared from angry crowds by Roman officials. Then God would use the Roman armies to render judgment upon covenant-breaking Israel with the destruction of the temple and Jerusalem. God thus used these four nations during this time of transition when the kingdom was taken away from Israel under the Old Covenant and before it would be restored to the faithful, Jews or Gentiles, under the New Covenant during the days of Jesus' Return when He received the kingdom and would reign forever.

8

THE PERIOD OF THE SEVEN TRUMPETS

Let us see if we can determine a chronological pattern for the seven trumpets in the Book of Revelation. Chapters 8, 9, and 11 of Revelation report seven trumpet blasts with corresponding events. The last three trumpets, according to Revelation 8:13 and 9:12, occasion three major woes upon the earth. The magnitude of such events prompts us to begin our search here. At the fifth trumpet, angels release from the abyss the beast and his hosts who inflict suffering for five months. Revelation 13:7-15 tells about his further activity in persecuting the Christians. Revelation 17:16-17 may imply the beast also causes the burning of Rome that precedes the persecution. The sixth trumpet sees the release of four angels empowered to kill one-third of mankind. At the seventh trumpet, Michael and his angels defeat the devil and his hosts, casting them forever out of heaven.

We discover historical occurrences corresponding to these events in just the right sequence. The fifth trumpet announces the imminent release of the beast from the abyss whose activity will lead to the persecution of Christians and perhaps the burning of Rome. Tacitus tells us that on July 19, A.D. 64 fire breaks out in Rome and destroys a good part of the city.[20] When suspicion points to Nero as instigator of the fire, he diverts attention away from himself by blaming the Christians and initiating their persecution. They were arrested, thrown to wild animals, and burnt alive as torches.[21] Though Christians were misunderstood and despised by the Roman populace, believers came to be pitied as they were seen to be victims of the emperor's cruelty.

Next, we look for an epidemic or plague causing many deaths. The sixth trumpet introduces the second major woe with the release of four angels destined to slay one-third of mankind (Rev. 9:13-19). Tacitus describes a devastating plague sweeping through the vicinity of Rome during A.D. 65 and killing all ranks of people and leaving houses filled with dead bodies and streets with funerals.[22] Suetonius reports that 30,000 deaths were recorded at an ancient temple resulting from a plague that struck one autumn.[23] While he does not specify the year, it occurs around this time in his history of Nero, probably referring to the same prophesied plague. The historical records of the sixties again provide the kind of information predicted by the Revelation given to John. Early in this investigation, my initial timeline estimates pointed to this year as the time for this massive plague to have struck. I can still remember the very day when I went to the library stacks and opened Tacitus' records for this year. There was the forecasted plague. I stood there in a kind of silence, further convinced that I was being led upon the right trail.

We then come to events related to the seventh trumpet. War breaks out in heaven as angels cast Satan and his hosts to earth. While this occurs in heavenly regions, Josephus relates a strange event observed by persons in A.D. 66 prior to the beginning of the war with the Romans. It sounds incredible to us, and seemed incredible to Josephus. Could this be a rare glimpse into some part of this heavenly warfare not normally seen by human eyes?

> Besides these, a few days after that feast, on the one-and-twentieth day of the month Artemisius, [Jyar,] a certain prodigious and incredible phenomenon appeared; I suppose the account of it would seem to be a fable, were it not related by those that saw it, and were not the events that followed it of so considerable a nature as to deserve such signals; for, before sun-setting, chariots and

troops of soldiers in their armour were seen running about among the clouds, and surrounding of cities.[24]

This is consistent with the Old Testament understanding as heavenly messengers rode in chariots. One took Elijah to heaven (2 Kings 2:11) and Elisha saw chariots bearing heavenly hosts coming to his rescue (2 Kings 6:17). After Michael and his angels cast Satan from heaven, Revelation 12:13 says the devil pursues a woman. As we shall see in chapter 11 of this book, she represents the Jewish Christians. The attack begins at the point of her origin at Jerusalem. Revelation 12:14 says the woman flees from Satan to safety in the wilderness. Eusebius says the Christians flee the doomed city in A.D. 66 prior to the war. They go to Pella in the wilderness where they wait until their Lord comes to take them off the earth. Figure 6 presents these historical events on a time line.

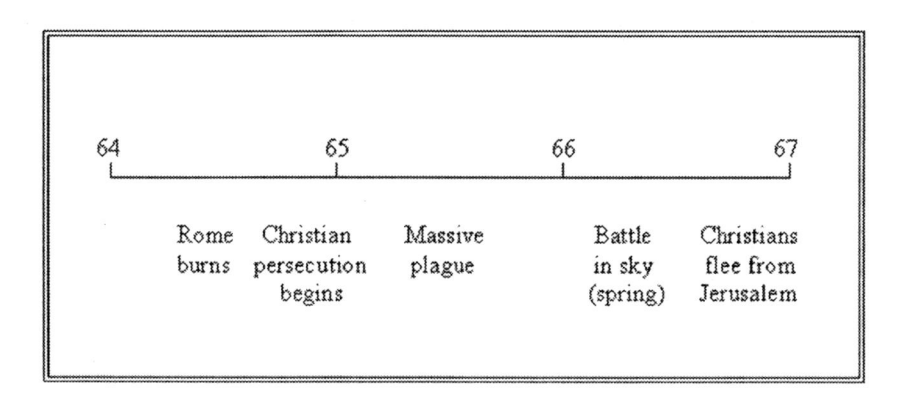

64	65		66	67
Rome burns	Christian persecution begins	Massive plague	Battle in sky (spring)	Christians flee from Jerusalem

Figure 6 Historical Events Related to Last Three Trumpets

Not only are there historical events reflecting these woes associated with the last three trumpets, when we lay this out on a time line, we see that these events occur about a year apart. The Feast of Trumpets, an annual Jewish festival observed during the harvest season in the fall, is the logical date for the time when these trumpets sounded. We shall see the rationale for this in the next chapter. Let us therefore assume that the trumpets occur on *Tishri* 1, the date for the Feast of Trumpets, during seven consecutive years. Based on the data, the seventh trumpet would have occurred on *Tishri* 1, A.D. 65, the sixth trumpet on *Tishri* 1, A.D. 64, and so on to the first trumpet blast on *Tishri* 1, A.D. 59. The Jewish month of *Tishri* corresponds to our September or October.

This does not mean the event related to each trumpet necessarily happens on the exact date of the trumpet blast. Rather, the period of time begins when the prophesied events would take place. The Book of Revelation talks about "the days of the sounding [trumpet] by the seventh angel" (Rev. 10:7) when the mystery of God announced to the prophets would be fulfilled. This means the seventh trumpet would begin the period when the mystery of God would occur. According to this hypothesis, the events corresponding to a particular trumpet would take place on Tishri 1 or during the days following the trumpet. Figure 7 summarizes this hypothesis for the seven trumpets.

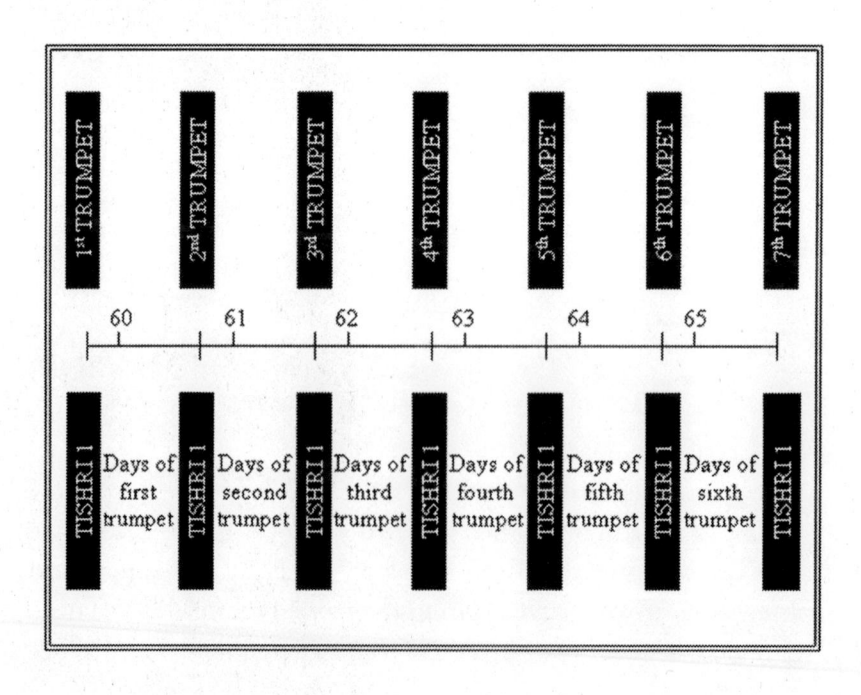

Figure 7 Hypothesis for Time Framework of the Seven Trumpets

Let us go over our hypothesis again as it relates the Book of Revelation to the historical events that occurred back then. The days of the fifth trumpet would begin on *Tishri* 1, A.D. 63 and would include the days following. As we saw in the last chapter, the beast from the abyss is released on May 11, A.D. 64 that would take place during these days of the fifth trumpet. His prophesied activity includes persecuting the Christians that begins sometime after the burning of Rome that started on July 19, A.D. 64.

Tacitus tells about a plague that strikes during A.D. 65 and Suetonius likewise reports a massive plague around this same time as we saw earlier. The days of the sixth trumpet would begin on *Tishri* 1, A.D. 64 and would include the days following in A.D. 65 when the plague struck. It is the kind of event predicted by the Book of Revelation as many persons die as a result of the woe associated with this trumpet blast.

The days of the seventh trumpet would begin on *Tishri* 1, A.D. 65 and would extend into A.D. 66. Early in His reign, Jesus sends Michael and the righteous angels to engage Satan and his hosts in heavenly warfare resulting in the latter being thrown down from heaven to earth. Josephus reports a strange event that could be this heavenly warfare in the spring of A.D. 66 that would place it during the days of the seventh trumpet. Satan then pursues the woman in Revelation 12. In this same year Jewish Christians flee Satan's wrath as they abandon the doomed City of Jerusalem and go to a refuge in the wilderness.

The first four trumpets occasion minor events, less apparent and sometimes not easy to understand. Yet it is interesting to note the following observations. The first trumpet would sound in the fall of A.D. 59 with hail and fire mixed with blood thrown on the earth, resulting in a third of the earth, grass, and trees being burnt (Rev. 8:7). Tacitus says that the Roman armies suffer during the summer of A.D. 60 because of the blazing heat, shortage of water, and inadequate food.[25] As a result of the second trumpet that would sound in the fall of A.D. 60, "A third of the sea became blood" and "a third of the living creatures in the sea died" (Rev. 8:8-9). Tacitus reports around this time a strange incident where the ocean appeared to be like blood and the likeness of human forms were seen as the tide ebbed.[26] This may have nothing to do with the second trumpet, but it is interesting to observe that it is recorded at this time. Many strange events indeed took place during those last days.

The seven trumpets sounded the time of God's judgment upon the hosts of heaven and the human race. The last three trumpets occasioned three major woes. In the midst of all the suffering and persecution, Peter and Paul encouraged and guided the faithful to the climax of the prophetic promises. Just after reporting the woes associated with the Second Coming, Luke inspired by the Holy Spirit writes the following encouraging words for the faithful. "Now when these things begin to happen, look up and lift up your heads, because your redemption draws near" (Luke 21:28). The time of judgment was also the time of reward for the saints. The faithful in Christ welcomed those last days that brought about the fulfillment of God's promises for His people. The prophetic countdown would have begun in the fall of A.D. 59 with the sounding of the first trumpet and would have climaxed during the days of the seventh trumpet begun in the fall of A.D. 65. Though figured independently, the reader will see that this hypothesis for the seven trumpets fits well with the chronology of Daniel's Seventieth Week. The Period of the Testimony of the Two Witnesses would span the time of the three major woes related to the last three trumpets. In the midst of all the persecution and suffering associated with the last days, the two witnesses would be guiding the faithful to their promised reward.

9

FOUR SIGNIFICANT DAYS OF ATONEMENT

From the time of Adam and the first sin, human beings were banished from the Divine Presence according to the Bible. For a while during the Old Testament period, that Presence dwelt in the midst of ancient Israel over the Ark of the Covenant in the Most Holy Place behind the veil separating the rest of the tabernacle or temple from the Most Holy Place. The sacrifices offered on the Day of Atonement (*Yom Kippur*) made this possible. On that special day, the Jewish high priest would enter the Most Holy Place and make atonement for the sins of the people. The people did not enter that Presence. The high priest alone could do that on this one day only after first making atonement for his own sins. This Day of Atonement made it possible for the Divine Presence to dwell in the midst of ancient Israel. That was as close as human beings ever got after our first ancestors sinned against God.

Jesus came on a mission to save us from sin, so at long last we could be restored to the Divine Presence. At the conclusion of His life on earth, He died for our sin and initiated a New Covenant providing for cleansing from sin and the gift of the Holy Spirit. He returned at the conclusion of that generation to complete the faithful and raise them into the Divine Presence in heaven. Finally, persons from this earth were again permitted to live in the presence of their Creator who had been there in the Garden of Eden where it all began.

The last book in the Bible reports this climax to Christian faith and experience. What our first ancestors lost through sin was regained during the Second Coming. It is interesting to observe that four times in the Revelation given to John, he reports seeing heaven opened leading into the Divine Presence seated upon the throne (4:1, 11:19, 15:5, 19:11). After Revelation 4:1, a door is opened in heaven and John is taken up before the throne to receive the Revelation. Heaven is again opened in Revelation 11:19 right after the seventh trumpet sounds when the mystery of God is fulfilled and those completed in Christ are raised spiritually before the throne while still dwelling in a body on earth. Heaven is opened again in Revelation 15:5 as the climactic Day of the Lord takes place with the pouring out of God's wrath (Rev. 15:6-16:21), the viewing of its effects upon Babylon the Great (Rev. 17:1-18:24), and the rejoicing of the saints invited to "the marriage supper of the Lamb" (Rev. 19:1-10). This was the grand climax of the biblical prophecies as the faithful were raised from the dead with a new body and Christlike nature and brought into the Divine Presence to live forevermore. Heaven is once again opened in Revelation 19:11 as the armies of heaven come forth from the throne to engage in the final battle of Armageddon and inflict upon the powers of darkness their just punishment.

I believe these four references to the opening of heaven where dwelt the Divine Presence point to four separate Days of Atonement during the decade of the sixties. This will help in the chronology of the second-coming events as recorded in Revelation. The Epistle to the Hebrews tells us that Jesus was a far superior High Priest who entered before the presence of the Father in heaven with His own blood, a far superior sacrifice, that took care of all sin for all people for all time. This made it possible for Jesus our Lord from heaven to come at the trumpet and be joined to His bride and then raise her into the presence of the Father before the throne in heaven. The power released in this world through the priestly ministry of Jesus, His efficacious blood, and the sanctifying work of the Holy Spirit prepared the faithful for this climax to Christian faith and experience. I believe the Jewish Day of Atonement was the day during particular years in the decade of the sixties when heaven was at long last opened for persons to enter the Divine Presence. This provides an important key to understand the chronology of second-coming events.

Let us look at the Jewish feasts of which the Day of Atonement was a part. There were three annual festivals for the Jewish people: the Feast of Unleavened Bread (Passover) in early spring, the Feast of Weeks (Pentecost) in late spring, and the Feast of Booths in the fall. The Day of Atonement was part of the third Jewish festival. The first two festivals provided dates for significant events related to Jesus' first coming. He was crucified and rose from the dead during the time of the Feast of Unleavened Bread, and He poured out the Holy Spirit during the second festival, the Feast of Weeks. This leads us to look to this third festival related to the fall harvest to provide dates for the Second Coming when Jesus returned to reap a spiritual harvest of the saints now ripened and matured. The Day of Atonement was one of three events observed during the seventh month of *Tishri* as part of the third Jewish festival. The Feast of Trumpets occurred first on *Tishri* 1 followed by the Day of Atonement on *Tishri* 10. These were followed by the time of rejoicing with the celebration of the Feast of Booths during *Tishri* 15-22. These three events comprised the third of three festivals observed annually by the Jewish people. Table 1 summarizes this information.

Table 1 Three Annual Jewish Festivals

Feast of Unleavened Bread	Feast of Weeks	Feast of Booths
(Spring of the Year)	(50 Days Later)	(Fall of Year)
Month of *Nisan*		Month of *Tishri*
14 – Passover		1 – Feast of Trumpets
15-21 – Feast of Unleavened Bread		10 – Day of Atonement
		15-22 – Feast of Booths

The Scripture points to parallels between the Old Testament feasts and significant events in Jesus' life. The Feast of Unleavened Bread in the spring with the Passover and Waving of the First Fruits celebrated God's delivering His people from Egyptian slavery related to the Old Covenant. Jesus delivered us from our bondage to sin through His Crucifixion and Resurrection that took place at the time of the events associated with the Feast of Unleavened Bread as He instituted the New Covenant. The second Jewish festival, the Feast of Weeks, during early harvest was the time to remember how God had blessed them and make freewill offerings to the Lord (Deut. 16:10). One of those blessings was His faithful provision for their physical needs as witnessed by the manna gathered in the wilderness and the crops harvested in the Promised Land. Jesus poured out the Holy Spirit at the time of this festival witnessing to His provision for the spiritual needs of His people as they made their spiritual journey, not to the physical Land of Canaan, but to the spiritual land of the Divine Presence on the heavenly Mount Zion.

The Feast of Booths in the fall celebrated God's meeting His people after deliverance from Egypt and taking them through the wilderness into the Promised Land of Canaan. It was a time for rejoicing (Lev. 23:40) as they remembered how the Lord had blessed them in their harvest and in all the work of their hands (Deut. 16:14-15). It was a time to remember that God commanded the people to live in booths for seven days so all future generations "may know that I made the children of Israel dwell in booths when I brought them out of the land of Egypt" (Lev. 23:43). They were totally dependent upon God's mighty hand for deliverance from Egypt and making their journey through the wilderness. They needed to regularly remember that. The events that were part of the third Jewish festival season associated with the fall harvest provide dates for the second-coming events when Jesus would return to meet His people and with a mighty hand climax their spiritual journey by raising them into the Promised Land of the Divine Presence. They would learn to dwell not in booths but in the Divine

Presence into which they were raised at the Return of Jesus. Let us look at the significance of the three events that were part of this third festival season during the seventh month of *Tishri*: the Feast of Trumpets, the Day of Atonement, and the Feast of booths.

The Feast of Trumpets was held on *Tishri* 1. It is described in Leviticus 23:23-25 and Numbers 29:1-6. The people made proper offerings and abstained from work making it a day of rest. We are not told about the significance of the feast in these passages, but we do know about the significance given to the trumpet at that time. A loud trumpet announced the Lord's coming to meet the people at Mount Sinai. "When the trumpet [ram's horn] sounds long, they shall come near the mountain" (Ex. 19:13). Moses was then permitted to go up the mountain into the Divine Presence where he received the Ten Commandments along with other instruction regarding the people's part in the covenant, making it possible for God to dwell in their midst. When they were ready to leave Sinai and begin their journey to the Promised Land, God gave a lasting ordinance about the priests blowing the trumpet in the future. "When you go to war in your land against the enemy who oppresses you, then you shall sound an alarm with the trumpets." (Num. 10:9). God assures that He will hear and give His people victory over their enemies as would be evidenced at the future battle at Jericho. The trumpet was used to announce the coming of the Lord, prepare for battle, and appeal to God for help. The seventh trumpet sounded in Revelation 11:15 announced the Return of Jesus for His people when He would raise the faithful in a mystery so they would be able to dwell in the Divine Presence while still on earth. It also was a call to battle the powers of darkness and overcome in God's strength, much like the Israelites would have to overcome hostile people and claim their Promised Land. Though no trumpet is mentioned in Revelation 14:14-16 regarding the later event of the *Parousia*, I believe it also occurred on the Feast of Trumpets during that particular year. It announced Jesus' coming to remove His people prior to receiving their final reward of the glorified body and entrance into the marriage supper of the Lamb.

The Day of Atonement was observed on *Tishri* 10. When God met the people at Mount Sinai, He spelled out the importance of this day in order for a holy God to dwell in the midst of an unholy people. After making the appropriate sacrifices for himself, the high priest would enter into the Most Holy Place on this one day, the Day of Atonement, to make the necessary sacrifices in order to atone for the sins of the people. Jesus served as our High Priest going into the very temple in heaven where dwelt the Divine Presence and with His own blood securing many benefits for His people. The climax of what Jesus made possible for the faithful while they were still on earth would be the mystery of a spiritual resurrection that would enable the faithful to live in the Divine Presence.

I believe this Jewish Day of Atonement was the day when heaven was opened and persons were raised into the Divine Presence on high during those last days. First, John was raised there to receive the remainder of the Revelation. Second, the faithful of the apostolic generation were spiritually raised there at the seventh trumpet as part of a great mystery while still on earth witnessed to especially in Ephesians, Colossians, and Hebrews. Third, the Day of the Lord occurred when God's wrath was poured out and the resurrected faithful who were taken from the earth at the *Parousia* entered the marriage supper of the Lamb where they would dwell forever in heaven.

The Feast of Booths celebrated during *Tishri* 15-22 was a time of rejoicing before the Lord their God (Lev. 23:40). They were to be joyful in Him because of God's blessing "in all your produce and in all the work of your hands" (Deut. 16:15). They were to remember how God made them dwell in booths as He brought them on that journey through the wilderness into their Promised Land of Canaan. They were totally dependent upon Him not only for deliverance from Egypt but also for survival in the wilderness and then claiming the Promised Land. The Feast of Booths was a time for rejoicing during those second-coming days as God brought to fulfillment the promises made to the prophets. At long last, descendants of Adam were admitted again into the Divine Presence, now to dwell there forevermore.

We saw in chapter 7 that Daniel's Seventieth Week began in the fall of A.D. 63 just after the autumn feast events. This leads us to look to those events as the time when John received the Revelation. God's purpose would be to alert the church that Daniel's Seventieth Week was about to commence when the Old Testament prophecies would be fulfilled. In addition, as John records the Revelation, he twice refers to the imminence of the release of the beast from the bottomless pit (Rev. 11:7, 17:8) indicating that John received the Revelation shortly before this. The persecution of the Christians, activity attributed to the beast, began in A.D. 64 following the burning of Rome in July of that year. This also supports John's receiving the Revelation in the fall of A.D. 63. It would be prior to the release of the beast from the abyss and just before the beginning of Daniel's Seventieth Week.

The chronology of the "Period of the Seven Trumpets" in the previous chapter presents the basis for determining that the seventh trumpet sounded on *Tishri* 1, A.D. 65. Hence, the second Day of Atonement would have occurred on *Tishri* 10, A.D. 65 when the mystery of God was completed in the faithful. Jesus then comes to remove the faithful from the earth during the time of the autumn festivals in A.D. 68. The key to this dating is based upon Revelation 17:10 that talks about seven kings associated with the last (Roman Empire) of Daniel's four nations to whom God subjected His people. We discussed this in the chapter dealing with "The Real Enemy." We saw that Galba was the seventh and last king mentioned because the saints are removed during his brief reign from July A.D. 68 to January A.D. 69. The departure of the saints during the *Parousia* in A.D. 68 would have removed the Jewish faithful from this world and ended the time of subjectivity to Daniel's four Gentile nations for the remnant of God's people. It is easy to determine the last Day of Atonement when the Battle of Armageddon began, as there is only one more occurring within the period of Daniel's Seventieth Week. That took place during *Tishri* A.D. 69. We shall see that history reflects what the Revelation describes. Daniel's Seventieth Week would be concluded just before *Tishri* A.D. 70.

Figure 8 summarizes this information following which we shall examine how this hypothesis works. We shall see if the order of these four Days of Atonement and what is taking place in the Book of Revelation fits with the witness of the epistles of the New Testament and the historical records.

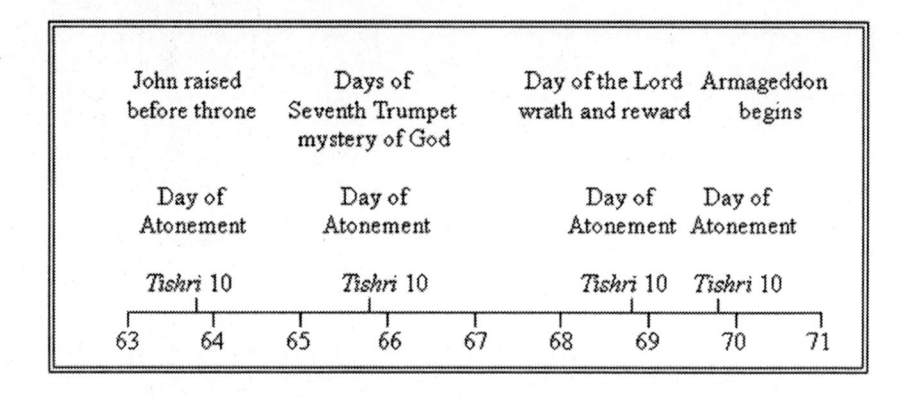

```
John raised         Days of           Day of the Lord   Armageddon
before throne    Seventh Trumpet     wrath and reward     begins
                  mystery of God

  Day of            Day of              Day of          Day of
Atonement         Atonement           Atonement       Atonement

 Tishri 10         Tishri 10           Tishri 10       Tishri 10
    |                 |                   |               |
----+-----+-----+-----+-----+-----+-----+-----+-----+
   63    64    65    66    67    68    69    70    71
```

Figure 8 The Years of Four Significant Days of Atonement

Now let us look in more detail at each of these years when heaven was opened remembering the key that *the Day of Atonement was that day when heaven was opened for these special events related to the Second Coming during these particular years in the decade of the sixties.*

JOHN RECEIVES THE REVELATION—*Tishri* A.D. 63

Authorities imprisoned John on Patmos, an island in the sea west of Ephesus. Jesus appears to His disciple during this month of *Tishri*. I believe John received the Revelation during two separate occasions. Jesus reveals Himself to John there in his cell on Patmos and gives him messages for the seven Asian churches. "After these things" (Rev. 4:1) suggesting a later time, John is taken out of his cell before the throne in heaven where the remainder of the Revelation unfolds as God reveals to His servant the events that are about to transpire.

Feast of Trumpets, *Tishri* 1, A.D. 63

Jesus appears to John as "One like the Son of Man" (Rev. 1:13) resplendent in glory. John simply tells us that the voice he hears at first is like "a trumpet" (Rev. 1:10). I believe this points to the very day, the Feast of Trumpets on *Tishri* 1, when John sees this vision of the glorified "Son of Man." The trumpet announces the visit from the Lord who manifests Himself to John as recorded in Revelation 1:12-20 and gives counsel to the angels of the seven Asian churches. "And I have the keys of Hades and of Death" (Rev. 1:18). The promises are about to be fulfilled when Jesus will deliver His people from this deadly prison. This would have been the fifth in a series of seven trumpets and announced the first of three major woes to accompany the last three trumpets.

First Day of Atonement, *Tishri* 10, A.D. 63

Just nine days later, heaven is opened to John and he is taken up before the throne where he receives the remainder of the Revelation. "After these things [the vision of Jesus and His counsel for the angels of the seven Asian churches] I looked, and behold, a door standing open in heaven" (Rev. 4:1) and John is raised into the Divine Presence. John soon observed that in the midst of the throne there stood "a Lamb as though it had been slain" (Rev. 5:6). This scene portrays Jesus who has served not only as John's sacrifice for sin but also as his High Priest. The Epistle to the Hebrews likewise points out that Jesus has opened the way into the Divine Presence through His high priestly ministry. Before John returns to his prison cell on Patmos, he will have been shown what is about to occur in heaven and on earth during the imminent second-coming days. He will then write about the seven seals, the seven trumpets, and the seven bowls of God's wrath and all that will soon happen in fulfillment of the prophetic promises. John concludes the Revelation with a vision of the new heaven and earth that will result from all of this.

Feast of Booths, *Tishri* 15-22, A.D. 63

This would be the last Feast of Booths to be observed before Daniel's Seventieth Week would begin. This would initiate the time when the prophetic promises would be fulfilled and the faithful would be raised up before the throne and the Divine Presence. The Feast of Booths in A.D. 63 would have ended with the great Day on *Tishri* 22, or October 3 (see table 2) of that year. Daniel's Seventieth Week would have begun on October 4 indicating the accuracy of the dating. The first sixty-nine weeks of years in Daniel's prophecy about Seventy Weeks of Years ended with Jesus' entrance into Jerusalem on Palm Sunday just before His Crucifixion. Now, just after the Revelation of Jesus Christ given to John, Daniel's prophecy resumed with the beginning of Daniel's Seventieth Week. The Feast of Booths was a time of rejoicing and in this particular year, John and any others privy to what he had learned rejoiced because the waiting period was over. Daniel's Seventieth Week was about to begin when Jesus would return to fulfill the promises.

THE MYSTERY OF GOD—*Tishri* A.D. 65

Paul refers to this trumpet in 1 Thessalonians 4:16 and 1 Corinthians 15:52. The latter also tells about a mystery to occur at this time when both the dead and those on earth will be changed "in the twinkling of an eye." This is the first great and wondrous sign (Rev. 12:1) in Revelation and describes the spiritual resurrection for the perfected faithful while yet on earth when Jesus returned. This mystery remains to this day to be appropriated by the faithful.

Feast of Trumpets, *Tishri* 1, A.D. 65—Seventh Trumpet

The seventh trumpet sounds in Revelation 11:15 announcing the long-awaited coming of the Lord. Loud voices in heaven proclaim: "The kingdoms of the world have become the kingdom of our Lord and of His Christ, and He shall reign for ever and ever." At this last of the seven trumpets, Jesus takes authority over this earth. Revelation 11:18 tells us that this was the time to "reward Your servants the prophets and the saints, and those who fear Your name, small and great" (Rev. 11:18). We know from 1 Thessalonians 4:16 and 1 Corinthians 15:52 that Jesus raised the dead at this trumpet. We have also seen from 1 Corinthians 15:52 that those on earth undergo a change at the same time "in the twinkling of an eye," along with the dead in Christ. Hebrews 11 confirms that the Old Testament faithful were perfected at the same time as those of the apostolic generation. This was the trumpet when God raised the dead and at the same time perfected the faithful on earth as part of this great mystery. We shall be looking more in the next chapters at this victory to which those faithful of the apostolic generation came during those days when Jesus returned.

The kingdom of God operated in this world under the kings in ancient Israel. Because of the disobedience of the kings to the rule of God over their lives, there was very little evidence of the power of God's kingdom in their midst. Some of that power was in evidence during the times of King David who did obey the Lord. God promised David that the Messiah would be born to his line and this Messiah would receive the kingdom and reign forever. Daniel foresaw those days.

> "I was watching in the night visions, and behold, One like the Son of Man, coming with the clouds of heaven! He came to the Ancient of Days, and they brought Him near before Him. Then to Him was given dominion and glory and a kingdom, that all peoples, nations, and languages should serve Him. His dominion is an ever-

lasting dominion, which shall not pass away, and His kingdom the one which shall not be destroyed." (Dan. 7:13-14)

Satan was in the position of authority over this earth during the days that God's kingdom was present in the midst of ancient Israel under the terms of the Old Covenant. At the seventh trumpet, Jesus received the kingdom that had operated in Israel under David and the other kings, but Jesus' government extended throughout the entire earth. He also replaced Satan who came into his authority over the earth as a result of our rebellion against God through sin. Now the kingdom was in the hands of God's choice extending over the whole earth, and He would reign forever.

Second Day of Atonement, *Tishri* 10, A.D. 65— Mystery Completed

"Then the temple of God was opened in heaven, and the ark of His Covenant was seen in His temple" (Rev. 11:19). The Ark of the Covenant shows that God is about to act in fulfillment of the promises He made during the days of the Old Covenant through the prophets. This Ark of the Covenant in heaven, in contrast to the one on earth, was where Jesus came as our High Priest with His own blood to secure an eternal redemption.

Just after heaven is opened, John sees a great and wondrous sign (Rev. 12:1). This is part of God's great mystery. The angel told this to John as recorded in Revelation 10:7. "But in the days of the sounding of the seventh angel, when he is about to sound, the mystery of God would be finished, as He declared to His servants the prophets." This first "great and wondrous sign" seen in Revelation 12:1-6 portrays this mystery and the victory to which those first faithful came. We shall look more at this mystery in chapter 11, "God Has an Exciting Mystery to Reveal." It reveals how those first saints were raised into the Divine Presence. This victory opened to disciples of Jesus at the seventh trumpet is the key to bringing heaven to this earth, possible because we live in a world where Jesus has returned.

Feast of Booths, *Tishri* 15-22, A.D. 65

This festival was a time of rejoicing for the Jewish people as they celebrated God's bringing them through the wilderness into the Promised Land. The faithful Christians would have been celebrating a similar fulfillment of promises through the New Covenant. While the Christian's final Promised Land would be in heaven where they would go after removal at the *Parousia*, now, as a result of the mystery of God, they were now celebrating their entrance into the Promised Land of the Divine Presence while still on earth. They also would have to learn to dwell in that spiritual tabernacle of the Divine Presence while they continued on their journey through this sinful and evil world. They would have to claim that spiritual ground by overcoming spiritual foes just as Israel had to defeat physical enemies to claim their Promised Land.

Jesus spoke of this in John 15 regarding the branch abiding in the vine, and Paul speaks of this in Ephesians and Colossians where he counsels those "raised with Christ" to "set your mind on things above, not on things on the earth" (Col. 3:1-2). This first "great sign" (Rev. 12:1) is the basis for bringing heaven to earth, because it describes the victory possible while still in a body. Paul was looking into the future and the glorious implications for this when he wrote to the Ephesians. God "raised us up together [with Christ] and made us sit together [with Christ] in the heavenly places in Christ Jesus, that in the ages to come He might show the exceeding riches of His grace in His kindness toward us in Christ Jesus" (Eph. 2:6-7). We today have access to the same discoveries made by the apostolic generation when Jesus returned.

PAROUSIA AND DAY OF THE LORD—*Tishri* A.D. 68

The prophets spoke about a future day when God would reward the saints and punish the wicked. This Day of the Lord would occur during the days of the Second Coming when the Messiah would return to render such judgment upon the opponents of God and reward the faithful. Originally intended to take place on the 1,335th day of Daniel 12:12 at the conclusion of Daniel's Seventieth Week, God shortened the days for the sake of the elect, moving the grand climax of the Day of the Lord to this Day of Atonement in A.D. 68.

Feast of Trumpets, *Tishri* 1, A.D. 68 – *Parousia*

I believe the two events in Revelation 14:14-20 took place on this *Tishri* 1 in A.D. 68 since they occur prior to the Day of Atonement indicated in Revelation 15:5 when heaven was opened. Though no trumpet is mentioned in the Revelation in conjunction with these events, the Feast of Trumpets preceding the Day of Atonement would be the logical time. The sounding of trumpets announced the coming of the Lord as He would remove His faithful from the earth (Rev. 14:14-16) and place unfaithful Israel in the great winepress of His wrath (Rev. 14:17-20). These two events prepare the way for the Day of the Lord to occur on the Day of Atonement when the grand consummation of the promises will take place.

Revelation 14:14-16 tells us about the first event. John sees "One like the Son of Man" seated upon a cloud wielding a sickle to gather in the ripe harvest. In what the New Testament calls the *Parousia*, Jesus removes the faithful, likened to a reaper gathering in His ripe crop, where they now receive the glorified body. This is the date envisioned by Paul in 1 Thessalonians 4:17 when Jesus comes with the dead who were previously resurrected at the trumpet and takes the faithful off the earth at which time they also receive the resurrection body. Jesus said these were like the days of Noah (Luke 17:26-27). After Noah entered the ark, the rains came. After the faithful were taken off the earth at the *Parousia*, God's wrath would be poured out shortly thereafter on the Day of the Lord.

Revelation 14:17-20 tells us about the second event on *Tishri* 1 when Israel is thrown into "the great winepress of the wrath of God." Psalm 80 likens God's people to a vine. "You have brought a vine out of Egypt; you have cast out the nations and planted it" (Ps. 80:8). Israel represented God's vine on this earth as He bound Himself through the Old Covenant to His people and lavished His love upon them. The people spurned His love and broke the covenant. God warned them through the prophets about His judgment if they rejected their Lord. Those dire prophecies were now about to take place. The covenant-breaking and Messiah-rejecting people are likened to grapes upon that vine and are cast into the winepress of the Divine wrath (Rev. 14:19). Daniel foretold this time when "the power of the holy people" would be "completely shattered" over a three-and-one-half-year period (Dan. 12:7). The beast from the abyss, whose authority began January 1, A.D. 67, had already by this time been at work corrupting the worship of God at the temple. Roman armies were in position to finally destroy Jerusalem and its temple. Things were now ready for the Day of the Lord when God's wrath would be poured out upon the powers of darkness and judgment would come upon the Jewish people.

Third Day of Atonement, *Tishri* 10, A.D. 68—Day of the Lord

John sees another great and marvelous sign (Rev. 15:1). He views the seven angels with the seven plagues of God's wrath, and the faithful just harvested from the earth standing beside the sea of glass (Rev. 15:2) and singing the song of Moses (Rev. 15:3). The angels have not yet delivered the wrath and the saints have not yet entered the marriage supper of the Lamb which we shall hear about after the fact in Revelation 19:7. Everything is now ready for the grand climax which for the sake of the saints was moved from August 27, A.D. 70 to this time in A.D. 68. So terrible were those days that God shortened them for the sake of the elect.

In Revelation 15:5, the temple in heaven is again opened and the seven angels proceed out of the temple to pour out God's wrath upon the earth in final judgment. John describes this in chapter 16 and then tells in chapters 17 and 18 about what this means for Babylon the Great who had corrupted the earth since the time of the flood. After describing the rejoicing in heaven (Rev. 19:1-6), John tells us that the saints have entered the marriage supper of the Lamb, though the actual entrance is not portrayed (Rev. 19:7-9). Here perfected people with glorified bodies exist in the Presence of the Lord God Almighty and the Lamb forever more. The Day of the Lord on the Day of Atonement in A.D. 68 and its results are described in Revelation 15:5-19:10 with God's people receiving their full reward and the powers of evil receiving their judgment with the outpoured wrath of God.

Feast of Booths, *Tishri* 15-22, A.D. 68

The previous Feast of Booths in A.D. 65 saw God's people celebrating the spiritual resurrection associated with "the mystery of God" as they entered into the Tabernacle of the Divine Presence as a result of resurrection power raising up those perfected in Christ. Now the saints were rejoicing as they had received the glorified body to go along with the completed Christlike nature and dwell in a heaven purged of all powers of evil. The Bridegroom and His bride now had begun to share in the marriage supper of the Lamb where they would dwell eternally in the presence of God, the Father, Son, and Holy Spirit. Here they were sitting with Abraham, Isaac, and Jacob at the heavenly banquet prepared for the Jewish elect and the expanded gathering including the faithful "of all nations, tribes, peoples, and tongues" (Rev. 7:9). The Feast of Booths in A.D. 68 witnessed to this heavenly celebration as the faithful finally enjoyed the complete fulfillment of the promises as they celebrate in heaven the marriage supper of the Lamb. The journey begun when first betrothed to Christ at conversion was now complete as Jesus returned and brought them, now as His bride, into their Promised Land of heaven.

ARMAGEDDON—*Tishri* A.D. 69

In ancient Israel, when a young man got married, he was exempt from any military involvement for one year to enjoy His wife (Deut. 24:5). As we continue through the chronology of Daniel's Seventieth Week, this appears to be the case with Jesus and His bride. Jesus returned in A.D. 68 and removed the remainder of the faithful, His bride, from the earth as it continued under the 1,260-day Period of the Authority of the Beast. After enjoying the marriage supper of the Lamb for one year, on the next Day of Atonement, *Tishri* 10, A.D. 69, John again sees heaven opened and Jesus emerges with the armies of heaven ready to engage in the final battle of Armageddon and begin their millennial reign. While this battle would carry over upon the earth through the Gentile armies converging upon Jerusalem, yet the primary importance of Armageddon took place between heavenly combatants. The armies of heaven defeat the powers of darkness and render final judgment upon those eternally rebelling against God's authority.

Feast of Trumpets, *Tishri* 1, A.D. 69

This trumpet signaled the alert for the great and final battle of Armageddon when Jesus and the armies of heaven go forth with the authority to carry out God's final judgment upon His spiritual enemies. They would be confined forevermore in the lake of fire. God's wrath had already been poured out at this point, but there would be more. Those who had deliberately disobeyed the living God and persisted in their rebellion would burn eternally in the lake of fire. There would be no escape as the sentence was irrevocable. The beast and the false prophet were about to receive their just punishment. The armies of heaven were ready to carry out God's sentence.

Fourth Day of Atonement, *Tishri* 10, A.D. 69

After the marriage supper of the Lamb in Revelation 19:7-9, John sees heaven opened for the fourth and last time, signaling another Day of Atonement, and ushering in the last mighty acts from heaven to complete the prophecies concerning Daniel's Seventieth Week, and the establishment of all things. Heaven is opened before John and he sees a white horse with a rider who is called "Faithful and True" (Rev. 19:11). Written upon His robe is "KING OF KINGS AND LORD OF LORDS" (Rev. 19:16). "And the armies in heaven, clothed in fine linen, white and clean, followed Him on white horses" (Rev. 19:14). The marriage of the Bridegroom and bride had been celebrated for a year. Now it was time to march to battle and take care of unfinished business in the plan of God.

The powers of darkness had headed for the showdown as usual by opposing God's work on earth, and so they had converged upon the City of Jerusalem, the site of the Old Covenant and the ministry of the Jewish Messiah. "And I saw the beast, the kings of the earth, and their armies, gathered together to make war against Him who sat on the horse and against His army" (Rev. 19:19). This described the scene in the fall of A.D. 69 as Roman armies surrounded Jerusalem. This battle between the powers of darkness and the living God would be different. Here at Armageddon, Jesus and His heavenly hosts cast the beast and the false prophet into the lake of fire and Satan into the abyss in warfare not seen by human eyes. The Revelation then says: "The rest were killed with the sword which proceeded from the mouth of Him who sat on the horse" (Rev. 19:21) which was the word of God. It had foretold in its prophecies the destruction of Jerusalem by Gentile armies, and the Romans would fulfill this in the months ahead. Vespasian would become emperor late in A.D. 69 and would charge Titus to finish the war against the Jews resulting in the prophesied destruction of the temple and the city by late summer of the next year. We shall look at this in more detail in the next chapter.

Feast of Booths, *Tishri* 15-22, A.D. 69

This was again a time of rejoicing for God's people. John sees a new heaven and a new earth (Rev. 21:1). The earth was new because Jesus replaced Satan as ruler over this world. Heaven was new because Satan and all rebellious angels were cast down from heaven, leaving the righteous angels along with those redeemed from the earth. John also sees the bride of Christ as "the holy city, New Jerusalem, coming down out of heaven from God" (Rev. 21:2). He hears a loud voice from the throne say: "Behold, the tabernacle of God is with men, and He will dwell with them" (Rev. 21:3). John adds "the nations of those who are saved shall walk in its [New Jerusalem's] light, and the kings of the earth bring their glory and honor into it" (Rev. 21:24). "And they shall bring the glory and the honor of the nations into it" (Rev. 21:26). Here we see what God has opened to us as a result of the Incarnation and Return of the Jewish Messiah, Jesus. Exciting discoveries lie ahead for the Body of Christ as it prepares faithful disciples to become the bride of Christ and appropriate the fulfillment of the prophetic promises as they carry out on this earth the will of the One on the throne who works to "make all things new."

> And the Spirit and the bride say, "Come!" And let him who hears say, "Come!" And let him who thirsts come. And whoever desires, let him take the water of life freely. Revelation 22:17

The invitation is open and the gift is free. Yet, it will cost us everything, in fact the death of our old selves. In return we shall gain everything, everything that counts, everything that is eternal.

10

DANIEL'S SEVENTIETH WEEK AS IT HAPPENED

The Gospels reveal Jesus to be the Jewish Messiah as He lived on this earth. The Revelation given to John reveals this same Jesus, now as the first-born from the dead, the glorified Son of Man, coming to raise His people to the same victory over death. When John first sees the light-radiating Jesus in His glory, the apostle falls on his face before the Lord. Note carefully His words

> "Do not be afraid; I am the First and the Last. I am He who lives, and was dead, and behold, I am alive forevermore. Amen. And I have the keys of Hades and Death." (Rev. 1:17-18)

Jesus in His Return during Daniel's Seventieth Week would unlock the prison of death and hell that held us in their unrelenting grasp. Jesus remains the only One with the authority and power to free people from sin, the powers of darkness, and death. This revelation would be for all people in the future, but it was first for John and his generation. When Daniel received his visions about the last days, the angel told him "seal up the vision, for it refers to many days in the future" (Dan. 8:26). John is told to do exactly the opposite and the reason for this. "Do not seal up the words of the prophecy of this book, for the time is at hand" (Rev. 22:10).

John is clear. His generation that received the visit of the Jewish Messiah was about to receive His Return. "The Revelation of Jesus

Christ, which God gave Him to show His servants things which must shortly take place" (Rev. 1:1). John leaves no doubt. He concludes his opening words in this way: "The time is at hand." What time? The time for rewarding the saints with the long-promised victory over death and punishing the powers of darkness was about to take place (Rev. 11:18). The Old Testament faithful such as Enoch, Noah, Abraham, Isaac, Jacob, Moses, and Elijah waited for this time. They along with the faithful of the apostolic generation still alive on earth would come into the fulfillment of the promises. Gentile converts to the new faith birthed by the Jewish Messiah likewise looked for this fulfillment of the promises made to Israel over the past centuries. After Jesus' life on earth, it was only a matter of time while those of the generation who received His ministry would have time to mature and spread the Good News throughout the world in preparation for those wonderful and terrible last days.

We shall proceed to go through each year in Daniel's Seventieth Week and bring together the time framework set forth in the previous chapters with the events recorded in history.

A.D. 63—Daniel's Seventieth Week Begins

Daniel's sixty ninth week of years ended on Palm Sunday in A.D. 33, when Jesus, the anointed One, appeared at the temple in Jerusalem as God's chosen One. Daniel's Seventieth Week would begin on October 4, A.D. 63, computed by going back in time 2,520 days (seven prophetic years of 360 days each) from the end of Daniel's Seventieth Week on August 27, A.D. 70. This gap in time between Daniel's first sixty-nine weeks of years and the Seventieth Week amounted to thirty years. This provided the necessary time for that first generation of Christians to mature in preparation for the Second Coming.

Jesus first appeared to John on *Tishri* 1, September 12, the date for the Feast of Trumpets[27], revealing that He was coming with the "keys" to unlock the prison door of death and Hades holding all human beings in its deadly grip. He also relays messages to the angels of the seven Asian churches so they might prepare the people for the imminent Return of Jesus. Then on *Tishri* 10, the Day of Atonement, John is taken up to heaven where he receives the revelation of the second-coming events. The Jewish people then celebrated the Feast of Booths whose last day, the great day of the feast, was held on October 3.

Paul and Peter, the two witnesses, undertake this final stage of their ministry on earth with this three-and-one-half-year period of testimony on October 4, A.D. 63 as Daniel's Seventieth Week begins. This would prepare the faithful for the revelation of Jesus Christ and the manifestation of His glory in a marvelous mystery, the imminence of which had just been shown to John. This fits with the chronology provided by the Book of Acts that concludes with Paul's imprisonment at Rome around A.D. 60-62. If Paul continued on to Spain as he intended according to Romans 15:28, then he would have been ready in A.D. 63, along with Peter, to begin the final period of testimony to prepare the saints for the Return of Jesus Christ.

What an appropriate date in the wisdom of God to begin Daniel's last week and the Period of the Testimony of the Two Witnesses. The Feast of Booths, the third of three festival seasons commanded by God through Moses, celebrated the harvest season at the end of the year. Peter and Paul were commencing the witness that would prepare God's people for a spiritual harvest whereby they would receive the promised inheritance and take their place in the heavenly tabernacle of the Divine Presence. Revelation 14:14-16 describes this ingathering, as Jesus likened to a reaper gathers the ripe harvest. Peter and Paul prepare the saints to pass through the suffering and persecution ahead and be ready to receive the revelation of their Returning Lord and appropriate "the mystery of God" preparatory to exiting the earth at the *Parousia* for their eternal reward.

Those first disciples would have to contend with the powers of darkness like no other generation either before them or after them. The last three trumpets occasion three major woes upon the earth that included the release of the beast from the abyss (bottomless pit) with his imprisoned hosts, and the casting down of Satan and his hosts from heaven. Daniel's Seventieth Week would include a 1,260-day period when the powers of darkness would be given authority over the people of the earth, even the authority to kill the saints. These were truly those once-and-for-all days the like of which there will never be again upon the face of the earth.

A.D. 64—Faithful Prepare for Seventh Trumpet

The fifth trumpet, sounding in the fall of A.D. 63 on *Tishri* 1 when Jesus appeared to John, foretold the first major woe upon the earth. This trumpet announced the days when *Apollyon* or *Abaddon*, the beast locked in the abyss, would be released. The 2,300-day time interval of Daniel 8:14 gives us a clue regarding when *Apollyon* was released from the abyss. It tells about a power of evil who will magnify himself to be as great as God, take away the daily sacrifice, and bring about the destruction of the temple (Dan. 8:9-12). If his release from the abyss marks the beginning of this period, and the end coincides with the end of Daniel's Seventieth Week on August 27, A.D. 70, then he would have been released on May 11, A.D. 64. This fits with the days of the fifth trumpet beginning in the fall of A.D. 63 and extending until the sixth trumpet in the fall of A.D. 64. This also agrees with what happened historically as we shall see. This evil being was released from the abyss during this period and would work terrible things on this earth throughout the remainder of Daniel's Seventieth Week. He would initiate the persecution of the Christians, corrupt the worship of God at the temple in Jerusalem, and finally bring about the end of the continual burnt offering along with the destruction of the temple and the city. All of these things forecasted for the second-coming days occurred at the conclusion of the apostolic generation during the period A.D. 64-70.

This power of evil goes for the Roman Emperor Nero who is the ruling head of the Roman Empire. We read that in the spring of A.D. 64, Nero entertains aspirations to pursue his singing career on the stage.[28]

He wants to go to the contests in Greece, but begins at Neapolis, a Greek community in Italy. From there he continues to Beneventum on the way to Greece. Something happens at Beneventum causing him to change his mind. Nero returns to Rome but still entertains thoughts of possible eastern travel to Egypt. He goes to the pagan temple of Vesta to seek guidance in this matter. He suddenly begins to tremble like a seizure.[29] His participation in this occult practice opened himself to this entrance by the beast from the abyss, released on May 11, from his long imprisonment.

Nero abandons all plans to travel and remains at Rome. He begins to throw lavish parties that are nothing more than sexual orgies. Rome breaks out in fire on July 19, and ten of the fourteen districts are burned.[30] Suspicions soon turn to the emperor who diverts attention away from himself by fixing the blame on the Christians[31] who had been talking about a kind of judgment by fire to come upon the world. Persecution of Christians begins sometime after this before the end of the year. In light of the Scripture, it was probably *Apollyon*, the beast from the abyss, who turned Nero's attention away from the eastern travel to the parties and sexual orgies at Rome. Then in this atmosphere of excess, this power of evil puts the thought into Nero's mind to burn the city and rebuild it to his own glory. At least some Roman citizens suspected Nero and the beast from the abyss had accomplished one of his goals: to begin the destruction of God's people on the earth.

Peter and Paul are carrying on their witness to prepare the faithful for the Return of Christ. The suffering and persecution would help God's people to turn wholeheartedly to seek the Lord. Paul gives us insight into His ministry through 1 Timothy and Titus that I believe were written during this year but evidently before the persecution had begun. He writes to Timothy encouraging him to remain at Ephesus (1 Tim. 1:3). Paul hopes to come to him soon (1 Tim. 3:14), but in case that does not work out, he has written the letter containing helpful counsel. Paul writes to Titus instructing his coworker left on the island of Crete to come to Paul after a replacement arrives (Tit. 3:12). Paul by this time has decided to spend the winter in Nicopolis (Tit. 3:12).

What would have caused Paul to spend the winter at the out-of-the-way location of Nicopolis, a coastal town across the sea to the east of Italy and Rome? He has never spoken of that place in his missionary travels nor does Luke mention it in the Acts of the Apostles. It is strategically located at this particular time between Rome, the headquarters of Nero, and the area where Paul has conducted most of his missionary work. Paul, I am sure, is aware of the release of *Apollyon*, the beast from the abyss, and the imminent persecution that he will vent on Christians using Nero. I am sure that Paul has also heard of the burning of Rome in July A.D. 64, as such news undoubtedly spread rapidly throughout the empire. In Nicopolis, just across the sea east of Italy, Paul can closely monitor what is occurring at Rome. From there he can discern the Spirit's leading for the remaining year before the seventh trumpet, so He can further prepare the saints for the Return of Christ in the midst of a world being greatly shaken, indeed to its very foundations.

These epistles written in this year give us insight into what Paul is doing to prepare the saints to pass through those terrible days. Paul organizes Christians at the local level by appointing leaders. He establishes a network of relationships that will help believers "stick together" as one body helping one another to withstand the terrible onslaught of the powers of darkness. Paul spells out the qualities such leaders should possess. Regarding overseers, Paul writes the following.

> A bishop then must be blameless, the husband of one wife, temperate, sober-minded, of good behavior, hospitable, able to teach; not given to wine, not violent, not greedy for money, but gentle, not quarrelsome, not covetous; one who rules his own house well, having his children in submission with all reverence (for if a man does not know how to rule his own house, how will he take care of the church of God?); not a novice, lest being puffed up with pride he fall into the same condemnation as the devil. Moreover he must

have a good testimony among those who are outside, lest he fall into reproach and the snare of the devil. (1 Tim. 3:2-7)

People can look up to and follow such leaders who "walk the walk." Paul also mentions the *epiphaneia* in 1 Timothy and Titus. Associated with the Second Coming of Jesus, this is the hope of the believer. "I urge…that you keep this commandment without spot, blameless until our Lord Jesus Christ's appearing, [*epiphaneia*] which He will manifest in His own time" (1 Tim. 6:13-16). Paul also reminds Titus of this significant event.

> For the grace of God that brings salvation has appeared to all men, teaching us that, denying ungodliness and worldly lusts, we should live soberly, righteously, and godly in the present age, looking for the blessed hope and glorious appearing [*epiphaneia*] of our great God and Savior, Jesus Christ, who gave Himself for us, that He might redeem us from every lawless deed and purify for Himself His own special people, zealous for good works. (Tit. 2:11-14)

In his earlier correspondence to the Thessalonians, Paul had referred to the *epiphaneia* of Jesus' coming (*Parousia*) (2 Thess. 2:8) and this appearing associated with the Second Coming would overcome the works of the evil one who would also be revealed during those last days. This *epiphaneia* or appearing resulting from the revelation of Jesus Christ and the manifestation of His glory in His people would enable them to overcome the forces of evil during those last days and appropriate the promised kingdom and salvation. With the persecution of believers soon to be launched by this power of evil, the appearing or *epiphaneia* of their returning King offered great hope. When Paul writes 2 Timothy a little over two years later and near the end of his life, he uses the word *epiphaneia* three times, all from the perspective that this event has happened.

In addition to organizing the saints at the local level as he appoints overseers or bishops along with elders and deacons, we read about a new word, *eusebeia*, Paul employs for the first time in his writings. He uses it eight times in 1 Timothy and once in Titus. The word translates as religion, godliness, or piety. Literally, it means "well-worshiping" or "good worship." The prefix *eu* in Greek means "well." Combined with the root *seb* meaning "worship" suggests this basic understanding. I believe Paul takes this word from the Greek to express what he is learning and what his people must learn: how to look to the Lord and worship Him. Those admitted into the Divine Presence where the kingdom and salvation are discovered must learn to worship not only in their gatherings, but in their private lives, and that privilege was unfolding through the light being given to those first Christians.

In the Old Testament, when the people drew near to the Divine Presence, they worshiped. "Enter into His Gates with thanksgiving, and into His courts with praise" (Ps. 100:4). The Levitical priesthood led the people in worshiping the Lord who dwelled in their midst over the Ark of the Covenant. Jesus taught during His ministry how earnestly the Father wanted His people to worship Him in spirit and truth "for the Father is seeking such to worship Him" (John 4:23). As a result of the ministry of the Messiah, and the gift of the Holy Spirit provided through the New Covenant, God was creating a people on this earth who would finally worship Him in spirit and truth. During the approaching days of the Second Coming, God was about to reveal to Jesus' followers that not only did they have the Holy Spirit within, they were about to be joined in spiritual union with Jesus, their Divine Bridegroom, and raised up into the Father's presence. Worship is the order of the day for those granted this privilege. I believe the word *eusebeia* meant something like that for Paul, accounting for its emergence at this point.

The persecution of Christians begins during the latter part of this year. Large numbers of Christians were arrested and put to death. They were crucified, killed by wild animals, and burnt alive as human torches.

The victims were pitied because the citizenry perceived that the Christians were the objects of the emperor's wrath.[32] The Revelation given to John affirms such an assessment indicating that such activity was indeed attributed to the brutality of the Roman Emperor Nero marked with the 666. Scripture also revealed what was going on in the spiritual realm behind the physical scene. *Apollyon*, recently released from the abyss, was the driving force behind Nero's actions, seeking to destroy God's people. The Roman emperor had no idea that he was merely a pawn in a far greater scenario that was playing itself out in this climactic period in history. The living God was accomplishing His purpose of ending the Old Covenant with the Jewish people and establishing a New Covenant open to all the peoples of this earth. God was also in the process of removing Satan as ruler over this world and establishing His Son in this position of authority. The terrible persecution related to these last days foretold by Jesus had begun.

A.D. 65—Year of the Seventh Trumpet

Paul undoubtedly leaves his winter haven at Nicopolis as soon as he can in the spring of A.D. 65 eagerly seeking to minister to the faithful as they prepare for Christ's Return. He will eventually arrive at Ephesus desiring to see Timothy as indicated in 1 Timothy 3:14, but probably stopping to minister along the way at such places as Corinth, Thessalonica, and Philippi. The Christian persecution under Nero would be well under way at this point by the spring of A.D. 65 and spreading throughout the Roman Empire. The actual persecution at Rome may have subsided somewhat in early A.D. 65 as an assassination attempt upon Nero's life prompts the emperor to go after anybody in Rome he might suspect.[33] His tutor, Senaca, comes under such suspicion and dies during this time.[34] This is an important date because Jerome tells us that Peter and Paul are put to death two years later, which correlates with the completion of their 1,260-day period of testimony. Paul reaches Ephesus probably around the summer of A.D. 65 and is imprisoned shortly after that.

Ephesus was a hotbed of opposition to early Christianity. Paul was driven out of this city in the mid-fifties, escaping with his life (Acts 19:23-41, 2 Cor. 1:3-11). John lived there and was imprisoned at Patmos, just out to sea from Ephesus. There he received the Revelation in A.D. 63. With the Neronian persecution begun by the beast from the abyss spreading throughout the Roman Empire, imprisonment would be expected for Paul, the spokesman for the gospel to the Gentile world.

The Philippians whom Paul had probably recently visited on the way from Nicopolis to Ephesus hear of Paul's imprisonment and send Epaphroditus to minister to the apostle. I believe Paul writes Philippians from this Ephesian imprisonment in the fall of A.D. 65, just before the seventh trumpet that sounded on *Tishri* 1. "The Lord is at hand" (Phil. 4:5) witnesses to this nearness. He vividly reflects second-coming expectations as he tells about his desire to be made perfect and to come to the knowledge of the power of the Resurrection, things which he clearly expects to happen in this life as Christ returns.

Paul tells us in Philippians 1:19-26 that death is a real possibility for him, accurately reflecting the background of a world where Christians were reeling under Nero's persecution. The apostle knows that God has more work for Paul, and that he will emerge from this imprisonment to continue in his ministry. His release probably happens in the spring of A.D. 66 as we shall see. The stress of these times is also reflected in the near-death of Epaphroditus who brought the gifts from the church at Philippi to Paul in prison. Paul rejoices as he writes to the Philippians that Epaphroditus has recovered.

I believe Peter writes his First Epistle from Rome to the Jewish exiles of the dispersion during this time of the persecution and just before the seventh trumpet to be sounded in the fall of A.D. 65. Peter writes to Jewish believers east of Ephesus in Pontus, Galatia, Cappadocia, Asia and Bithynia (1 Pet. 1:1). We see that the persecution had spread eastward through the Roman Empire. Peter talks about "the fiery trial" through which they are suffering (1 Pet. 4:12). He refers later on to

Babylon (1 Pet. 5:13) indicating that he has been exposed to the Revelation given to John, word of which I am sure spread rapidly through Christian circles.

The sixth trumpet that sounded in the fall of A.D. 64 indicated the period had begun when angels would be released to kill one-third of mankind (Rev. 9:15). As we saw in chapter 8, Tacitus reports such a plague in the vicinity of Rome occurring in A.D. 65 that devastated the entire populace. Suetonius is probably referring to the same plague when he reports around this time during the days of Nero that 30,000 deaths were recorded at a pagan temple. Luke appropriately described these terrifying days by saying how men's hearts would be "failing them from fear and the expectation of those things which are coming on the earth" (Luke 21:26). Yet, he admonishes believers as they see these terrible things taking place to "look up and lift up your heads, because your redemption draws near" (Luke 21:28).

Peter writes similarly in his First Epistle encouraging believers facing persecution. He exhorts them to look for the following things in the days ahead: the salvation soon to be revealed (1 Pet. 1:5), the testing of their faith by fire (1 Pet. 1:7), and the grace that will be given them at the revelation of Jesus Christ (1 Pet. 1:13). They are about to take part in the glory to be revealed during those last days (1 Pet. 4:13, 5:1). Peter leaves no doubt what is taking place as he tells his fellow Christians that "the end of all things is at hand" (1 Pet. 4:7). His testimony awakens his readers to be alert for great things to be coming during the last days as Jesus returns to reveal and manifest His glory in His faithful. We shall see shortly, these expectations are being realized when Peter writes his Second Letter, shortly before his martyrdom, but after the seventh trumpet.

It is interesting to observe Peter's mention that Mark is with the apostle (1 Pet. 5:13) there in Rome during late summer as he writes to the Jewish brethren east of Ephesus. We then hear of Mark in the spring of A.D. 66 in Paul's Letters to the Colossians and to Philemon. It may have been that Mark delivered Peter's letter and then came back to the area of Ephesus.

The seventh trumpet sounds on *Tishri* 1, September 19, A.D. 65 (see table 2 for this dating). "The kingdoms of this world have become the kingdoms of our Lord and of His Christ, and He shall reign for ever and ever!" (Rev. 11:15). Jesus replaced Satan as the ruler over this world. Now God was ready to fulfill the promises made during the Old Testament period resulting in rewarding the prophets, the saints, and those who reverence His name (Rev. 11:18). The time of wait was over. At this trumpet, the reward came to the dead as they were resurrected, meaning they received the perfected Christlike nature and the glorified body. Part of the reward came to those on earth as they were perfected in "the twinkling of an eye" along with the dead in Christ. Jesus would then join Himself to His bride on earth and raise her spiritually before the throne in heaven as part of this great mystery. What happened during the days of the seventh trumpet to the living on earth is the basic victory to be appropriated while still on earth and the key to finally bringing heaven to this earth.

A.D. 66—Faithful Appropriate Mystery of God

Hebrews 11:40 tells us that the dead Old Testament faithful from the past were perfected along with the Jewish faithful alive on earth. Appropriating this reality was more difficult for those on earth because Satan and his hosts converged upon them in great opposition not experienced by those in heavenly regions. Peter and Paul must continue to interpret to the saints on earth what has transpired, so they may see, believe, and appropriate these mighty works. Paul reflects this as he writes Ephesians and Colossians in the spring of A.D. 66 prior to his release from prison. This was not an automatic transport to bliss, but the biggest challenge those first followers ever faced, requiring their dependence upon all they learned about God's word in order to keep their faith strong. Those who overcame in the midst of great fear and terror would appropriate the victory.

It is one thing to have the Christlike nature completed "in the twinkling of an eye." It is another thing to believe that has happened within and appropriate it through daily living in an evil world. Luke records Jesus as saying during His ministry on earth that when He returned, would He find faith? (Luke 18:8). Would His people have grown in the knowledge of Scripture that alone supports faith so when the midnight hour came, they would be ready to meet all the fear and terror of the enemy with overcoming faith? When John views the first great sign in Revelation 12:1-6 depicting a woman birthing a male child that we shall discuss in the next chapter, Satan is portrayed as a dragon just waiting to destroy that child. The powers of darkness were deeply entrenched to do everything they could to destroy the faith of those first believers and prohibit them from appropriating this great mystery. They had to overcome or conquer by faith, and that meant keeping their "lamps burning" with a full supply of the oil of truth from Scripture. As John says in his First Epistle (5:4), faith is the victory that overcomes the world and faith depends upon God's word.

Paul tells about this mystery in Ephesians and Colossians hidden from all previous generations but now revealed through the apostles and the prophets. He shares valuable wisdom on how to overcome and appropriate this victory. It is clearly not automatic. Since they have now been raised with Christ, they must set their hearts and minds on things above (Col. 3:1-2). Prior to the experiential dimension of the Second Coming, they could vacillate between the two. Now, maintaining this Divine life required a disciplined mindset upon heavenly things while still living in a world filled not only with distractions but also with hostile opposition.

Now that they had this completed life within, they had to take special care to practice the love and ways of this life in daily living. They must now be sure to put off the old self (Eph. 4:22) that they still carried around in the body and put on the new self created in the likeness of God (Eph. 4:24). Paul says the same things to the Colossians in 3:5-14. They must take every care to put off the old man and its ways in sexual immorality, impurity, lust, evil desire, greed, anger, wrath, malice, blasphemy, and filthy language. While still living in this evil world, they must also take care to put on the ways of the new man in compassion, kindness, humility, gentleness and patience. They are to bear with one another and forgive one another, and above all else, put on the *agape* that is God's love.

They must also go out each day with their spiritual armor in place in order to be victorious in this spiritual warfare (Eph. 6:10-20). If they had been careless before, they soon learned their spiritual existence in this evil world depended upon it now. The mystery of God thrust those first faithful into such spiritual warfare requiring now the "putting on" of spiritual armor each day. Prayer is also an essential. After admonishing the Ephesians to put on such armor, he exhorts them to be "praying always with all prayer and supplication in the Spirit, being watchful to this end with all perseverance" (Eph. 6:18). He also admonishes them when they get together to share with each other "psalms and hymns and spiritual songs" (Eph. 5:19). They must learn to take charge of their interior life as they learn to sing and make melody in their hearts to the Lord (Eph. 5:19). In the next verse, he admonishes them to give "thanks always for all things to God the Father in the name of our Lord Jesus Christ" (Eph. 5:20). Appropriating the mystery of God required those first faithful to "overcome" the powers of darkness in these ways, and Paul encourages those first saints along this kingdom path.

I believe Paul writes Ephesians and Colossians in the spring of A.D. 66 reflecting what he and the first faithful were going through. Some marvelous physical signs accompany these extraordinary spiritual events. Halley's Comet would have been blazing across the sky during this time from the fall of A.D. 65 to the spring of A.D. 66,[35] as Jesus returned to reveal His glory in His saints through this great mystery. I believe this was the sign of the Son of Man referred to in Matthew 24:30. Some other unusual things occurred at this time prior to the Jewish rebellion and the war with the Romans. Josephus tells us that on *Nisan* 8[36] (Nicephorus dates it *Nisan* 9)[37] of A.D. 66, a light glows over the altar of the temple in Jerusalem for thirty minutes during the night. The huge iron gates facing east open of their own accord during the same Passover Feast.

> Thus also, before the Jews' rebellion, and before those commotions which preceded the war, when the people were come in great crowds to the feast of unleavened bread, on the eighth day of the month Xanthicus, [Nisan,] and at the ninth hour of the night, so great a light shone round the altar and the holy house, that it appeared to be bright day-time; which light lasted for half an hour. This light seemed to be a good sign to the unskilful, but was so interpreted by the sacred scribes as to portend those events that followed immediately upon it…Moreover, the eastern gate of the inner, [court of the temple,] which was of brass, and vastly heavy, and had been with difficulty shut by twenty men, and rested upon a basis armed with iron, and had bolts fastened very deep into the firm floor, which was there made of one entire stone, was seen to be opened of its own accord about the sixth hour of the night. Now, those that kept watch in the temple came thereupon running to the captain of the temple, and told him of it; who then came up thither, and not without great difficulty was able to shut the gate again. This also appeared to the vulgar to be a very happy prodigy, as if God did thereby open them the gate of happiness. But the men of learning understood it, that the security of their holy house was dissolved of its own accord, and that the gate was opened for the advantage of their enemies. So these publicly declared, that this signal foreshewed the desolation that was coming upon them.[38]

Josephus and the learned Jews saw these events as signs pointing to the city's imminent doom. "The unskilful" so designated by Josephus are most likely those Jewish Christians who understood these signs as indeed a "very happy prodigy" pointing to the truth that God was opening to them the heavenly places of His Divine Presence.

It is interesting to note the following. Joshua led the children of Israel under the Old Covenant into the Promised Land of Canaan on *Nisan* 10 (Josh. 4:19), and they were sanctified on the previous day, *Nisan* 9

(Josh. 3:5). Could these physical signs at the doomed temple in Jerusalem be witnessing to the spiritual resurrection that was taking place in the new temple of the Body of Christ as the mystery was being appropriated by the faithful remnant? The light glowing over the altar, if it were on *Nisan* 9 as Nicephorus reports, would witness to the perfecting of the Christlike nature within the faithful that occurred at the seventh trumpet. The opening of the huge eastern gate would witness to the returning Lord raising His people spiritually through the provisions of the New Covenant out of the corruption of this world into the Christian's Promised Land of the Divine Presence where they would discover His kingdom and salvation. These signs during *Nisan* would witness to the saints appropriating the mystery of God. This requires taking Nicephorus' date as the time when the light shone over the altar at the temple, and assumes that the opening of the huge iron gates facing east occurred on *Nisan* 10. Josephus only indicates that the latter happened during this same festival without giving the exact date.[39] At any rate, it is interesting to observe that such strange occurrences took place in the physical temple at Jerusalem at this time and their possible significance.

I believe Hebrews, James, 2 Peter, and 1 John are also written around this time after the seventh trumpet, for they reflect these same truths of the perfected or completed life being appropriated among God's people and now looking ahead to Jesus taking them off the earth. Hebrews 12:23 talks about "the general assembly and church of the firstborn" and "the spirits of just men made perfect" and how they "are receiving a kingdom which cannot be shaken" (Heb. 12:28). He also says that in just a little while, "He who is coming will come and will not tarry" (Heb. 10:37). James exhorts his readers in 1:4 to let "patience have its perfect work, that you may be perfect and complete, lacking nothing." He also says: "The coming of the Lord is at hand" (James 5:8) and "the Judge is standing at the door!" (James 5:9). Second Peter 1:3-11 relates about how God's great and precious promises have enabled those first Christians to "be partakers of the Divine nature" (2 Pet. 1:4) and receive "an entrance…into the everlasting kingdom of our Lord and Savior

Jesus Christ" (2 Pet. 1:11). Peter does not admonish his readers to look for any more revelation as in his First Letter. He now exhorts them to appropriate what God has opened to them.

Paul's silence about names in the earlier Letter to the Ephesians (mentioning only Tychicus in 6:21) suggests that his imprisonment is in that area, and does not wish to implicate any of his brethren. To the further removed community of Colossae, and with the time of his release appearing to be near, he mentions quite a few names. Written a little after Colossians from this same imprisonment, Paul's Letter to Philemon, verse 22, indicates his release from prison is near as he says: "Prepare a guest room for me, for I trust that through your prayers I shall be granted to you."

Paul was probably released from prison in the spring as he writes. He proceeds to encourage the brethren in the churches and will eventually make his way to Rome where Paul is imprisoned in the fall of A.D. 66. He writes his Second Letter to Timothy from here and indicates that he expects his martyrdom from this imprisonment. Paul's letter reflects the stress of those days. All who are in Asia have turned away from Paul (2 Tim. 1:15). Demas has deserted and gone to Thessalonica (2 Tim. 4:10). Others have dispersed. Crescens has gone to Galatia and Titus to Dalmatia (2 Tim. 4:10), while he left Trophimus sick in Miletus (2 Tim. 4:20). Luke alone remains at Paul's side there at Rome (2 Tim. 4:11). Paul has fought the good fight and the time for his departure is at hand. He encourages Timothy to come before winter of A.D. 66-67 and to bring Mark along.

It is interesting to observe Paul's use of the word *epiphaneia* in 2 Timothy. In his earlier uses of the word in 2 Thessalonians 2:8, 1 Timothy 6:14, and Titus 2:13, all in regard to the Second Coming, he refers to an event that is still in the future. It has now occurred when he writes this letter. God's marvelous grace given to us in Christ Jesus from the beginning "has now been revealed by the appearing [*epiphaneia*] of our Savior Jesus Christ, who has abolished death and brought life and immortality to light through the gospel" (2 Tim.

1:9-10). Death was indeed abolished at the seventh trumpet when God raised the dead and Paul witnesses to this triumph in 2 Timothy. We learn in this letter that a certain Hymenaeus was saying during these very days that the resurrection was past (2 Tim. 2:16-18). Paul referred to this man earlier in 1 Timothy 1:20 as one rejecting conscience and a blasphemer whom the apostle turned over to Satan. Satan again was using Hymenaeus now to confuse believers by leading them to think they had missed the resurrection. Paul does not answer by explaining the details of that unique period between the seventh trumpet and the Parousia. The apostle simply dismisses such talk as "profane and vain babblings" and witnesses that the *epiphaneia* abolishing death has occurred and encourages the faithful to hold the course during those second-coming days till the *Parousia* when they will come into the fullness of their inheritance of glory.

If Timothy heeded Paul's direction to come before winter and brought with him Mark, this would have given opportunity for contact with Luke in the writing of their respective Gospels, as well as supervision from Paul and Peter prior to their martyrdom the next year. Mark and Luke were in the vicinity of Ephesus according to Colossians 4:10,14 and Philemon 24 during the spring of A.D. 66, and now in Rome later on that same year if Mark accompanied Timothy. It is interesting to observe that Paul instructed Timothy on his way to Rome to not only bring Mark but also the scrolls and the parchments (2 Tim. 4:13). We do not know what those documents contained, but there may well have been information used in the Gospels among other things. The two witnesses of Christ knowing that their 1,260-day period of testimony was coming to an end as well as their subsequent deaths undoubtedly wanted to leave a record of the life of Jesus. Peter says as much in 2 Peter 1:15. The New Testament epistles say nothing about Matthew, but we know from the inter-relatedness of the synoptic Gospels, that he had either personal contact with Mark and Luke, or at least shared some common sources, perhaps among the documents picked up from Carpus at Troas.

Early documents tell us that John survived those last days and continued on earth for several decades. Eusebius reports that John lived until the days of Trajan, the Roman emperor who ruled from A.D. 98 to A.D. 117.[40] This may have been part of the message of the angel to John in Revelation 10:11. "And he said to me, 'you must yet prophecy about many peoples, nations, tongues, and kings.'" While his brethren surviving martyrdom and remaining faithful would be taken off the earth to be with the Lord in about two years, John's lot was to remain through these events and minister to the church on earth. I believe he writes his Gospel after these second-coming events thereby giving him time to assimilate all this light. Scholars through the years have recognized a difference between John's Gospel and that of Matthew, Mark, and Luke thereby grouping the three together as the synoptic Gospels because they reflect a similar perspective. John's writing after the Parousia in contrast to their writing before would account for the difference.

Revelation 12:7-9 reports that after the mystery revealed in 12:1-6, Satan is cast out of heaven. Josephus records a strange appearance in the clouds around May A.D. 66, shortly after the Feast of Unleavened Bread that year.[41] Josephus is aware of the unusual event he is reporting as he refers to it as "a prodigious and incredible phenomenon; I suppose the account of it would seem to be a fable, were it not related by those who saw it." He includes it in his history in this same passage because of the witness of persons who claimed to see "before sun-setting, chariots and troops of soldiers in their armour...running about among the clouds, and surrounding of cities." This strange event occurs at the right time and may reflect this heavenly warfare.

After expulsion from heaven, Satan goes after the woman of Revelation 12:1-6, the Jewish Christian faithful appropriating the mystery of God. If you follow Josephus, Jewish zealots attack Masada and kill the Romans there sometime around June.[42] In the next month, they are stirring up trouble at the temple in Jerusalem.[43] Toward the end of August, they slay Roman soldiers who had laid down their arms having been promised security.[44] On the very same day, the Cesaerians rise up and kill the Jews occupying their city.[45] This begins the wars between the Jews and their neighbors. In October, Cestius, a Roman officer, kills the Jews in a certain town who did not go down to the Feast of Booths at Jerusalem.[46] Shortly thereafter, the zealots retaliate and inflict defeat upon Cestius.[47] He sends representatives to report to Nero about the rebellion in Judea. Many Jews at Jerusalem flee the doomed city around November and December.[48] Eusebius tells us that the Christians did likewise around this time just prior to the beginning of the war.

Satan in these few months had succeeded to divide the Jews internally, alienate them from their Gentile neighbors, and provoke Rome to war. I believe Revelation 12:15 reports this activity of Satan. "So the serpent spewed water out of his mouth like a flood after the woman, that he might cause her to be carried away by the flood." The next verse tells us "the earth helped the woman, and the earth opened its mouth and swallowed up the flood which the dragon had spewed out of his mouth" (Rev. 12:16). Neither the Jews, nor the Romans, nor the Gentiles understood that those faithful Christian Jews were the real target for all this activity. Satan's efforts, likened to a flood, were absorbed on earth in the resultant warfare that actually enabled the Jewish Christians to flee Jerusalem and escape to Pella.[49] This village was laid waste by the Jews during the warfare and left vacant. This became the wilderness refuge referred to in Revelation 12:14 where the Jewish Christians waited for their Lord to take them off the earth.

Josephus in his "Wars of the Jews" takes one paragraph to cover the events from A.D. 59 to A.D. 66. It requires eighteen pages to cover A.D. 66 during this year when Satan was cast out of heaven. While heaven rejoices to be rid of this enemy, the earth is about to reel from his anger.

> Woe to the inhabitants of the earth and the sea! For the devil has come down to you, having great wrath, because he knows that he has a short time. (Rev. 12:12)

The stage is set for the 1,260-day period when the beast will be given authority to accomplish great evil, and Satan will put his weight behind this initiative for destruction (Rev. 13:4).

I believe Galatians is Paul's last letter written either late in A.D. 66 or early in A.D. 67. Timothy may have reported the news about what had happened in Galatia as Timothy was from that region. In this letter, Paul travails over the Galatians as a mother with child "until Christ is formed in you" (Gal. 4:19). Paul concludes this letter with something he has not said before. "From now on let no one trouble me, for I bear in my body the marks of the Lord Jesus" (Gal. 6:17). I get the picture that Paul knows his ministry is near its end and martyrdom awaits him. He is truly ready to depart this earth. He witnesses to the imminence of his death also in 2 Timothy 4:6-7 as he talks about having fought the good fight and the time is near for leaving this earth.

I believe Peter writes his last epistle around the same time Paul writes Galatians as both of the witnesses complete their 1,260-day "Period of Testimony." He does not exhort the people to look for any further revelation of Jesus Christ as in the First Epistle (1:7,13), but rather to appropriate the Divine nature (2 Pet. 1:4) and look for the entrance into the eternal kingdom (2 Pet. 1:11). He now witnesses to what they have received and encourages them to hold on faithfully until Jesus returns to remove them. Peter indicates his death is imminent as he writes, "shortly I must put off my tent [physical body] just as our Lord Jesus showed me" (2 Pet. 1:14).

A.D. 67—Authority of Beast Begins

The Period of the Authority of the Beast begins on January 1, A.D. 67. Revelation 13:6-7 describes what he is permitted to do on this earth during a 1,260-day period.

> Then he opened his mouth in blasphemy against God, to blaspheme His name, His tabernacle, and those who dwell in heaven. And it was granted to him to make war with the saints and to

overcome them. And authority was given to him over every tribe, tongue, and nation.

Here is a description of what transpired in history during the next three-and-one-half years. God, His Name, His worship, and His temple in Jerusalem would be desecrated and the persecution of the saints would continue. Tradition tells us that all of the apostles were martyred except John. The city and its temple would finally be destroyed in A.D. 70.

Paul and Peter's testimony ends in the spring of A.D. 67, overlapping by a few months the 1,260-day Period of the Authority of the Beast. They are martyred sometime after this. Jerome tells us that they were put to death two years after the death of Senaca[50] that occurred in A.D. 65. This would place their deaths in A.D. 67 supporting this chronology. The challenge for those not suffering martyrdom would be to remain faithful during those days of gross darkness and hold on until Jesus returned to remove them from the earth.

One primary activity this year regarding second-coming events is the advance of the Roman armies against the Jews. Nero upon hearing word from Cestius about the Jewish rebellion proceeds to commission Vespasian to head up the war.[51] He meets his son, Titus, a Roman officer, around March at Ptolemais. They plan the campaign and begin to march around May against Gadara that is easily taken.[52] They then proceed to Jotapata where the Romans encounter stiff resistance. They take the city by early July.[53] The Romans take Tarichae[54] around September and Gamala[55] around October as they move toward Jerusalem.

While the Romans are advancing through Judea this year, Josephus reports that the Jewish zealots have challenged the duly appointed High Priest Ananus and chosen a replacement.[56] They have begun to pervert the worship of God, ignoring the instructions He had given His people though Moses. The abominations to occur at the temple in Jerusalem during the last days had begun. *Apollyon* confined to the abyss for his bold rebellion against God has still not learned. He now boldly heads for the temple at Jerusalem to corrupt the worship of the living God. Even Satan was wiser than this. Despite his being cast out of heaven, he did not attack the worship of God at the temple, but went after God's people as we have seen. *Apollyon* goes now for the temple.

Josephus reports the activity of this abomination that makes desolation. The rebels made the temple "a stronghold for them" and "the sanctuary was now become a refuge, and a shop of tyranny."[57] They chose a high priest favorable to themselves. "This horrid piece of wickedness was sport and pastime with them, but occasioned the other priests, who at a distance saw their law made a jest of, to shed tears, and sorely lament the dissolution of such a sacred dignity."[58] The High Priest Ananus remarked about the state of affairs at the temple: "Certainly it had been good for me to die before I had seen the house of God full of so many abominations, or these sacred places that ought not to be trodden on at random, filled with the feet of these blood-shedding villains."[59] These seditious "walk about in the midst of the holy places, at the very time when their hands are still warm with the slaughter of their own countrymen."[60] Another Jewish leader remarked about these rebels. "They are robbers, who by their prodigious wickedness have profaned this most sacred floor, and who are to be now seen drinking themselves drunk in the sanctuary, and expending the spoils of those whom they have slaughtered upon their unsatiable bellies."[61] Warfare took place at the temple. The Zealots assisted by the Idumeans invade the holy place. "And now the outer temple was all of it overflowed with blood; and that day, as it came on, saw eight thousand five hundred dead bodies there."[62] The High Priest Ananus is slain around this time as the rebels take over at the temple.[63] Josephus then remarks about this desolation of the abominable beast from the abyss, the spiritual power at work behind the scenes. "These men, therefore, trampled upon all the laws of man, and laughed at the laws of God; and for the oracles of the prophets, they ridiculed them as the tricks of jugglers."[64] The prophesied corruption of the worship of

God at the temple foretold for the last days was now clearly evident at the temple. Final judgment upon the Jewish people and the ending of the Old Covenant would soon follow.

A.D. 68—The *Parousia* and the Day of the Lord

With Nero's death in June[65], Galba reigns as the last head of the beast in Revelation 13:1-10. More emperors followed, but he is the last mentioned because during his reign, the *Parousia* will take place when Jesus removes from the earth the faithful Christian Jews along with the faithful Gentile Christians. This ended the days of subjection for the remnant of the Jewish faithful to those four Gentile nations foretold in Daniel. Since the time of Nebuchadnezzar, the faithful and all Jews had been subject to the rulers of four nations: Babylon, Media-Persia, Greece, and finally Rome. Galba was the last such ruler as the saints were removed from the earth during his reign.

The stage was now set for two big events in second-coming prophecy: the *Parousia* and the Day of the Lord. Galba, the seventh head, had become emperor indicating the time had arrived for this grand climax. The authority of the beast for accomplishing destruction and desolation was taking place. Roman armies now surrounded Jerusalem awaiting word for the final move, which would actually not come until early A.D. 70 because of all the uproar that would occur at Rome during those last days as Galba would be followed by three other emperors in A.D. 69. The abominations to occur at the temple during the last days were taking place. In addition, the two witnesses, Peter and Paul, and probably most of the rest of the apostles had been martyred. These were those days that God shortened for the sake of the elect. Originally set for August 27, A.D. 70, God moved the grand climax to these feast days in A.D. 68. All of the signs pointed to these long-awaited days in biblical prophecy when finally the faithful throughout the ages would sit down with Abraham, Isaac, and Jacob and dine together in the kingdom of heaven.

The Feast of Trumpets on *Tishri* 1, A.D. 65 announced Jesus' Return to raise the dead and perfect the faithful. Now, it announced the *Parousia* or the Return of the Lord. This was the time that Jesus came with those raised from the dead at the earlier event of the seventh trumpet and removed his remaining faithful who had survived martyrdom. Revelation 14:14-16 portrays this event as a harvester reaping his ripe crop. John views this happy throng in Revelation 15:1-4. They rejoice together as the first fruits now sharing the Christlike nature and the glorified body. They only wait for the imminent Day of the Lord on *Tishri* 10 when they will enter the marriage supper of the Lamb.

I believe Revelation 14:17-20 also occurred on *Tishri* 1, A.D. 68 further preparing the way for the Day of the Lord. Here Israel, referred to as the earth's vine, is thrown into the winepress of God's wrath. The corruption of the worship of God at His temple forecasted for the last days had occurred and God places unfaithful Israel in the winepress of His wrath that will be poured out during the imminent Day of the Lord and the Old Covenant will shortly come to an end.

There is no historical evidence regarding the *Parousia*. This should not surprise us. What actually happened at that moment when Jesus removed the faithful from the earth? They would have simply discarded their bodies and at once received their new glorified body. People left behind would have thought that they simply died. At Pella to which the Jewish Christians at Jerusalem fled at the end of A.D. 66, there would have simply been a large number of dead bodies remaining. That would have been no unusual event in those days during the wars between the Jews and their Gentile neighbors beginning the latter part of A.D. 66. Pella, in fact, had been left uninhabited because of those very wars preparing a wilderness refuge to which those Jewish Christians in Jerusalem escaped from the wrath of Satan.

The New Testament does not teach that bodies went flying into the air. The faithful left those bodies behind and received their new bodies. Paul deals with this matter in 1 Corinthians 15:35-44. He gives an analogy to describe the relationship between our old body that perishes in the grave and the glorified body that will last forever. He refers to the planting of a seed in the ground that gives rise to a plant. Paul likens our physical bodies to the seed that is sown and the glorified body to the plant that emerges. The outer husk of the seed, the part that we see, perishes in the ground. Paul's analogy suggests that in like manner, our physical bodies will perish giving rise to the glorified body. It is not necessary for God to gather the remains of the bodies of His saints and transform them into the glorified body. If Paul had used the analogy of a caterpillar becoming a butterfly in connection with the body, then this would be the case. The physical body would be transformed into the glorified body. This was true for Jesus who lived without sin. By God's grace, we shall end up with the same kind of glorified body, but not through the physical metamorphosis Jesus underwent. Our physical bodies, condemned to death because of our sin, like a seed that is sown in the ground, will perish and return to the earth. God does not need to gather the decayed or destroyed bodies of the faithful who suffered different fates and whose ashes or remains have been scattered about. A new glorified body awaited the faithful when Jesus returned to take them off the earth and join those previously raised from the dead at the trumpet.

Let us look further at this matter by examining the Greek verb Paul uses in Philippians 3:20-21 to tell what happens to the body at the Return of Jesus. "For our citizenship is in heaven, from which we also eagerly wait for the Savior, the Lord Jesus Christ, who will transform our lowly body that it may be conformed to His glorious body, according to the working by which He is able even to subdue all things to Himself." The word "transform," is a misleading translation. This is not the Greek word, *metamorphoo*, from which our word "metamorphosis" derives that would mean the old body is transformed into the new glorified body. The Greek word here is *metaschematidzo* and simply means to change the fashion or form of something. Paul uses this word in 2 Corinthians 11:13 to refer to false apostles appearing as apostles of Christ and again in 2 Corinthians 11:14 to refer to Satan appearing as an angel of light. Paul is simply saying in this Philippian text that when the dead are raised, the form in which they are seen will be changed from the old physical body to the new glorified body. The old body was not transformed into the new glorified body any more than those false apostles were transformed into apostles of light or Satan was transformed into an angel of light. In other words, *metaschematidzo*, opens the door to the understanding presented here. At the Parousia, the saints merely changed the form of the bodies in which this new Christlike life resided. They shed their physical bodies, and the person within would have been raised to a new glorified body. Thus, the bodies of the saints still in their graves or wherever their remains may have been scattered poses no problem from the biblical perspective. This also helps us to understand, in contrast to some of the spectacular portrayals depicting bodies flying up into the air in what is popularly called the Rapture, why this event actually took place without leaving any trace in the historical records of the day.

The *Parousia* on *Tishri* 1 with the removal of the faithful and the casting of Israel into the winepress of God's wrath prepares the way for the Day of the Lord that occurs on the Day of Atonement, or *Tishiri* 10. This is also referred to as the second great sign in Revelation. The first sign witnessed to the victory made possible on earth through the events related to the seventh trumpet in A.D. 65. This second great sign witnessed to the grand climax and final reward of the inheritance promised to the faithful. John sees heaven opened in Revelation 15:5 following which God's wrath is poured out (15:5-16:21) and the saints enter the marriage supper of the Lamb referred to in 19:6-9. Chapters 17 and 18 tell about how Babylon the Great has finally received her just punishment with this outpoured wrath.

After God has delivered His wrath in final judgment upon sin and evil, we then hear about the final victory for the faithful and their rejoicing in Revelation 19:5-9. The long awaited celebration of Jesus and His bride was taking place. There is little detail, but the grand climax is clear. In this second great sign of Revelation, the promises made through the prophets to God's people find their complete fulfillment. Now they have come into their full inheritance of the new nature and new body and will abide forever in God's presence. He did not require them to endure the entire 1,260-day Period of the Authority of the Beast, but removed the faithful about two years earlier than the original "grand climax" of Daniel 12:12. God shortened those terrible last days for the sake of the elect.

A.D. 69—Armageddon Begins

While the elect are enjoying this first year of marriage with the Lamb in heaven, we see the effects of this Divine judgment through historical events in A.D. 69 as the powers of darkness absorb the outpoured wrath of God. The normally stable Roman Empire has four emperors over the course of this year. Five emperors ruled over the Roman Empire during the period from about 28 B.C. to A.D. 69. Five emperors occupy the throne during the short period from A.D. 68 to A.D. 69. Galba will follow Nero and rule from June A.D. 68 until January A.D. 69. Otho, Vitellius, and Vespasian will follow Galba, hence four emperors rule in A.D. 69. The heavens and the earth were clearly reeling from God's wrath during this tumultuous year just after the Day of the Lord in the fall of the preceding year resulting in this Divine judgment.

Toward the end of this year, one year after the marriage supper of the Lamb, John sees heaven opened for the fourth and last time in Revelation 19:11. We have identified such openings of heaven with the Day of Atonement. John sees Christ riding upon a white horse (Rev. 19:11) followed by the armies of heaven (Rev. 19:14). John describes the enemy. "And I saw the beast, the kings of the earth, and their armies, gathered together to make war against Him who sat on the horse and against His army" (Rev. 19:19).

Note the accurate historical description regarding what was happening on earth at this time in A.D. 69 as the final warfare associated with Armageddon is about to commence. The powers of darkness had gathered Roman armies into Judea. Vespasian and Titus were stationed around Jerusalem since June A.D. 68 when they learned of

Nero's death. The Roman officers were awaiting word from the new emperor that never came because of the turmoil at Rome and the rapid succession of emperors after Nero. The powers of darkness were waging their war against God as they always had done, by opposing His work among His people on earth.

This battle would be different. Before the war plays out through the human contestants involved, the armies of heaven are dispatched to carry out the long-awaited sentence upon the powers of evil. They cast the beast and the false prophet into the Lake of Fire, and then throw Satan into the abyss where he will be confined for one thousand years. This was the most important part of this final warfare, this "otherworldly" dimension not usually visible to human observation. Here the powers of darkness that had opposed God for centuries received their just punishment.

I want to share one thought about the word, "Armageddon." It means literally the Mount of Megiddo. I am inclined to think that it was never intended here in Revelation to refer to any specific location but to commemorate something that happened at Megiddo centuries earlier. It was there that Pharaoh Necho killed King Josiah. The powers of darkness squelched the life of this great king. "Now before him there was no king like him, who turned to the Lord with all his heart, with all his soul, and with all his might, according to all the law of Moses; nor after him did any arise like him" (2 Kings 23:25). God yearned for such kings in the years that went before. Yet, Josiah was a man born at the wrong time and all his efforts at reformation would be for naught. The great evil done by King Manasseh had sealed the doom of the nation. Josiah's leadership was too late. It may be that God honored this great king by commemorating the place of Josiah's death at the hands of the powers of darkness by thus naming the battle where God would defeat these evil foes and inflict final judgment upon them. Remember, the primary battle of Armageddon involved non-human combatants. Righteous angels wielding the mighty power of God cast the beast and the false prophet into the lake of fire, and hurl Satan into the abyss.

Revelation tells us that the powers of darkness are now in their final state of punishment in the lake of fire. It is clear that they still have access to this earth. It was the abyss or bottomless pit that removed rebellious angels from contact with this earth. Revelation 17:8 describes *Apollyon* as the beast who "was, and is not, and will ascend out of the bottomless pit and go to perdition." "And is not" describing his existence in the abyss following his rebellion refers to the fact that those confined there have no contact with this earth. For all practical purposes, they do not exist in that regard. I believe that is why Satan is thrown into the abyss at Armageddon while the others are thrown into the lake of fire. God chose to remove this ancient foe for one thousand years from any contact with this earth. That would allow sufficient time for Jesus in His millennial reign with His saints to rescue this earth from the brink of destruction and head it on its new course under the New Covenant and its new ruler. After that, Satan is released and then thrown into the lake of fire with all the other rebels. Even this master opponent of God at this point could not turn back the tide of the ever-increasing kingdom that is spreading around this world.

The rest of the battle of Armageddon took place on earth and is simply described in Revelation where we read, "the rest were killed with the sword which proceeded from the mouth of Him who sat on the horse" (Rev. 19:21). This describes the final days at Jerusalem as Roman armies destroy the temple and the city in A.D. 70 just as God had foretold in Scripture, where His word is likened at times to a sword. The Old Covenant would come to an end and His people who rejected the Messiah and the New Covenant would die at the hands of the Gentile armies. Such was the grim conclusion to this period of biblical history foretold by the sword of God's word.

Tacitus' *Annals* break off at the end of A.D. 66 and he resumes with the *History* in A.D. 69 as he gives us an account of a world reeling from the outpoured wrath of God during that dark period in history. He describes civil wars and the different wars raging throughout the empire and fires taking their toll in Rome and destroying other towns. Terror reigned through the empire, especially at Rome as the political scene was thrown into chaos with four different emperors, people leveling accusations, and seizing positions for gain. Virtuous behavior seemed to guarantee certain death.[66] Tacitus concludes this dark period in Roman history by saying that it proves that the gods do not care for human welfare but only for punishment.[67] Here is a non-Christian's assessment of events as they unfold. Without the truth of sacred Scripture and the inspiration of the Holy Spirit, the unenlightened mind discerns no more than this gloom. The faithful who had responded to God's grace offered through the New Covenant had been taken from the earth in the fall of A.D. 68. They were removed from the earth during this period of judgment upon the world when God poured out His wrath and brought the Old Covenant to an end.

I believe the millennial reign of Christ with His saints began this year on the Day of Atonement, *Tishri* 10. I am assuming that the millennial reign coincides with the thousand-year imprisonment of Satan in the abyss or bottomless pit that I believe occurred as the heavenly part of the warfare identified with Armageddon. All of the prophecies about the Second Coming would then have been fulfilled by the time Daniel's Seventieth Week ends on August 27, A.D. 70. Then it could be said that Daniel's Seventy Weeks of Years that began in 444 B.C. had come to an end as God proved again His faithfulness to act in accord with His promises.

A.D. 70—Daniel's Seventieth Week Ends

Vespasian becomes emperor in December A.D. 69, and at once charges his son Titus to finish the Jewish war.[68] Continuing in Josephus, we read that Titus surrounds the city by Passover thereby containing a large number of people who gathered there for the feast. This sets in motion the conditions that will lead to starvation for the people trapped inside. Jesus foretold these terrible days on Palm Sunday as he wept over the city because it did not know the time of its visitation.

> For the days will come upon you when your enemies will build an embankment around you, surround you and close you in on every side, and level you, and your children within you, to the ground; and they will not leave in you one stone upon another. (Luke 19:43-44)

Those days came in A.D. 70. Starvation can do terrible things, moving people to acts of violence against those about them. The stronger and younger robbed and plundered the weaker and the elderly. One mother even ate her own infant in desperation. If you wish to read more about the tragic details of those days, go to Josephus, Books V and VI of "The Wars."

The continual burnt offering ends on July 13, A.D. 70, the inevitable result of the corruption of the worship of God and the siege by the Romans. As Josephus writes, it was not offered because there was nobody left to offer it. The famine was exacting its terrible toll. Roman armies burn the temple around August 5 and complete the desolation of Jerusalem around September 1. The abominable power of evil had accomplished the prophesied desolation.

Josephus records the last days of the temple at Jerusalem as Roman soldiers set fire to the place where the living God dwelt for a time in history over the Ark of the Covenant that resided in the Most Holy Place. The Old Covenant was indeed coming to an end. Listen to Josephus' account.

> While the holy house was on fire, every thing was plundered that came to hand, and ten thousand of those that were caught were slain; nor was there a commiseration of any age, or any reverence of gravity; but children, and old men, and profane persons, and priests, were all slain in the same manner; so that this war went round all sorts of men, and brought them to destruction, and as well those that made supplication for their lives, as those that

defended themselves by fighting. The flame was also carried a long way, and made an echo, together with the groans of those that were slain; and because this hill was high, and the works at the temple were very great, one would have thought that the whole city had been on fire. Nor can one imagine any thing either greater or more terrible than this noise; for there was at once a shout of the Roman legions, who were marching all together, and a sad clamour of the seditious, who were now surrounded with fire and sword. The people also that were left above were beaten back upon the enemy, and under a great consternation, and made sad moans at the calamity they were under; the multitude also that was in the city joined in this outcry with those that were upon the hill; and besides many of those that were worn away by the famine, and their mouths almost closed when they saw the fire of the holy house, they exerted their utmost strength, and brake out into groans and outcries again: Perea did also return the echo, as well as the mountains round about, [the city,] and augmented the force of the entire noise. Yet was the misery itself more terrible than this disorder; for one would have thought that the hill itself, on which the temple stood, was seething-hot, as full of fire on every part of it, that the blood was larger in quantity than the fire, and those that were slain more in number than those that slew them; for the ground did nowhere appear visible, for the dead bodies that lay on it; but the soldiers went over heaps of these bodies, as they ran upon such as fled before them.[69]

This description fulfills what John foresaw in the Revelation when the earth's vine, referring to those Jews who rejected the Messiah, would be placed into the winepress of God's wrath (Rev. 14:17-20). "And the winepress was trampled outside the city, and blood came out of the winepress, up to the horses' bridles" (Rev. 14:20). Roman armies burn the temple on *Ab* 10, around August 5, and destroy the City of Jerusalem on *Elul* 8, around September 1. Though the 1,260-day Period of the Authority of the Beast ends on June 13, A.D. 70, the momentum of the evil acts already done bring about the destruction of Jerusalem. Thirty days later, on July 13, A.D. 70, 1,290 days after the authority of the beast began, the continual burnt offering ends. The Romans then destroy the temple and complete the devastation of Jerusalem.

Daniel's prophecy about Seventy Weeks of Years was now fulfilled with the completion of Daniel's Seventieth Week in A.D. 70. God had fulfilled His promises to His people by bringing the faithful into their inheritance of the Christlike nature and glorified body. They would live forever in the Presence of the living God with the dark night of sin, death, and the powers of evil forever behind them. Jesus took authority over this earth from Satan, and then began His reign with the saints. God poured out His wrath and the powers of darkness received their final punishment. Everything was now in place to put this earth back together. God preserved the record of these mighty acts through the apostolic witness that has come down to us in the New Testament. Therein lies the light we need in order to know how to cooperate with Him in His great undertaking that will someday result in peace upon the earth.

Let us conclude this chapter by discussing the millennial reign of Jesus with His saints that began in A.D. 69. Remember that Jesus assumes authority over all things in A.D. 65. This is not the beginning of His millennial reign with the saints. He will shortly grant authority to the powers of darkness for 1,260 days to work terrible destruction during those last days of the Old Covenant period as Jerusalem and the temple will be destroyed and even the New Covenant people will undergo persecution and martyrdom. He begins His millennial reign with the faithful in A.D. 69 over a world reduced to shambles after centuries of satanic rule and this 1,260-day Period of the Authority of the Beast granted during those last days. The Roman Empire falls to pagan nations about halfway through the millennial reign. Probably the most important accomplishments during the millennial reign of Jesus with His saints were the preservation of the church and the clarification of the New Testament canon. With the faithful removed from the earth at the *Parousia*, the Body of Christ was not the dynamic church we see reflected in the Book of Acts and New Testament letters, yet it survived the dark ages following the fall of Rome and preserved the witness of Scripture.

The millennial reign of Jesus with His saints begins according to our reckoning in the year A.D. 69. Figuring one thousand years of 360 days each brings us to A.D. 1055. Several large pilgrimages to the Holy Land occur by A.D. 1054 with one that year numbering around three thousand participants.[70] The pilgrims encounter no trouble in these earlier crusades. That changes after Satan is released from the abyss in A.D. 1055. More than seven thousand persons embark on another pilgrimage in A.D. 1064. They were motivated by popular opinion that the Day of Judgment would come at Easter of A.D. 1065. Recently released from the abyss, Satan stirs up some Bedouins in the holy land who inflict suffering and persecution upon the invaders.[71] Revelation 20:7-8 tells about this. "Now when the thousand years have expired, Satan will be released from his prison and will go out to deceive the nations…to gather them together to battle." The deceiver who is also the destroyer proceeds to do his thing. He takes what is already in progress, the pilgrimages of Christians to the Holy Land, and stirs up war. Toward the close of A.D. 1074, Pope Gregory VII conceives of an armed expedition against the "enemies of God."[72] It remains for Pope Urban II to organize the Christians to undertake the first crusade[73], one reason being to rescue Jerusalem from the pagans. The leaders of the church were ignorant of the witness of Holy Scripture at this point. Jesus stopped Peter from taking the sword against those who came to seize Jesus in Gethsemane. He warned His followers that those who take the sword would perish by the sword. The Crusades witness to the truth of Jesus' words, as well as Satan's prophesied activity following his release from the abyss.

According to our time scheme, the millennium ends around A.D. 1055. After one thousand years under the reign of Christ and His saints, even the master deceiver and destroyer cannot stop the tide of the ever-increasing kingdom. He still stirs up trouble, but the advance of the kingdom he cannot stop. Then Satan is cast into the lake of fire. We cannot say exactly when this event takes place, but we can be sure the lake of fire provides appropriate punishment for this ancient enemy of God. He can still tempt us from there, but he cannot harm those who learn to live in Christ. Satan is powerless before our risen and reigning Lord. This ancient foe of truth and all that is good has been made a footstool for the feet of Christ through His mighty acts. As we learn to appropriate all that God has made possible for us through the Incarnation and Return of Jesus, Satan will become a footstool for our feet. In the power of the One now occupying the throne, we shall learn to tread upon Satan and build the new earth as the Sovereign Lord works to make all things new. May God be praised forevermore!

11

GOD HAS AN EXCITING MYSTERY TO REVEAL

Mystery religions flourished throughout the New Testament world. They involved participants in pagan rituals that were supposed to bring them to new life and immortality. Each had its own strange mystery by which such was accomplished. Against this background, God revealed His own mystery opening to fully cooperating disciples the eternal life perfected in Christ and raising such before the throne in heaven. The apostles had a considerable advantage over us in believing such things. They witnessed first-hand the ministry and miracles of Jesus, the Lord of heaven come to earth. They saw how this life from above manifested itself in relating to people, holding fast to truth, and yet loving those who lived in sin and error. Then after a little more than three decades of the sanctifying work of the Holy Spirit, Jesus returned to complete within the faithful the same kind of life and raise them to heavenly places while still on earth, a great mystery indeed.

Though not using the word "mystery" in Hebrews as he did in his letters to Gentile audiences, Paul talks about the perfecting of the faithful. He writes from the perspective that Jesus would soon take His faithful from the earth. "For yet a little while, and He who is coming will come and not tarry" (Heb. 10:37). Before the Lord removes them from the earth at the *Parousia*, Hebrews witnesses to what has already been happening during the post-seventh trumpet days while they were still on earth. Those first disciples of Jesus were perfected along with those Old Testament heroes of the faith who waited for centuries for this moment when the Jewish Messiah would return. We have observed this testimony in Hebrews 11:40 about how the faithful from the Old Testament period were perfected along with the faithful of the apostolic generation. One thing is certain. Persons have been perfected at the time Hebrews was written bearing witness to the occurrence of the seventh trumpet.

I believe these perfected people are the same persons John refers to when he talks about those "born of God" in his First Epistle. Remember, John also writes during the last days. "Little children, it is the last hour; and as you have heard that the Antichrist is coming, even now many antichrists have come" (1 John 2:18). Because of these antichrists, John repeats his conviction in the same verse: This is how "we know it is the last hour." During those second-coming days, John witnesses about how the mature have come to perfection in being "born again." He is not talking about the beginning of the disciple life as this verse is usually interpreted. He talks about the other end of Christian experience, or the experiential dimension of the Second Coming or the "mystery of God," because this person no longer sins. This is certainly not the case for the new convert. The beginning believer will have as one of his biggest struggles overcoming sin through the power of the indwelling Holy Spirit. Listen to what John says about those "born of God." "Whoever has been born of God does not sin, for His seed remains in him; and he cannot sin, because he has been born of God" (1 John 3:9). I believe John refers to the same persons Hebrews talks about when it refers to "the spirits of just men made perfect" (Heb. 12:23).

Both John and Paul speak about the grand consummation of faith and experience possible on earth, truly amazing discoveries made by the apostolic generation during the Second Coming. God had finally completed His life within His people. Now at last, He had persons on this earth who by nature would love and obey God in contrast to their previous days when by nature they fell to sin. Just after talking about the power of the blood of Christ to perfect believers, Paul quotes from the Old Testament.

> "This is the covenant that I will make with them after those days, says the Lord: I will put My laws into their hearts, and in their minds I will write them." (Heb. 10:16)

With the completing of those first faithful disciples, God had demonstrated the sufficiency of this New Covenant made through the Jewish Messiah, Jesus Christ. He had created new people and written His law on their hearts and minds. Such would obey God with all their heart, the kind of people God has been looking for from the very beginning. During those second-coming days, the Old Covenant was about to vanish forever from this earth with the prophesied destruction of the temple and Jerusalem leaving the covenant made through Jesus Christ as God's final pact with us on this earth. Hebrews 8:13 says that the very reference to the covenant made through Jesus as "new" means that the first one has become obsolete. The author continues in the same verse to then say: "Now what is becoming obsolete and growing old is ready to vanish away." The Jewish Messiah returned, completed those first faithful disciples, and removed them from the earth to join the resurrected dead and live forever in God's presence. The Old Covenant came to an end, and the New Covenant remains, and will continue forever as flawless in producing the results God seeks in faithful disciples—persons who will love Him with all their heart, soul, mind, and strength.

Sin opened the door to corruption in this world. Its blight spoiled our human nature made in the image of God (Eph. 4:22). The corruption spread to our thoughts (2 Cor. 11:3), to our morals (1 Cor. 15:33), and to our bodies (1 Cor. 15:42). Jesus Christ came on a mission from our heavenly Father to bring us an incorruptible inheritance, the first part of which involves the very nature of God, just like that which was in Jesus. The writers of the New Testament let us know that God did not leave unfinished His promised work, but brought it to completion for those on earth during this approximately three-year period between the seventh trumpet and the *Parousia* when Jesus returned to remove the faithful from the earth.

Just as the Lord revealed to Paul the fulfillment of a mystery at the last trumpet, the angel also tells John about a mystery to be revealed in the days of the seventh trumpet (Rev. 10:7). Right after the seventh trumpet in the Revelation, John sees this mystery as a great and wondrous sign (Rev. 12:1). Both Paul and John anticipate the fulfillment of a mystery during the days of the Second Coming. A close look shows both are speaking about the same mystery only in different ways. John talks about a mysterious sign, while Paul relates in pastoral terms.

A mystery by its very nature remains hidden until revelation is given. God kept some things hidden until the time of the apostolic generation, those exposed to the ministry of Jesus and the outpouring of the Holy Spirit, signs that the last days were at hand. The revelation of this mystery found its fulfillment and climax during the Second Coming of Jesus Christ as the Lord returned to manifest His glory in His people who responded to the sanctifying work of the Holy Spirit. As we look at Paul's mystery revealed in pastoral terms and John's mystery revealed in terms of a great and wondrous sign, it becomes clear that they are talking about the same mystery.

In chapter 4, "Tracking Paul's Thoughts on the Second Coming," we observed how Paul anticipated the faithful on earth would be changed at the same moment that the dead were raised as part of a mystery to be experienced at the trumpet. Paul witnesses in Philippians to his desire to be perfected in Christ and experience resurrection power. Then we observed how these expectations have been realized when he writes Ephesians and Colossians as part of a mystery revealed to the apostolic generation prior to the *Parousia*.

Now let us look at the mystery disclosed to John. The revealing angel tells John in Revelation 10 that "in the days of the sounding [trumpet] of the seventh angel, when he is about to sound, the mystery of God would be finished, as He declared to His servants the prophets"

(Rev. 10:7). The seventh trumpet sounds in Revelation 11:15 and John sees heaven opened in Revelation 11:19. In the next verses, John sees a great and wondrous sign (Rev. 12:1-6). The mystery announced by the angel to be accomplished during the days of the last or seventh trumpet is here depicted as a light-radiating woman who gives birth to a male child who is snatched up to God's throne to avoid harm from Satan portrayed as a dragon. Not until Revelation 14:14-16 does Jesus return to remove His faithful from the earth, likened to the harvesting of a ripe crop. What does this mystery represent in Revelation 12:1-6 immediately following the last trumpet, but before Jesus removes His faithful from the earth in Revelation 14:14-16?

Isaiah provides a clue. The prophet likened Israel under the Old Covenant to a woman who was pregnant with child but unable to deliver.

> As a woman with child is in pain and cries out in her pangs, when she draws near the time of her delivery, so have we been in Your sight, O Lord. We have been with child, we have been in pain; we have, as it were, brought forth wind; we have not accomplished any deliverance in the earth. (Is. 26:17-18)

The Old Covenant failed to produce the desired result of salvation. The Revelation shows that the New Covenant does not fail. This woman in Revelation 12 is also pregnant but proceeds to give birth to a child. She wears a crown of twelve stars, pointing to the elect Jewish Christians on earth during the second-coming days. (Revelation 12:17 suggests that Gentiles find their inclusion in "the rest of her offspring.") As soon as the male child is born, caught up to God's throne, and the woman flees to the nurturing place after which Satan and his hosts are cast out of heaven, a great cry is heard from heaven. "Now salvation, and strength, and the kingdom of our God, and the power of His Christ have come." (Rev. 12:10). The Old Covenant failed through Israel to bring forth in this world the salvation God intended.

This New Covenant through the faithful succeeds during the second-coming days as beautifully portrayed in Revelation 12:1-6.

These verses express the profound truth about how God's working through the provision of the New Covenant climaxed during the Second Coming in the forming of the Divine life within His people and raising them to victory while still on earth. This fulfilled what the angel referred to in Revelation 10:7 as the mystery of God. John's mystery consists of two primary elements. Notice how similar these are to what Paul speaks about in Ephesians as part of the mystery revealed to him. In John's case, a male child is born and then taken up to God's throne. For Paul, the Christlike nature is formed and resurrection power takes the completed person up to God's throne. John's "male child" would correspond to Paul's "Christlike nature" and John's "snatched up" would correspond to Paul's "resurrection power" as both take the completed believer to the same place—to the presence of God and His throne on high (Rev. 12:5, Eph. 2:6).

Revelation 12:1-6 helps us to understand the mystery experienced by the apostolic generation when Jesus returned. We have called this the experiential dimension of the Second Coming. The Christlike nature was completed within them and they were raised spiritually to the throne and God's presence. Revelation 12:1-6 illustrates this mystery as a woman gives birth to a male child who is taken up to God's throne. What we call birth is the moment a baby leaves the dark watery womb of the mother and enters the world of light and air. Just prior to birth and after about nine months since conception, the baby comes to a kind of completion or readiness to make this transition. In the case of those first Christians, the sanctification process begun at conversion came to completion at the seventh trumpet with the perfecting of the Christlike nature. They were now ready for this spiritual transition to live in God's presence. On the Day of Atonement, they were spiritually raised before God's throne, entering a new dimension just as a baby does at birth. The raising of that male child born to the light-radiating woman illustrates the spiritual resurrection experienced by those first

Christians. Jesus and the Holy Spirit prepared the way leading to this climax for the bride of Christ occurring during those last days.

Revelation 12:1 tells us that the woman is "clothed with the sun." What does this mean? I believe this indicates that Jesus, the King of glory, has joined Himself in spiritual union to His bride in whom the Christ-life had just been brought to completion at the seventh trumpet. When John first sees Jesus in Revelation 1:12-16, Jesus is a light-radiating person whose face shines like the sun. I believe the woman in Revelation 12, representing the faithful Jewish Christians on earth, similarly radiates such light because Jesus has joined Himself to her in spiritual union. He will shortly raise the new person within, portrayed by the male child, before God and His throne though His bride is still confined by the body to this earth. This great mystery enables His bride to live as citizens of heaven while still on earth. Figure 9 illustrates the mystery for the faithful.

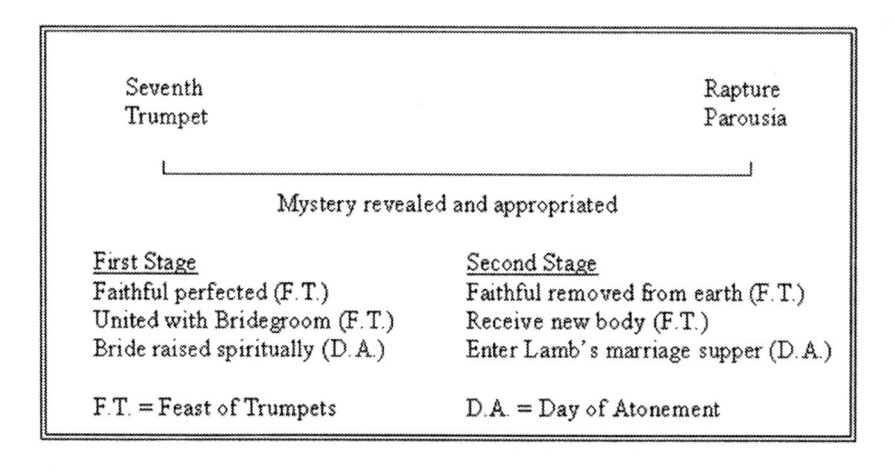

```
Seventh                                    Rapture
Trumpet                                    Parousia
    L_____J
              Mystery revealed and appropriated

First Stage                      Second Stage
Faithful perfected (F.T.)        Faithful removed from earth (F.T.)
United with Bridegroom (F.T.)    Receive new body (F.T.)
Bride raised spiritually (D.A.)  Enter Lamb's marriage supper (D.A.)

F.T. = Feast of Trumpets         D.A. = Day of Atonement
```

Figure 9 Time Interval between Seventh Trumpet and Parousia

Life on this earth would never be the same for this woman. These faithful in whom this new life was completed were raised up into God's presence. Paul refers to this in Colossians 1:13 when he says "He has delivered us from the power [authority] of darkness and translated us into the kingdom of the Son of His love." They were raised to the new spiritual environment of heaven while their bodies kept them at the same time surrounded by the spiritual atmosphere of corruption in this world. Paul seeks to help the faithful appropriate this through wisdom in Ephesians and Colossians. "If then you were raised with Christ, seek those things which are above." (Col. 3:1). He continues in the next verse. "Set your mind on things above, not on things on the earth." They must do this to maintain their link with heaven while still living in the corruption of this world. They must now become established in the realities of this new heavenly environment.

I believe this mystery reveals the fulfillment of Christian faith and experience on this earth as well as God's strategy through the Body of Christ and the New Covenant to bring heaven to this earth and the long-awaited prophetic dream of peace. This mystery constituted the appearing or *epiphaneia* of Jesus Christ and His glory in His waiting people as He revealed Himself and manifested His life in them. They were taught such expectations. The pathway to maturity led to this climax for the first followers of Christ according to the New Testament. The apostles prepared the Body of Christ for this conclusion, and the Scripture bears witness to its happening. This is what lay ahead for the first followers of Jesus as they journeyed according to the word. I believe this is what lies ahead for the Body of Christ today. The journey of servanthood and discipleship leads to this climax for the faithful according to the apostolic witness.

It remains a mystery, how we can still live in a body on this earth and be raised up with Christ in heavenly places. How can the life of Christ be formed within ordinary people? This is a great mystery indeed, and possible only through the mighty, but hidden, working of God through the Holy Spirit in the lives of cooperative and submissive servants who are hearing and doing His word. I am sure some reading this are still overwhelmed by the idea of perfection, thinking that it is utterly impossible for you to accomplish. That is correct. You cannot do this. No human effort could ever pull this off. Let that realization, that this is something totally impossible through anything of yourself, only move you to a greater dependence upon God and an insatiable hunger for His word that inspires the faith we need. What is absolutely impossible for any human being is nonetheless possible for God. The Bible tells about His intention to do just exactly that in the lives of cooperative disciples and the New Testament clarifies how we cooperate. Jesus taught this from the first. "Therefore, you shall be perfect, just as your Father in heaven is perfect" (Matt. 5:48). God accomplished that at the Second Coming of Jesus.

The Spirit revealed such things to the first Christians during their last days on earth as Jesus returned to reveal His glory in His waiting people. When He later took the faithful off the earth, knowledge of this mystery remained in the apostolic witness that would be clarified and fixed around the fourth century as our New Testament. I believe the Spirit is finally bringing the church to similar spiritual ground to which the apostolic generation had come. I also believe God wants to move us beyond all the speculation about the cosmic dimension of the Second Coming that tries to correlate current events with biblical prophecies. This enables us to focus on the experiential dimension of the Second Coming, the climax of Christian faith and experience possible while still on earth. We need to embrace the witness of the apostles rather than centuries of tradition shaped by post-apostolic generations.

This means working with the Holy Spirit to build the Body of Christ through ministries and the related spiritual gifts. That will help the members go on to maturity as God works to head up all things in heaven and earth in Jesus Christ. It means turning from all sin as God reveals in His word so He may form in His faithful disciples the righteous and holy character of Christ. Such commit to seeking and doing the will of God and being His servants in this world. They lead the way as the Holy Spirit prepares such responsive followers for union with their Divine Bridegroom and bringing heaven to this earth. Preparing for the Return of Christ is not primarily an intellectual journey learning how historical events are fulfilling biblical prophecies, but a spiritual journey growing a new person within, and an outer journey of witness and good deeds. Such belief in and obedience to God's word revealed through Scripture enables the Holy Spirit to purify the heart. Jesus said that the pure heart would see God and thus would receive the revelation of Jesus Christ and the manifestation of His glory as part of God's great mystery.

12

DISCOVERING GOD'S ETERNAL JUBILEE

God instructed the Israelites through Moses to observe the year of Jubilee. Every fiftieth year, poor people who had sold their land or themselves as hired servants were released from their debt and servitude. Jubilee was the time when they could return to their land and family.

> "And you shall consecrate the fiftieth year, and proclaim liberty throughout all the land to all its inhabitants. It shall be a Jubilee for you; and each of you shall return to his possession, and each of you shall return to his family." (Lev. 25:10)

Jubilee was a kind of redemption releasing the poor from bondage and enabling them to return to their land and family. Jubilee occasioned great joy for such poor persons.

This was a type of the redemption God would accomplish in the spiritual realm for His people through the Incarnation and Return of Jesus Christ. Because of the debt of sin we incurred, we all were indeed the "poor in spirit" Jesus talked about in the first beatitude. "Blessed are the poor in spirit, for theirs is the kingdom of heaven" (Matt. 5:3). The actual Greek here means "utterly poor." Sin reduced human lives to such a spiritually impoverished state, so distant from the intended glory. Hopeless was our plight on earth because of this debt of sin that left us separated from the Divine Presence, in bondage to sin, and under the authority of the powers of darkness.

Our spiritual plight was similar to that of the materially poor in ancient Israel. First, we all incurred a debt of sin that we could never pay leaving us in hopeless bondage. Second, we lost the spiritual homeland of the Divine Presence for which we were created. This bondage to sin and separation from the presence of God left us in a futile spiritual environment consisting of the corrupting powers of darkness with Satan at the head possessing the power of death over us all. Divine intervention through the Incarnation and Return of Jesus Christ was our only hope for redeeming what had been lost. Let us look more closely at these two problems and how the real victory for each was secured during the days of the Second Coming as the faithful discovered freedom from sin and entrance into the Divine Presence.

Our first problem of sin leading to our spiritual bondage was twofold in nature. First, there was the power of sin that led us to disobey God and second, there was the penalty of sin, the guilt resulting from the trespass that separated us from God. When we first become Christians, God reckons righteousness to us because of the Cross and cancels the sin reckoned to our account that condemns us. This grace frees us from guilt and the penalty of sin. When Paul writes in Romans 6:18,22 about being freed (*eleutheroo*) from sin, he refers to this penalty of sin. The power of sin, however, is still clearly evident for Paul at this point in his life. He writes in Romans 7:14-23 that he still keeps on doing the evil he hates because of the power of sin that dwells within. While forgiven and provided with a new start when we begin the Christian life, we are by no means yet free from sin, because we still have an old nature from which sin exerts its power. The new nature being formed within by the sanctifying work of the Holy Spirit is not yet sufficient to be free from the power of sin. It would not be until the Second Coming that the sanctification process would come to completion within the faithful forming the Christlike nature. Not until we possess this perfected nature can we be victorious over the power of sin and achieve the freedom from sin God desired.

Jesus came from the Father on the Divine mission to save us from the penalty and power of sin, to finally produce on this earth a people who could be victorious over sin. When Jesus stood up before His hometown people at Nazareth to read from the prophet Isaiah, He announced the launching of His ministry.

> The Spirit of the Lord is upon Me, because He has anointed Me to preach the gospel to the poor. He has sent Me "to heal the broken-hearted, to preach deliverance [*aphesis*] to the captives and recovery of sight to the blind, to set at liberty [*aphesis*] those who are oppressed, to preach the acceptable year of the Lord. (Luke 4:18-19)

The Greek word *aphesis* is a very important word in understanding the victory over sin that God provided for us through Jesus Christ. This word is closely related to the word Jubilee in the Old Testament, as we shall see. The word means deliverance, release, or freedom and conveys something more than just forgiveness. It is used in the Gospels and Acts to refer to the Good News and ministry of Jesus. It is always used in conjunction with sin. Jesus came to provide for release (*aphesis*) from sin that held us in bondage (Matt. 26:28, Mark 1:4, Luke 1:77, 3:3, 24:27, Acts 2:38, 5:31, 10:43, 13:38, 26:18). The only other uses of *aphesis* are from the letters of Paul in Ephesians, Colossians, and Hebrews. The apostle does not use this word until these letters written after the seventh trumpet when full deliverance or freedom from sin was accomplished resulting from the completed Christlike nature within the faithful.

The word Jubilee comes from the Hebrew word *yobel* meaning "ram's horn." Jubilee is a transliterated form of this Hebrew word. The *yobel* or *shophar*[74] was blown on the Day of Atonement every fiftieth year proclaiming deliverance for the slaves. While the trumpet is referred to in Leviticus 25:9 as the *shophar*, the rest of the references to a trumpet in the chapter are to the *yobel* and the event takes its name Jubilee from the latter. The horn itself came to signify this release and the Hebrew word *yobel* came to be translated as "deliverance." The Greek Septuagint in the translation of Leviticus 25 that tells about the year of Jubilee renders the Hebrew word *yobel* three different ways. In this important chapter, it is first translated in verses 10,11,12, and 13 as *apheseos semasia* meaning "the trumpet blast of liberty."[75] In verse 15, it is simply translated as *semasia* meaning "trumpet blast." In the remainder of the chapter, *yobel* is rendered as *aphesis*, meaning "release" or "liberty" in verses 28,30,31,33,40,50,52, and 54. We see here the progression from translating *yobel* as "trumpet blast of liberty" to simply "liberty." In other words, the meaning or significance of what was taking place when the *yobel* sounded its trumpet blast announcing the year of Jubilee determined its translation into the Greek. The poor were set free and the Greek word *aphesis* signified this anticipated release or liberty. The English usually translates *yobel* by its equivalent transliteration of Jubilee signifying this liberty or release announced by the blowing of the trumpet on the Day of Atonement every fiftieth year.

It is interesting to note that when Paul talks about God's remedy for our sin-problem, he does not use this word *aphesis* until Ephesians, Colossians, and Hebrews as the mystery hidden for ages is being revealed to the apostles during the days of the Second Coming. *Aphesis* never appears in his earlier correspondence to the Thessalonians, Corinthians, or Romans. He uses the word *charidzomai* that can be translated to forgive and *eleutheroo* when talking about being freed from the penalty of sin. He also expounds on justification and the reckoning of righteousness through faith. "Blessed are those whose lawless deeds are forgiven, and whose sins are covered; blessed is the man to whom the Lord shall not impute sin" (Rom. 4:7-8). Not until the Second Coming does he use the word *aphesis* indicating that complete deliverance from sin had now come within the grasp of the faithful. In addition to being freed from the penalty of sin accomplished at the

Cross resulting in our justification, the new Christlike nature completed in the saints during the days of the Second Coming now produced on this earth people who were able to be victorious over the power of sin. The possibility of freedom from this terrible blight upon human life had now opened to the faithful.

Paul now uses *aphesis* in the post-seventh trumpet Letters of Ephesians and Colossians. "In Him we have redemption through His blood, the forgiveness [*aphesis*] of sins, according to the riches of His grace." (Eph. 1:7). He writes similarly in Colossians 1:13-14. "He has delivered us from the power of darkness and translated us into the kingdom of the Son of His love, in whom we have redemption through His blood, the forgiveness [*aphesis*] of sins." I believe the reason Paul does not use this word with regard to sin until the post-seventh trumpet letters is because such liberty or freedom from sin has not been realized until we have the new nature completed within that does not sin. Then it can be said that freedom from bondage to sin is finally possible. Jubilee is truly here.

Paul also uses *aphesis* twice in the Epistle to the Hebrews written after the seventh trumpet. In this climactic theological treatise about Jesus as the final sacrifice for sin as well as our great High Priest before the Father, the word *aphesis* occurs in 9:22 and 10:18. The former reference simply says that there is no release from sin without the shedding of blood. The second reference follows immediately after the quote from Jeremiah 31:33-34.

> "This is the covenant that I will make with them after those days, says the Lord: I will put My laws into their hearts, and in their minds I will write them...Their sins and their lawless deeds I will remember no more." (Heb. 10:16-17)

Following this, the writer says where there is *aphesis* for sin, "There is no longer an offering for sin" (Heb. 10:18). God foretold through Jeremiah a future day when He would remember the sins of the people no longer (justification), and when He would write His laws on their hearts and minds (sanctification). The sanctification process was completed at the Return of Christ as perfected persons emerged with God's law written on their very hearts and minds. Here were finally people on this earth, fashioned after the Second Adam, our Lord Jesus Christ, for whom obedience to God was as natural as sin was to the First Adam. *Aphesis* or deliverance from sin had been realized on earth. This was the first part of Jubilee experienced by the faithful.

The second part was related to the separation from our spiritual homeland of the Divine Presence. Made in the image and likeness of God and designed to live in His Presence, our spiritual ancestors lost this as a result of the debt of sin. Jesus through His Incarnation and Return delivered us completely from sin enabling us to return to our true spiritual home. God's presence was there in the Garden of Eden. Little did Adam and Eve know what they had before they sinned, because they had never known otherwise. When once they lost His precious Presence, I am sure they deeply regretted the foolishness of their sin against God. God's presence is everything. "You will show me the path of life; in Your Presence is fullness of joy; at Your right hand are pleasures forevermore" (Ps. 16:11). After their sin, they were banished from the Divine Presence and came under the authority of Satan. What a tragic exchange! From that moment on, all the descendants of Adam and Eve have remained separated from the spiritual homeland for which they were created, the Divine Presence. That changed at the Second Coming when resurrection power raised the completed faithful.

The Epistle to the Hebrews makes it clear that during those days before Jesus removed the faithful from the earth, they had been given the privilege of entering into the Divine Presence as a result of the blood of Christ and His high priestly ministry. Written to Jewish Christians, Paul knows how difficult the idea of persons entering into the Divine Presence would be. Only the high priest in ancient Judaism, with the appropriate blood sacrifices, could enter into "the Most Holy Place" where the Divine Presence dwelt over the Ark of the Covenant. Hebrews tells us that Jesus is a superior High Priest, and the blood of

Jesus issues from a vastly superior sacrifice. Because of these two things, those who have come to Jesus, cooperating completely with God's word and Holy Spirit in the sanctifying process, may now enter into the Divine Presence. "Therefore, brethren, having boldness to enter the Holiest by the blood of Jesus…and having a High Priest over the house of God, let us draw near with a true heart in full assurance of faith." (Heb. 10:19-22). This entrance into the Divine Presence is why John writes at the beginning of the Revelation that Jesus "has made us kings and priests to His God and Father" (Rev. 1:6). Priests in ancient Israel were the ones who were permitted to come before the Divine Presence and minister before the Lord God Almighty.

This was the presence of the Father. The New Testament tells about God revealing Himself as the Father, Son, and Holy Spirit. In the Book of Revelation, the Lord God Almighty refers to the Father. When John is taken up to God's throne, the One on the throne is worshiped as the "Lord God Almighty" (Rev. 4:8). In the next chapter, John then sees the Lamb of God also there at the throne (Rev. 5:6). Jesus as the Lamb of God provided for access again into the Father's presence because of His sacrifice upon the Cross. At the seventh trumpet, "The kingdoms of this world have become the kingdoms of our Lord and of His Christ" (Rev. 11:15). Jesus is distinguished from the Father who is referred to as the Lord. Then near the end of the Revelation, this distinction continues.

> But I saw no temple in it, because the Lord God Almighty and the Lamb are its temple. And the city had no need of the sun or of the moon to shine in it, for the glory of God illuminated it, and the Lamb is its light. (Rev. 21:22-23)

Jesus came from the Father, as did the Holy Spirit, down to this earth. Their ministries prepared the way for us to be brought into the presence of the Father, the Lord God Almighty. This was the prize awarded to the faithful during Jesus' Return. Those born again, having the Christlike nature completed within, were spiritually raised up before God's throne on high and given entrance into the Divine Presence.

The heavenly Mount Zion was the dwelling place for the Divine Presence of the Lord God Almighty. Isaiah 35 told about a highway of holiness leading up that heavenly mountain.

> But the redeemed shall walk there, and the ransomed of the Lord shall return, and come to Zion with singing, with everlasting joy on their heads. They shall obtain joy and gladness, and sorrow and sighing shall flee away. (Is. 35:9-10)

When Paul writes to the Hebrews, he tells them they had come not to an earthly mountain like the Israelites did at Mount Sinai, but to the heavenly Mount Zion.

> But you have come to Mount Zion and to the city of the living God, the heavenly Jerusalem, to an innumerable company of angels, to the general assembly and church of the firstborn who are registered in heaven, to God the Judge of all, to the spirits of just men made perfect, to Jesus the Mediator of the new covenant. (Heb. 12:22-24)

Here those completed in Christ though still surrounded by the corruption of this world entered the Divine Presence, the spiritual homeland in which they were redeemed to live. When Paul writes to Gentile audiences, he says that they have been raised up before God's throne in heavenly places as he witnesses in Ephesians and Colossians. During those last days, Jesus came back for those first faithful disciples who received His word, believed the promises, and submitted to God's way. He completed the Divine life within the faithful and by the power of the Resurrection raised them out of the corruption of this world into the Divine Presence and kingdom.

God had indeed provided Jubilee for the faithful saints during those second-coming days. Remember their spiritual plight, likened to that of the materially poor in ancient Israel. First, they all incurred a debt of sin that they could never pay leaving them in hopeless bondage. Second, they lost the spiritual homeland of the Divine Presence for which they were created, leaving them under the authority of the corrupting powers of darkness. God intervened through the Incarnation and Return of Jesus Christ providing for an eternal Jubilee. He freed them from bondage to sin by removing its guilt and forming the Christlike nature within the faithful saints so they could conquer sin. Jesus joined Himself to His perfected bride and raised her in a spiritual resurrection into the presence of the Father, the Lord God Almighty. All of these realities, the perfected Christlike nature, union with Jesus, and resurrection power opened to those first faithful the possibility to be free from and victorious over sin. The Jubilee that will last forever finally occurred during those days of Jesus' Return. God wants to reveal to His faithful today the same eternal Jubilee.

13

FROM BETROTHAL TO MARRIAGE

Christians frequently mention the beloved hymn "In the Garden" when asked about their favorites. The chorus witnesses to an intimate relationship with Jesus whereby we may walk and talk with Him in our daily lives. "Footprints in the Sand," a more recent poetic writing, similarly portrays this closeness with Jesus likened to a walk along the beach. It has also become very popular with Christians. I believe the reason for this is that both the old hymn and the more recent poetic writing touch one of the deep longings of the human heart: intimacy with the living God who created us in His own image and likeness. Sin disrupted the Divine blueprint, but Jesus restored God's original plan to have such intimacy with His creatures. In fact, we shall see that when God looked into our world to help us understand the kind of closeness He desired to have with us, He used the example of the marriage relationship with which we were familiar. The intimacy between a man and woman in holy matrimony is a type of the higher spiritual union God envisioned between Himself and His creatures, and to which He calls us in Christ.

Paul was God's spokesman to the Gentile world and had this end in sight from the beginning. He proclaimed the gospel seeking to bring people to Christ. When they did repent and trust in Jesus, Paul likened what he was doing to espousing them to Christ. "I have betrothed you to one husband...to Christ" (2 Cor. 11:2). They would receive the Holy Spirit who would begin the sanctifying process preparing them for their returning Bridegroom. The end result was to produce persons who could be joined in spiritual union with the Divine Bridegroom, our Lord Jesus Christ. Paul witnessed in Ephesians to the emergence of such persons as the Christlike nature was being completed in the faithful. He also relates in that same letter as part of a great mystery that they were united to Jesus in a kind of spiritual union, likened to the union of a man and woman in marriage. I believe His betrothed is again ready to appropriate the discoveries made by the apostolic generation. Let us retrace the steps that led to this climax.

John the Baptist stepped onto the stage of history preparing the way for the Jewish Messiah by calling the people to repentance. The Gospel of John records the testimony of this forerunner of the Messiah.

> He who has the bride is the bridegroom; but the friend of the bridegroom, who stands and hears him, rejoices greatly because of the bridegroom's voice. Therefore this joy of mine is fulfilled. He must increase, but I must decrease. (John 3:29-30)

John the Baptist was one of the first to recognize the significance of Jesus and the ministry of the Jewish Messiah. This was the Lord of heaven, the Divine Bridegroom, coming to choose His bride from this earth and make spiritual provision for His people through the New Covenant for this Divine-human marriage. John prepared the way for the Lord by calling people to repentance. Jesus would follow by teaching and demonstrating the ways of the dawning kingdom. He would die for the sin of those destined to be His bride. They would be forgiven and receive the Holy Spirit who would prepare them for union with the Divine Bridegroom and entrance into the kingdom.

According to John's Gospel, Jesus worked His first miracle at the wedding in Cana of Galilee. Jesus' mother tells Him they have run out of wine. Jesus at first seems uncertain whether His heavenly Father wants Him to get involved in this. He simply instructs the servants to place water in the containers. He pronounces no words over the water, but entrusts the working of any miracle into the hands of His Father.

When the servants draw from the container, the water has become wine. The head of the marriage celebration says to the bridegroom: "Every man at the beginning sets out the good wine, and when the guests have well drunk, then that which is inferior; but you have kept the good wine until now" (John 2:10). The Father was clearly in this and used this first miracle to point to the ministry His Son was beginning.

God likewise saved the best for last by offering us His kingdom and a great salvation through the New Covenant. The preparation for that begins as the Father launches His Son upon His ministry to teach about the kingdom and its righteousness and finally offer Himself as a final sacrifice for sin, the great barrier alienating us from God. Jesus' first miracle at the marriage feast pointed to the spiritual marriage between the Lord and His people that would happen someday in the future as a result of the ministry of the Messiah. The Divine Bridegroom had come from heaven to bring to His prospective bride the new wine of the kingdom. God indeed saved the best for last to offer us through the New Covenant of grace.

Jesus understood Himself to be this Bridegroom coming to claim His bride. When disciples of John the Baptist asked Jesus why his disciples did not fast, He responded.

> Can the friends of the bridegroom mourn as long as the bridegroom is with them? But the days will come when the bridegroom will be taken away from them, and then they will fast. (Matt. 9:15)

Jesus understood the uniqueness of who He was. He Himself was the long-awaited Bridegroom, the Jewish Messiah. His disciples did not fast because they abode in His Presence. They were with the Bridegroom. The One with whom they would dwell someday in heaven was right there with them on earth. There was no need for fasting at that time. After His Crucifixion and Resurrection, Jesus would return to heaven and send the Holy Spirit. Then, there would be times for fasting, as they would grow to maturity, preparing to be a bride worthy for union with this holy Bridegroom who would return for them at the conclusion of their generation.

Hebrews admonishes its readers that they need to move beyond the diet of milk in spiritual infancy to the solid food of Scripture that trains them to tell good from evil (Heb. 5:11-14). Chapter 6 continues the same thought. "Therefore, leaving the discussion of the elementary principles of Christ, let us go on to perfection." (Heb. 6:1). The first disciples took such maturing and spiritual growth very seriously. As we noticed earlier, they devoted themselves to four spiritual disciplines in order to disentangle their lives from the sinful world and become a bride set apart for the Lord. The Holy Spirit worked in those first Christians to prepare them for the Return of their Lord when they would be perfected or changed into His likeness and be joined with the Divine Bridegroom. Such would be the spiritual union enjoyed by the faithful while still on earth, likened to a marriage between the Lord and His people, a profound mystery indeed.

Jesus spoke about this in the parable of Matthew 25:1-13. "Then the kingdom of heaven shall be likened to ten virgins who took their lamps and went out to meet the bridegroom" (Matt. 25:1). Spiritual growth takes time. The virgins needed time to gather a sufficient supply of oil. That is why the Bridegroom left, and sent the Holy Spirit into the hearts of His people. That breath of life from heaven would prepare those responding to the gospel for that future day when they would be ready to enter into spiritual union with the Lord.

Finally, the long-awaited moment comes. "And at midnight a cry was heard: 'Behold the bridegroom is coming; go out to meet him!'" (Matt. 25:6). Five of the virgins failed to take sufficient oil to keep their lamps burning at that dark hour. As shared earlier, I believe that oil was the word of God learned through the apostolic witness and the ministry of the Holy Spirit. The faith, wisdom, righteousness, and love it inspires would enable the inner lamp of the spirit to keep aglow through all the spiritual warfare that arises from the powers of darkness who will do all they can to rob us of such victory. The faithful stored up the oil of the word and they were ready for this moment. The five foolish virgins neglected to do this and missed the Return of their Lord because they were unprepared. "And while they went to buy, the bridegroom came, and those who were ready went in with him to the wedding; and the door was shut" (Matt. 25:10).

The faithful who through the years of waiting took the preparation seriously were ready to be united with their returning Lord and Bridegroom. Paul in Ephesians 5:14 admonishes his readers on a similar note: "Awake, you who sleep, arise from the dead, and Christ will give you light." "Give you light" is the translation of the Greek word, *epiphausko*, used only here in the New Testament where Paul witnesses to a great mystery. When Christ gives us this light (*epiphausko*) or thus shines on His people, the *epiphaneia* or "appearing" occurs. Years of learning and applying God's word learned through Scripture prepare the way for this climactic appearing of the Returning Lord as He comes to be united with His bride. I believe it is already beginning to happen in the church as the faithful are awakening to the Divine Bridegroom and moving toward the spiritual union Jesus seeks with His bride that is at the heart of the experiential dimension of the Second Coming.

As we noted at the beginning of this chapter, Paul similarly understood the church as the future bride of Jesus. "For I have betrothed you to one husband, that I may present you as a chaste virgin to Christ" (2 Cor. 11:2). The apostle saw his ministry as bringing people to Christ thereby introducing them to the Lord destined to be their spiritual Bridegroom. Paul is also aware of the many temptations awaiting God's people. He continues in the next verse. "But I fear, lest somehow, as the serpent deceived Eve by his craftiness, so your minds may be corrupted from the simplicity that is in Christ" (2 Cor. 11:3). Such is the battle we face in this world from the first. It continues as the powers of darkness try to deceive us and spoil our preparation to be the bride of Christ. The knowledge of and the faith inspired by the word of God alone can enable us to escape the confusion created by the powers of darkness and continue in the light of God's kingdom way for His people. The Lord waited until those betrothed to Jesus came to maturity. When He returned, they were perfected and joined in spiritual union with Jesus.

When we come to Paul's late Letter to the Ephesians, the apostle speaks about the marriage of the church with its Lord as if it is in the midst of happening while Paul writes in the afterglow of the completion of the mystery. The faithful among the people he betrothed to Christ throughout his ministry now have been completed, joined in spiritual union with Jesus, and raised up into the Divine Presence. Let us look at Paul's witness about this marriage and mystery.

> Husbands, love your wives, just as Christ also loved the church and gave Himself for it, that He might sanctify and cleanse it with the washing of water by the word, that He might present it to Himself a glorious church, not having spot or wrinkle or any such thing, but that it should be holy and without blemish…"For this reason a man shall leave his father and mother and be joined to his wife, and the two shall become one flesh." This is a great mystery—but I speak concerning Christ and the church. (Eph. 5:25-27, 31-32)

In the context of talking about the biblical concept of marriage as the union of a man and a woman, Paul speaks about a "great mystery" and here the apostle makes clear he is talking about "Christ and the church." He compares the intimate relationship of marriage between a man and a woman to the spiritual union of Jesus Christ with His church, and that is indeed a "great mystery." He refers to how Jesus "gave Himself" for His bride, the church, in order to "sanctify…and present it to Himself a glorious church, not having spot or wrinkle or any such thing, but that it should be holy and without blemish." Those maturing disciples were ready to receive the revelation of their Divine Bridegroom and the manifestation of His glory within them as He returned to complete His own incorruptible life within His betrothed and raise her up as His bride.

Here is the heart of the experiential dimension of the Second Coming. When we talk about the inheritance, the eternal Jubilee, the completing of the Christlike nature, and the resurrection power, these are all precious truths related to the experiential dimension of the Second Coming. When we talk about the great marriage, here is the heart of the matter, the personal dimension toward which the truths point. The climax of our relationship with Christ with whom we were betrothed at the beginning of our journey is that of this intimate spiritual union. The grand conclusion of our disciple journey is this ultimate love relationship with Jesus Christ.

The apostle Paul quotes from Genesis in giving us the basic biblical definition of marriage. "A man shall leave his father and mother and be joined to his wife, and the two shall become one flesh" (Eph. 5:31). Let us expand a little upon this. Marriage is the union of a man and a woman based on a commitment until death where they bring the persons they are and the resources they have to serve the needs of the other, and together accomplish God's purpose for their lives. In such a union, God designed the physical delight and pleasure of sexual love to be enjoyed by the man and woman entering into such a relationship. Here they might continue to grow in their love for one another, and provide the kind of environment and nurture necessary for human infants. We were created in the image and likeness of God and designed to be His servants, serving according to His will and plan, to build the marvelous world He envisions where people may live together in peace. Marriage is this union of a man and a woman bringing all they are and have to minister to the needs of the other and support each other in their service to God.

In the case of our marriage with Jesus as His bride, He offers Himself and all that He has to enable us to live victoriously. Paul tells at the beginning of Ephesians about how Jesus our Divine Bridegroom brings to His bride on this earth all of heaven's resources, part of a great mystery. "Blessed be the God and Father of our Lord Jesus Christ, who has blessed us with every spiritual blessing in the heavenly places in Christ" (Eph. 1:3). Then Paul refers to Jesus in Ephesians 1:6 as "the Beloved," an endearing term reminiscent of "The Song of Solomon" that prepares us for the light to be shared later on in Ephesians 5 about the marriage of the faithful with Jesus. He brings every spiritual blessing of heaven to His bride while she still lives on earth. The faithful now changed into His likeness offer themselves completely and everything they have to be His servants in this world. Yes, Jesus needs us, persons in this world who will obey the Father's will, opening the way for the very life of heaven to come to their part of the world. This union or marriage of Jesus and His Bride is the key to bringing heaven to earth. The bride lives to honor and glorify the Bridegroom who died to save her.

God desired from the first such intimacy with His people, like the spiritual union in a marriage that we understand in this world. He tried to reveal this to Solomon. At the beginning of his reign, the Lord appeared to Solomon in a dream saying: "Ask! What shall I give you?" (1 Kings 3:5). Solomon's answer pleased the Lord greatly: "Give to Your servant an understanding heart to judge Your people, that I may discern between good and evil" (1 Kings 3:9). Moved by Solomon's unselfish response, God said: "I have given you a wise and understanding heart" (1 Kings 3:12) and "I have also given you what you have not asked: both riches and honor" (1 Kings 3:13). I believe Solomon's unselfish response prompted God to reveal to Solomon something of the kind of intimacy God wants with His people expressed in "The Song of Solomon," this unusual Old Testament book couched in terms of the love between a man and a woman. It would not work without a perfected nature that Solomon did not have under the Old Covenant. God revealed such amazing truth to Solomon, blessed him abundantly in every way, yet Solomon could not handle it. Foreign wives, whom God forbade him to marry, turned Solomon's heart away to their gods, causing him to be unfaithful to the God of Israel who lavished such love upon Solomon.

God never made that mistake again during the days of the Old Covenant. He would share through the prophets such dreams about His marriage with His people in the future during the days of the

Messiah. "For as a young man marries a virgin, so shall your sons marry you; and as the bridegroom rejoices over the bride, so shall your God rejoice over you" (Is. 62:5). The apostle Paul witnesses to this in his Letter to the Ephesians during the days of the Messiah's Return. The way opened again to people on this earth for the kind of intimacy God wanted, likened to a spiritual union between Jesus, the Bridegroom, and His bride, the faithful among those betrothed.

Solomon did not have the Christlike nature within him. He was fortunate to have King David as his father and blessed through the anointing of the Holy Spirit to serve as King over God's people. His unselfish response as a young man prompted God to risk revealing Himself to Solomon beyond what He had done to David. It did not work. Sex, money, and power are all potential areas where the powers of darkness can topple God's servants. Such matters will be resolved through the sanctification process under the New Covenant in the faithful as they walk by the light of Scripture. Here God reveals what our attitudes and behavior should be in those vulnerable areas. The way will be opened for those who fully cooperate to enter into this spiritual intimacy with Jesus as reflected in Paul's Letter to the Ephesians.

From the very first, God has been looking for people who will walk with Him in faith and obedience. God's disdain for sin is clear from the first. Adam and Eve committed one sin at the beginning, and God banished them from His Presence, subjecting them to the authority of Satan and bringing them under the curse and the sentence of death. The experiment turns sour, causing God to grieve that He made man (Gen. 6:6). "Then the Lord saw that the wickedness of man was great in the earth, and that every intent of the thoughts of his heart was only evil continually" (Gen. 6:5).

God finally finds one man Enoch of whom it was said that he "walked with God." Though all others came under the sentence of death, Enoch was the first of only two persons in the biblical account who was spared this ending to his life according to Genesis 5:24. His great grandson Noah also walked with God (Gen. 6:9) and God chooses

Noah and his family to begin again on the earth. A flood destroys all flesh except Noah and his family whom God forewarns and preserves by guiding Noah to build an ark. Ten generations later, God binds Himself to Abraham in a covenant. Best known for his faith resulting in God reckoning righteousness to him (Gen. 15:6, Rom. 4:3), God also witnesses of Abraham that he "obeyed My voice and kept My charge, My commandments, My statutes, and My laws" (Gen. 26:5). In Isaiah 41:8, God makes the extraordinary statement referring to Abraham as My friend. Jesus clarifies what it means to be His friend. "You are My friends if you do whatever I command you" (John 15:14).

There is no doubt what God is looking for according to the Bible. He looks for people who will turn from sin, and walk with Him through a living faith that obeys His commands as revealed in Scripture. Such are the friends responding to the initiating love of God and who will become the Bride of Christ. They are described in Revelation 14:4 as those who "follow the Lamb wherever He goes." To such who submit to the Lordship of Jesus, taking seriously to turn from the sin He died for, and humbling themselves as servants of God, Jesus comes to be joined with them, completing the Christlike nature within, and raising them into the Divine Presence.

This great marriage, begun at the last trumpet during *Tishri* A.D. 65, revealing the spiritual union of Jesus with His saints while they still lived on earth, opened to them a whole new dimension of life. Unfortunately, they would not be able to enjoy it for long, as God would delegate authority to the beast beginning in January A.D. 67. Approximately two years later, the faithful would be removed, not being required to endure through the entire 1,260 days of gross darkness. However, for a brief time, as the Spirit unfolded the great mystery during those last days, they were able to receive and appropriate this experiential dimension of the Second Coming, and leave testimony to their discoveries in the New Testament. Nowhere else in the world will you read of such things, except in the Holy Scripture that God has preserved through the centuries to guide us in appropriating all He has done to conquer sin, death, and the powers of evil.

Our Bible concludes with John's vision of the new heaven and earth resulting from all the second-coming events. Listen to his testimony.

> And I saw a new heaven and a new earth, for the first heaven and the first earth had passed away. Also there was no more sea. Then I, John, saw the holy city, New Jerusalem, coming down out of heaven from God, prepared as a bride adorned for her husband. (Rev. 21:1-2)

John sees the New Jerusalem "coming down out of heaven from God." "Prepared as a bride adorned for her husband," the New Jerusalem is descending, suggesting a kind of accessibility to the people who still live on this earth. Listen further to his testimony.

> And I heard a loud voice from heaven saying, "Behold, the tabernacle of God is with men, and He will dwell with them, and they shall be His people, and God Himself will be with them and be their God. (Rev. 21:3)

We learn in subsequent verses that this One on the throne works to make all things new, and His inheritance awaits all who overcome in the spiritual warfare with the powers of darkness, conquering by God's word these foes of faith, love, and righteousness. We also learn that "the nations of those who are saved shall walk in its [the heavenly city's] light" (Rev. 21:24), and that "they shall bring the glory and the honor of the nations into it" (Rev. 21:26). The Holy Spirit works in the church on behalf of the Lord and Bridegroom dwelling in the New Jerusalem to prepare His people on earth for spiritual union with Jesus Christ. God makes His dwelling accessible to His bride on earth and raises her by the power of the Resurrection to heavenly places. Wow! What an amazing plan designed in the heart of God to head up all things in heaven and earth through His Son Jesus Christ. Everything is ready because we live in a world where Jesus has returned. "And the Spirit and the bride say, 'Come!'" (Rev. 22:17).

14

BUILDING THE NEW TEMPLATE

Prophetic speculation frequently focuses attention on rebuilding the temple at Jerusalem. Some persons look with eager anticipation to the day when by a miracle the Jews will be permitted to rebuild the temple upon the mount in Jerusalem. The temple had been rebuilt shortly before the birth of the Messiah. Jews responded to Jesus on one occasion by saying that it had taken forty-six years to build this temple. That temple would be destroyed during the second-coming days. The apostles were commissioned to build a new temple consisting of the Body of Christ. Paul talks in Ephesians 2:19-21 about how the Body of Christ is built upon the foundation of the apostles and the prophets. Jesus himself is the chief cornerstone "in whom the whole building, being joined together, grows into a holy temple in the Lord" (Eph. 2:21). During those last days when the stone temple at Jerusalem would be torn down, the faithful who under the New Covenant were part of the new temple of the Body of Christ would be raised before the Divine Presence in the true temple in heaven.

God is not concerned about temples of stone. God created a new temple through the New Covenant enabling Him to move more effectively to reveal Himself and communicate His love, life, and truth to people in the world. God is more concerned about building this living temple of the Body of Christ through the work of the Holy Spirit using ministries employing the related spiritual gifts. The Jewish Messiah demonstrated through His life what this God was like whom the Jews worshiped at the stone temple in Jerusalem. Unlike that old temple of stone, this new temple provides God with the lips, feet, and hands to continue what Jesus began and take His love and life to a hurting world. That is why this new temple is called the Body of Christ.

I remember years ago as a young pastor hearing a speaker address a large gathering of ministers. He made a comment I have never forgotten. He said the renewal of the church in the future would take the shape of recovering the New Testament form of faith and experience. He was right on target. Since that time, the Spirit is returning the church to the wisdom given to the apostles as they went about building this new temple of the Body of Christ. The church strayed from some of that original wisdom in the intervening years by setting up traditions not in harmony with the New Testament. Exciting things are happening where leaders and churches get beyond "business as usual" and seek to operate according to the wisdom reflected in the apostolic leadership as they built the first church. They had been taught by Jesus and were the first recipients of the Holy Spirit who built upon what Jesus had taught. They erected this new temple of the Body of Christ or what I like to call the New Testament church.

The foundation for the spiritual building of the new temple of the New Testament church is Jesus Christ. He is its head, the truth it lives by, and the life it embodies through the Holy Spirit. The New Covenant made by God through Jesus and open to anybody on this earth, Jew or Gentile, replaced the Old Covenant limited only to the Jewish people. Paul likened the church to a building God was erecting in this world through Paul's ministry and that of the other apostles. "For we are God's fellow workers; you are God's field, you are God's building" (1 Cor. 3:9). The church is the spiritual building of the living God in this world. Paul continues in the next verse saying: "As a wise master builder I have laid the foundation." We know from this same letter to the Corinthians that Jesus Christ is the only foundation for the church. "For no other foundation can anyone lay than that which is laid, which is Jesus Christ" (1 Cor. 3:11).

We leave the ranks of the world and become part of this new building when we respond to the gospel or Good News of Jesus Christ. Paul's gospel focused on preaching Christ. "For I determined not to know anything among you except Jesus Christ and Him crucified" (1 Cor. 2:2). Jesus died for our sins and rose from the dead. God made a New Covenant through the Jewish Messiah open to anybody on this earth. Jesus provides for forgiveness of sin and reconciles us to a Holy God from whom sin alienated us. The journey begins here, recognizing that we are sinners separated from God, but forgiven and restored through Jesus when we repent and trust in His mercy and love. As a result of this relationship with Jesus, God receives us into the New Covenant and gives us the Holy Spirit thereby incorporating us into the spiritual temple of Christ's Body.

In this New Testament church, the focus is upon making disciples, not church members. The New Testament defines disciples as persons who are learning how to conduct their lives according to God's word as revealed through Scripture. "Go therefore and make disciples of all nations, baptizing them in the name of the Father and of the Son and of the Holy Spirit, teaching them to observe all things that I have commanded you; and lo, I am with you always, even to the end of the age" (Matt. 28:19-20). Jesus first taught the apostles, and then teaches His disciples in each succeeding generation through the apostolic witness in the New Testament. Disciples learn the commands of Jesus preserved in the New Testament so they might no longer conform to the world but live the new way of God's kingdom. You can be a church member and rarely ever read your Bible or especially the New Testament. You cannot be a disciple of Jesus that way. By very definition, a disciple is one who is learning the commands of His Lord and obeying them. Such persons constitute the building blocks of this new temple.

Paul then tells us how the Holy Spirit builds this new temple upon the foundation of Jesus Christ. The apostle says that God gave "some to be apostles, some prophets, some evangelists, and some pastors and teachers" (Eph. 4:11). This endowment was "for the equipping of the saints for the work of ministry, for the edifying of the body of Christ" (Eph. 4:12). God erects the spiritual building of the church through the work of ministry. We are beginning to discover what Paul and the apostles clearly understood. When God gives the Holy Spirit to persons, He also gives at least one spiritual gift, frequently more, endowing the members of His Body for the work of ministry. God makes this Divine investment so that His people may serve the risen Christ in ministries related to building the Body of Christ, reaching the lost, and enabling each person in this Divine building to mature in Christ.

The New Testament church is not a "one-man show." Each member of the Body is called to some ministry under the direction of the Head of the Body, Jesus Christ. Here the members of the body are joined and knit together in relationships, and when each one is doing his or her part, the body grows and people are built up in love (Eph. 4:16). There is something for each member of the body in the New Testament church. It will not grow properly unless each member is challenged to discover his or her call from Christ and serve Him accordingly. There was no place in the understanding of the apostles for merely pew sitters. The risen Christ called each to serve in some capacity contributing to the building up of the Body of Christ.

It is through the ministry of the members of Christ's Body that God grows this living temple. Some ministries such as teaching and preaching interpret Scripture to help members learn God's promises to be believed, the truth that sets them free, and the wisdom and righteousness to be done. Other ministries take the form of leading worship as the Body gathers to offer praise and thanksgiving to the living God. Other ministries take the shape of organizing and administering God's plans to be implemented in the church. There are ministries that address various needs within the Body enabling its members to minister to one another. Some ministries reach out to touch persons in the world. It becomes a thing of beauty when members of the Body discover their individual gifts and ministries and serve as Christ the head directs. In this way, the amazing love of Christ flows between the members and bonds them together in the Body of Christ.

What is the end result or outcome of this ministry by the members of the Body of Christ? Let us look again at Paul's witness. "And He Himself gave some to be apostles, some prophets, some evangelists, and some pastors and teachers, for the equipping of the saints for the work of ministry, for edifying of the body of Christ, till we all come to the unity of the faith and the knowledge of the Son of God, to a perfect man, to the measure of the stature of the fullness of Christ." (Eph. 4:11-13). The sum total of all these ministries contributing to the growth and building up of the Body of Christ aimed at maturing the disciples of Jesus so that they might attain "to the measure of the stature of the fullness of Christ." There it is, just as clear as can be. What God is aiming at through the new temple of the Body of Christ is to produce Christlike people on this earth, persons who have attained "to the measure of the stature of the fullness of Christ."

What a vision of the church God has given us in Ephesians. Paul tells in Ephesians 1:9-10 about a mystery where God is bringing together all things in heaven and on earth in Christ. God is heading up all things in Christ. Paul continues in Ephesians 1 to tell us that everything God has done in Christ is for the sake of the church. "And He put all things under His feet, and gave Him to be head over all things to the church, which is His body, the fullness of Him who fills all in all" (Eph. 1:22-23). Paul sees the church as a living organism through which God changes people into the likeness of Christ. This is how He is bringing everything together under Christ. He has already united heaven under His authority as Satan and his hosts were cast out during the Second Coming and its sole occupants now consist of the righteous angels and the redeemed from the earth. He is now heading up all things in Christ on this earth by His plan to change people into the likeness of Christ that was also part of this mystery revealed during the last days as we have seen. Such people will submit to His authority and serve as He directs. We need a fresh vision of the church as Paul was given to see when he wrote to the Ephesians.

The apostles were privileged to live in the presence of Jesus. He called them to be His disciples and follow Him where He went. They saw how this Divine life functions in a world that has rebelled against God. Jesus involved them in His work so they learned by doing. They were granted a privilege that no other generation ever enjoyed or ever will. For about three years, they walked and talked with this unique person who was God in the flesh. He was back in the beginning when all was created. He knew all things and enjoyed a unique relationship with His Father. During those three years, they saw and learned things no other generation experienced. Years later, one of those apostles began his epistle this way.

> That which was from the beginning, which we have heard, which we have seen with our eyes, which we have looked upon, and our hands have handled, concerning the Word of life—the life was manifested, and we have seen, and bear witness, and declare to you that eternal life which was with the Father and was manifested to us—that which we have seen and heard we declare to you, that you also may have fellowship with us; and truly our fellowship is with the Father and with His Son Jesus Christ. And these things we write to you that your joy may be full. (1 John 1:1-4)

After His Crucifixion and Resurrection, Jesus poured out the Holy Spirit and those first followers continued the work Jesus began, only now on the basis of the New Covenant. Their writings witnessed to this new work God was doing in this world as He formed a new community of faith called the church or the Body of Christ, persons betrothed to Jesus. Their writings tell how they went about it. I believe God is moving the church to get back to this apostolic witness so as to be "on target" regarding the work God has for us to accomplish, building the Body of Christ so its members may become the bride of Christ.

John is the only New Testament writer who reports what has been called "the high-priestly prayer" of Jesus during his last night on this earth. The following was part of that prayer in which our Lord prayed for a kind of unity.

> I do not pray for these alone, but also for those who will believe in Me through their word; that they all may be one, as You, Father, are in Me, and I in You; that they also may be one in Us, that the world may believe that You sent Me. And the glory which You gave Me I have given them, that they may be one just as We are one: I in them, and You in Me; that they may be made perfect in one, and that the world may know that You have sent Me, and have loved them as You have loved Me. (John 17:20-23)

Notice the unity for which Jesus prays. Just as Jesus and the Father are one, so Jesus prays that His followers may be one with Him. He makes clear the nature of this unity as He repeats the petition: "That they may be one just as We are one: I in them and You in Me." Just as Jesus was one with the Father, so Jesus prays that His followers may be one with Him. This "complete unity" of Jesus and His followers is so that "the world may know that You sent me, and have loved them even as You have loved Me." Such an intimate union between Jesus and His followers will enable the world to see clearly the love and life of Jesus through His people. Quite clearly, the closer we approach such unity with Jesus, we shall experience greater unity with one another in the church. The focus, however, of Jesus' prayer was for unity between Himself and His followers and that climaxed as they were perfected and Jesus, the Bridegroom, joined Himself to His bride. This requires building the Body of Christ according to the apostolic wisdom in the New Testament.

I believe the challenge before the Body of Christ today is to rediscover the New Testament church as it was built by the wisdom given to the apostles. This has been happening throughout the world in all kinds of churches as they return to the wisdom in the New Testament. They lay the foundation of Jesus Christ where all must repent, trust in Jesus as Savior, and turn to follow and serve Him as Lord. They teach

Christians to become disciples, learning about Jesus in the New Testament, so they can obey His commands and walk in His ways. They help members of the Body of Christ to discover their spiritual gifts and corresponding ministries so they may serve the Risen Jesus and have some part in erecting the spiritual household of faith and spread His love through their witness and service. They meet in small groups for nurture, support, and accountability as they grow in loving relationships. They gather to joyously worship and praise the living God. Their fellowship is contagious and winsome as they joyfully witness and serve, drawing others into a living relationship with Jesus Christ. Such churches fashioned after the vision of the New Testament church are needed to sustain the faithful through the spiritual warfare along the journey to appropriate the experiential dimension of the Second Coming.

"You are the light of the world" (Matt. 5:14). Jesus referred to His disciples in this astounding way in what we call "The Sermon on the Mount" in Matthew 5-7. We want to ask Jesus if He has made a mistake. Take another look at these persons. Are you sure they are the light of the world? Let me ask you reading this book. Are you aware that you are also to be the light of the world if you are a disciple of Jesus? I am comfortable referring to Jesus as "the light of the world." Something within me at first recoils at the thought Christians are to be the light of the world. What would Jesus say about you and me at this point in our lives?

Was there something special about those first followers that caused Jesus to say that? No, they were ordinary human beings. They were, however, granted an extraordinary privilege. They lived at the very time when the Lord came down from heaven to live on earth. Jesus called those twelve disciples to follow Him. For a few years, they lived in His Presence, heard His teaching, and observed His miracles as they learned about the reality of the kingdom of God. They became His disciples, who, according to the New Testament, learn and obey the commands of Jesus. "Go therefore, and make disciples of all nations…teaching them to observe all things that I have commanded you" (Matt. 28:19-20). That is why they were the light of the world. They were learning from the Lord Himself and were committed to doing what He had commanded. That was why their writings became Holy Scripture. All was inspired by the life and teaching of this single person Christians claim was the Lord of heaven living in the flesh on earth. As disciples, they were learning God's higher thoughts and ways so different from ours, and committed to putting all this into action. Yes, because of this, they were indeed the light of the world.

You and I are "the light of the world" insofar as we learn what Jesus taught and implement it in the practice of our lives through the power of the Holy Spirit in a vital relationship with Jesus as Lord. Stumbling to sin does not necessarily hinder that if we are transparent, acknowledging our wrongdoing when it occurs, and apologizing when appropriate. This simply shows that we are not yet like Christ, but are totally committed to cooperating with the sanctifying work of the Holy Spirit to have that happen in our lives. The only way we as Christians today can be the light of the world is by learning God's ways from Scripture, especially the New Testament, and with the Holy Spirit's empowerment, doing them in our daily lives as we relate to God and others. Listen to Paul's admonition and witness to the Philippians. "Do all things without murmuring and disputing, that you may become blameless and harmless, children of God without fault in the midst of a crooked and perverse generation, among whom you shine as lights in the world, holding fast the word of life." (Phil. 2:14-16).

The apostolic witness contained in the New Testament provides the light we need in order to know how to build the living Body of Christ, as well as to know how to conduct our lives in a way that pleases God. That new temple is the focal point of the Holy Spirit's activity as He guides disciples to undertake the ministries Jesus has for them, grows the Body of Christ spiritually, and joins the members in love to one another. Such a temple provides the spiritual atmosphere and nurture faithful disciples need to appropriate the experiential dimension of the

Second Coming. The gates of hell will never stand against this temple built according to the wisdom of the living God given to the apostles and recorded in the New Testament.

15

GRACE AND ACCOUNTABILITY

Dr. James Dobson tells about a kind of vision given to his Christian father shortly before his death. Listen to this account as Dobson's father shared it with his wife just before the end of his life.

> "It happened in the early morning hours when I was neither awake nor asleep. I was lying there in my quiet hospital room, when I suddenly saw the most beautiful person I'd ever seen. His identity was not immediately revealed, but I now believe Him to have been Jesus. This was no dream, in the classic sense. I was conscious of my circumstances, and the figure was extremely vivid. It was apparent that I was being permitted to observe a kind of courtroom scene—a divine proceeding—but my being there was as an onlooker. No word was addressed to me directly. The 'person' was seated and was writing in a book. It seemed that he was considering an extremely important issue. Then I realized it was *my* case he was evaluating. The details of my life were being reviewed carefully. He stopped writing and began to plead my case directly to God. I have never heard such eloquent language as he described my circumstances, calling me by name repeatedly. Then he continued to write until he came to the bottom of the page, at which time he completed the last sentence and thrust his hand outward in a sudden gesture. Though no words were spoken, his motion and his countenance revealed his conclusion about my life. It said, 'For time and eternity, he is *acceptable*!'"[76]

We all will face such an evaluation at the conclusion of our lives. Jesus will judge our performance on earth. How have we responded to God's grace? In putting off the matter of the Second Coming of Jesus Christ, we may have dulled the awareness of our accountability before God. Let me ask you a question? How would you fare this day in Jesus' evaluation of your life so far? How would He rate your attitudes and actions in the areas of sex, money, and power? What or who is in control of your life? Have you turned from all sin of which you are aware? Are you serving Jesus in the ministries for which He has gifted you? Jesus' evaluation would make that clear whether we are living by our own agenda, the world's agenda, or that of the kingdom of God.

The Second Coming was a time of accountability when God judged the performance of those who entered into the New Covenant through their relationship with Jesus. Laboring for centuries under the condemnation of the law, God offered us a second chance through Jesus and the Cross. Our Savior brought us out from under the law's condemnation, reconciling us to His Father and endowing us with all we would need to turn from sin, follow in His ways, and serve Him. This grace comes to us as a result of His ministry and the New Covenant. The New Testament teaches that Jesus would return to judge those who rejected His grace offered in Christ, as well as evaluating the performance of those who responded. Did the latter follow through with their repentance, turning from the sin that dishonors God and serving Him, as they were able? Jesus would render that verdict at His Return and determine those who would enter heaven. Peter reflects the seriousness of this as Jesus' Return drew near: "For the time has come for judgment to begin at the house of God; and if it begins with us first, what will be the end of those who do not obey the gospel of God?" (1 Pet. 4:17).

We must be careful lest God's marvelous grace lulls us into a kind of complacency that loses sight of our accountability before God, that someday we shall stand in His Presence for His evaluation. It will have nothing to do with how visible or well known we may have been in the Body of Christ. In that awesome moment, standing before God by ourselves, we shall be evaluated regarding our faith in Christ, how we have turned from sin, embraced His righteous will, and served Him in accord with the spiritual gifts He gave us and the service to which He called us.

Some will say, but is not faith all we need? "For God so loved the world that He gave His only begotten Son, that whoever believes in Him should not perish but have everlasting life" (John 3:16). Faith is essential, but we need to be aware that the New Testament understands faith differently from how we often view it. Lest any think that saving faith is merely giving intellectual assent to the Good News that Jesus died for our sins, the Holy Spirit inspired James to write: "Faith by itself, if it does not have works, is dead" (James 2:17). James refers to Abraham whom Paul also used as the classic example of faith. James says that Abraham's faith in God was active, even responding obediently to the ultimate test of offering his son Isaac as a sacrifice. Therefore James asks his readers fully expecting a "yes" to his question. "Do you see that faith was working together with his works, and by works faith was made perfect?" (James 2:22). New Testament faith is living and dynamic. It responds to God's gracious offer of a second chance.

James at first sight appears to contradict Paul when the latter writes: "For by grace you have been saved through faith, and that not of yourselves; it is the gift of God, not of works, lest anyone should boast" (Eph. 2:8-9). Paul is writing to persons zealous for good works and warning them that the works do not save them and they should never be proud before God because of them. Jesus accomplished for us all we need at the Cross. Faith in His work reconciles us to His Father and keeps us in good stead before Him. We shall never have anything to boast about before God. Fruit-bearing works result from submitted persons depending upon God's blessing operating through their lives. The good works simply show that our faith is alive and that we are making good on the second chance God gave us through Jesus Christ. James writes to people who have become spiritually slothful, careless about "walking the walk," doing the good deeds that witness to a new life.

James issues a wake up call that such faith is a dead faith. I would hate to come before God for my final evaluation saying that I believed the Good News about Jesus, marveled at His accepting me as I was, and yet have the record show that I lived carelessly about the sin He died for, and refused to serve Him as the servant He redeemed me to be.

Jesus taught about this accountability at the Lord's Return through three parables in Matthew 25. In the first parable, Matthew 25:1-13, ten virgins go out to meet the bridegroom, but only five take enough oil with them to see their way at the midnight hour. The other five do not arrive in time and are barred from the marriage feast. In the second parable, Matthew 25:14-30, a master gives talents to three servants so they may serve him. Two obey and are rewarded accordingly. The third refuses to serve and is cast into darkness with weeping and gnashing of teeth. In the third parable, Matthew 25:31-46, persons are divided based on their willingness to serve and minister to human need about them. Those who serve inherit the kingdom, and those who refuse go away to eternal punishment. All three parables clearly teach accountability before God related to the Return of the Lord.

Why would God have delayed, now nearly two thousand years, to make such judgments about the performance of the first generation of Christians? Why would He have delayed rewarding the faithful? Remember, no one inherits the glory of God, the promised reward, until the Second Coming when Jesus returns and decides who has been faithful and hence worthy to share His glory. What would be the sense in putting those of the apostolic generation "on hold" and everybody since then? In addition, the people who would really be put "on hold" by our misconception regarding the time of the Second Coming were the Jewish people. Faithful Jews were waiting centuries for the coming of the Messiah and the fulfillment of the promises. Paul expresses this in Hebrews. In chapter 11, he recites past Hebrew heroes of the faith concluding the chapter with the following words.

> And all these, having obtained a good testimony through faith, did not receive the promise, God having provided something better for

us, that they should not be made perfect apart from us. (Heb. 11:39-40)

"All of these...did not receive the promise." Abraham, Moses, Gideon, David, and Samuel all had to wait until the Messiah came to earth, provided for a New Covenant, poured out the Holy Spirit, and then returned to fulfill the promises. Together with that generation, the apostolic generation, the Old Testament faithful would finally inherit the promised glory. Our "instant-satisfaction" generation would do well to ponder this fact. God does not rush things. He does it right, and there will be no sin in His heaven which corrupted life on this earth. Many generations since Christ have thought they were the special generation that would experience the Return of Jesus Christ. The apostolic generation was that special generation, those experiencing the long-awaited coming of the Jewish Messiah. His Return was the time for rendering judgment and fulfilling the promises for which the Old Testament faithful had been waiting for centuries.

The Revelation tells about two primary times for judgment. Apart from this last book of the Bible, one gets the picture in the parables of Jesus and His other teaching there would be one time for judgment related to His Second Coming. The last book of the Bible refines this by revealing two times for judgment separated by a thousand-year period. What is sometimes called the "great white throne" judgment occurred after this millennium. This was when all peoples of all nations up to that time stood before God in final judgment. Prior to the thousand years, at the time of the Second Coming, Jesus also rendered judgment among the living and the dead as to those who were ready to join Him in heaven at this earlier time. God renders judgment at these two times according to the Revelation.

At the first time of judgment taking place at the Second Coming, the Lord judges among His people regarding who is ready to join Him in heaven as His bride. The Book of Revelation refers to this as the first resurrection.

> But the rest of the dead did not live again until the thousand years were finished. This is the first resurrection. Blessed and holy is he who has part in the first resurrection. Over such the second death has no power, but they shall be priests of God and of Christ, and shall reign with Him a thousand years. (Rev. 20:5-6)

The second time of judgment occurs one thousand years later where all people of all time appear before God's throne for final judgment and a second resurrection takes place according to the Revelation given to John.

> Then I saw a great white throne and Him who sat on it...And I saw the dead, small and great, standing before God, and books were opened. And another book was opened, which is the Book of Life. And the dead were judged according to their works, by the things which were written in the books. The sea gave up the dead who were in it, and Death and Hades delivered up the dead who were in them. And they were judged each one according to his works. Then Death and Hades were cast into the lake of fire. This is the second death. And anyone not found written in the Book of Life was cast into the lake of fire. (Rev. 20:11-15)

These verses in Revelation 20 indicate that the faithful who were ready to meet the Lord when He returned took part in what John calls the first resurrection. Others would take part in a second resurrection one thousand years later.

It is beyond the scope of this book dealing with the experiential dimension of the Second Coming to explore the many questions this raises. Our concern here is to be sure that we are ready to take part in what those first prepared saints did when Jesus returned in what the Revelation calls the first resurrection. I do not believe persons had to be perfected in this life in order to take part in the first resurrection. I do believe they needed to show God true repentance by turning from sin and true obedience by serving Him in so far as it was within their power to do these things.

In 1 Timothy that I believe was written in A.D. 64 during the early part of Paul's final 1,260-day period of testimony, we see how the apostle prepared his people to get ready for the Return of Jesus. Right at the beginning, Paul tells us in 1 Timothy 1:1 that his authority is "by the commandment of God our Savior and the Lord Jesus Christ." Paul then tells us what he seeks to accomplish by his ministry: "Love from a pure heart, from a good conscience, and from sincere faith" (1 Tim. 1:5). Paul aims at this as he works with the Christians committed to His care, producing disciples overflowing with love issuing from pure hearts, good consciences, and sincere faith.

God lavished His love upon His followers through this New Covenant, and they are to be channels for such love through the power of the Holy Spirit working from within. This love fulfills the law, inspires a winsome demeanor to communicate Christ, and provides the glue enabling people to hold together in relationships. Here we reflect the heart of God as revealed in Christ. Paul admonishes the Ephesians as he helps them appropriate the experiential dimension of the Second Coming. "Be imitators of God, therefore, as dearly loved children and live a life of love, just as Christ loved us and gave himself up for us as a fragrant offering and sacrifice to God" (Eph. 5:1-2). God's love moves us to be servants relating to needs about us and keeps our tongues in check from tearing down other people. We love in word and deed. Such love fills heaven and shows our desire to take part in that ultimate fellowship by learning practically what it means to love in all our relationships in this life.

With this end result in mind, Paul works in his ministry to help people live with pure hearts, good consciences, and sincere faith. A pure heart no longer limps through life trying to serve God and please self and the world. It is one in choosing what it understands to be God's will. This effort is assisted by a good conscience that lives by what it understands to be right. All of this is assisted by a sincere faith, trusting the sanctifying and enlightening work of the Holy Spirit to guide us aright and supply what we lack. This enables the love of God to issue out of the hearts of Jesus' followers and spread through their lives out into the world so their witness and service may draw others to Jesus and this New Covenant where they meet the living God.

Jesus told a parable in Matthew 22:1-14 about a king who gave a marriage feast for his son. A person tries to get into the marriage celebration without wearing the appropriate garment for the big occasion. Revelation 19:7 tells us about this wedding garment.

> "Let us be glad and rejoice and give Him glory, for the marriage of the Lamb has come, and His wife has made herself ready." And to her it was granted to be arrayed in fine linen, clean and bright, for the fine linen is the righteous acts of the saints. (Rev. 19:7)

The bride wears "fine linen, clean and bright." So the reader may clearly understand, John says that the "fine linen is the righteous acts of the saints." "Righteousness" that is reckoned by faith is a different word. The word used here is clearly "righteous acts," the things we do in our walk with God as we seek to live in harmony with His will revealed through Scripture. This includes moral behavior and good deeds that minister to the needs of others. Let us be clear at this point. We must first have righteousness reckoned to us through repentance and faith in Christ. This grace afforded to us through the gospel was provided so we could then serve Him through "righteous acts" in the world about us.

Willing servants through a living faith expressing itself in good deeds are preparing the necessary wedding garments they will put on when the Bridegroom comes to take His bride to heaven. These faithful will have served just as their Lord and Bridegroom did before them. Such shows they possessed a living and dynamic faith translated into daily living. His Return marks the time of accountability and will reveal those who are ready to enter into all that God has prepared for those who love Him. All the righteous acts and good deeds we have done will attest to our love for Him. This time of accountability will come, sooner than we think. I believe that moment awaits each of us when we leave the earth. Will it be "Well done good and faithful servant!" or "I don't know you." That verdict is being shaped by how we live each day.

16

OVERCOMING THROUGH THE MIGHTY WARRIOR

Societal reform was not on the agenda of the first Christians in a world where Satan was still the ruler. The first believers focused on preaching the gospel, making disciples, and building up the Body of Christ in order that converts might mature. That is why the Spirit permitted Paul at that time to accept the institution of slavery, encouraging slaves to be the best workers they could be in those circumstances. God knew societal reform would be futile in a world where Satan was still in a position of authority. He also knew that those days would be terrible enough for His people with all that would occur during the Second Coming without adding any further "fuel to the fire."

Things changed in the years following Jesus' Return when He began His reign. Now, nearly two thousand years later, there is clearly a new stance for the Body of Christ. Societal reform is certainly part of the agenda of the new ruler, but He also recognizes the need for the change in human lives in order for this to work. His strategy is to transform the people of this world, gaining their willing cooperation as they work with and in dependence upon the new ruler who works to "make all things new." Since then, the Spirit has clearly revealed God's displeasure with the institution of slavery and His working toward its abolition. He has also elevated woman in the Body of Christ to a new position not enjoyed prior to and during the apostolic generation. This new stance of taking over this world as led by the Lord in His love and power will thrust the Body of Christ into even greater spiritual warfare in the days ahead. The powers of darkness are deeply entrenched and will not surrender without battle the ground they obtained through human sin. The apostle Paul makes it clear that many are the spiritual hosts that war against Christians. "For we do not wrestle against flesh and blood, but against principalities, against powers, against the rulers of the darkness of this age, against spiritual hosts of wickedness in the heavenly places (Eph. 6:12).

Spiritual warfare is heating up in the world about us. I believe the powers of darkness are aware that God is moving mightily to bring His people to the same victory discovered by the apostolic generation during the days of Jesus' Return and to tear down structures of evil in our world. As we go on to maturity walking in the straight and narrow way of His righteousness, serving Him in ministries to build up the Body of Christ, and tearing down barriers of injustice and evil in the world, spiritual warfare awaits us at every turn. The powers of darkness will resist social change and oppose our progress toward maturity. They want to keep us in darkness and bondage separated from the light and freedom God has for us in Christ. We need to learn how to deal with such spiritual foes. We need to learn to utterly depend upon Jesus, who is not only our Divine Bridegroom, but also our mighty Warrior as portrayed in Revelation.

> Then I saw heaven opened, and behold a white horse. And He who sat on him was called Faithful and True, and in righteousness He judges and makes war. His eyes were like a flame of fire, and on His head were many crowns. He had a name written that no one knew except Himself. He was clothed with a robe dipped in blood, and His name is called The Word of God. And the armies in heaven, clothed in fine linen, white and clean, followed Him on white horses. Now out of His mouth goes a sharp sword, that with it He should strike the nations. And He Himself will rule them with a rod of iron. He Himself treads the winepress of the fierceness and wrath of Almighty God. And He has on His robe and on His thigh a name written: KING OF KINGS AND LORD OF LORDS. (Rev. 19:11-16)

We are used to the Jesus who lived on earth as reported in the Gospels. He came as the Lord of heaven to this earth in human form to show the compassion of the Father through His miracles in feeding the hungry, healing the sick, freeing the demon-possessed, and raising the dead. In the most incredible event in all of history, this Lord of heaven suffered terrible shame and humiliation along with being brutally murdered as He bore the sins of humanity in an amazing display of Divine love. During the days of His life on earth, we see this gentle and compassionate Jesus, the Good Shepherd. To His faithful disciples during those last days, He revealed Himself as the Divine Bridegroom, entering into this most intimate love relationship, opening heaven to them where they would live in this spiritual union forever.

During the Second Coming, the Revelation also reveals this same Jesus now as the King of glory who not only rewards His faithful but as a mighty Warrior renders judgment upon the powers of darkness. No enemy can stand before Him. During all the persecution of those last days, Jesus brought His faithful through to their heavenly reward. The key for you and me to overcome in this spiritual warfare is to learn to let this mighty Warrior take care of those powers of darkness before which we are powerless on our own. The battle is real and you and I shall not be fruitful in our service until we learn to rely on this reigning King. We need to learn as did the faithful in the Bible that the battle is the Lord's, and He will fight for His people if, and this is a big if, we believe His promises and walk faithfully according to His word.

I have always been a sports fan, so God revealed to me this same truth years ago in terms I could better understand through a dream that came during the night after Christmas, 1975. I came to refer to this as "The Dream of the Magnificent Lineman." I was the quarterback on this football team and there was only one extraordinary lineman. He was the center, but on this team, he also called the plays in the huddle. On the opposite side of the line of scrimmage were these huge defensive linemen just waiting to flatten me to the ground. I ran in for touchdown after touchdown as I ran behind the blocking of this "magnificent lineman" in accordance with the plays He called. As the dream progressed, this all seemed pretty easy, so I decided to call a play on my own, a run around the end. One thing went wrong this time. The "magnificent lineman" did not run interference for me on the play I called, and I was smeared. The message was clear. Learn to huddle with Christ, discover His plays, and then run in dependence upon His interference.

This dream illustrated for me the real battle occurring in the spiritual realm, and pointed to the basic principles by which we win the warfare. First, we must learn to huddle with the Lord. It is important to take time for reading Scripture and waiting before the Lord in prayer. It is easy for us in our independent ways to rush out into the day and its activity simply forgetting to rely on the Lord. King David learned this lesson well. I don't know any other person in the Bible who better does this other than Jesus Himself who huddled with the Father to be sure to stay in His will. David would not undertake a battle unless he was confident that the Lord was with him in the venture. We see this in 2 Samuel 5. "Shall I go up against the Philistines?" (2 Sam. 5:19). The Lord answers David's prayer for guidance. "Go up, for I will doubtless deliver the Philistines into your hand" (2 Sam. 5:19). Once more the Philistines came up and David again huddled. The Lord counseled: "You shall not go up; circle around behind them, and come upon them in front of the mulberry trees" (2 Sam. 5:23). Not only do we receive Divine guidance as David discovered, but Isaiah also reminds us that such huddling renews needed strength. "But those who wait on the Lord shall renew their strength; they shall mount up with wings like eagles, they shall run and not be weary, they shall walk and not faint" (Is. 40:31). In such privileged fellowship, we tap Divine resources of wisdom and strength, essential to help us live in this world where we must battle the powers of darkness.

Second, this dream taught me the importance of following through with God's game plan. It is good to huddle and get God's direction. It is then essential that we follow through. My dream illustrated this. When I pursued God's plans and followed His interference, things went well. Then when I failed to pursue God's direction in favor of my own ideas, the Lord did not run interference, and I got smeared. King David also got smeared on the "end run" he called with Bathsheba. For the most part, however, King David took care to get God's direction, and then follow through to the letter. God eventually promised that the Messiah would be born to the line of David. King Saul, David's predecessor, failed at this point. On one occasion, God commanded Saul to utterly destroy every person and animal in a particular city. Saul spared the king and permitted the people to take spoil, claiming that the animals would be used for sacrificing to the Lord. Samuel shattered the king's rationalizations with the words: "Behold, to obey is better than sacrifice" (1 Sam. 15:22). Other such instances of failure to follow God's commands led the Lord to remove the kingship from Saul and replace him with David. If we are going to succeed in our battles with the powers of darkness, we must take care to get God's plan and then follow through. If the Lord fights the battle, we shall be victorious.

Third, I learned from this dream my utter dependence upon Christ. David learned this early in his life. We see this in his fight with the giant Goliath. David heard the giant defy the Israelite army and challenge someone to fight against him. David responded trusting that the God of Israel would give him victory. With only a slingshot in hand and facing a giant with a sword, a spear, and a javelin, David goes forth utterly relying upon God. "But I come to you in the name of the Lord of hosts, the God of the armies of Israel, whom you have defied" (1 Sam. 17:45). I am sure that everybody observing that strange battle was stunned, certain David had no chance. Being only a youth with no experience in war and carrying only a slingshot, what could he do against the Philistine giant experienced in warfare and wielding his trusted weapons? While the Israelites terrorized by Goliath were bound by fear, David kept his focus on God and His power. The truth was that Goliath did not have a chance because he was really going against God who had an obedient and trusting servant in that youth with the sling shot. God's people will triumph when the battle belongs to the Lord and they utterly depend upon Him.

One of our most important lessons to learn, and one that will probably take the longest to learn is this one of relying on the Lord for everything. We learn to do so when facing great obstacles, but we shall also learn that victory over temptation, sin, and fear are realized in total dependence upon the Lord. In fact, we shall learn that the privilege of abiding in continual fellowship with the Lord is only possible through the sovereign work of His grace and in reliance upon His Presence and power. The battles will be many en route to the victory of the experiential dimension of the Second Coming, but essential along this way of learning total trust and utter dependence upon God.

To live in a world where Jesus has returned means that the days are here for Christians to claim the earth for Christ. Satan is no longer in the position of authority over this world. The destroyer and deceiver has been replaced by Jesus Christ who declares concerning His rule. "Behold, I make all things new" (Rev. 21:5). He accomplishes that in this world through His people as they undertake the ministries He has for them, depending upon the Holy Spirit and using the spiritual gifts He gives them. He also accomplishes this as His people grow to maturity and claim the victory first discovered by the apostolic generation. We shall never go through what those first Christians went through who had to endure part of the 1,260-day period when the powers of darkness were given authority over all things, even to kill the saints. We shall, however, face great spiritual warfare. The powers of darkness that are now in their place of eternal punishment will give it all they have to still oppose God in this world. Their ultimate doom will be when "at the name of Jesus every knee should bow…and that every tongue should confess that Jesus Christ is Lord, to the glory of God the Father" (Phil. 2:10-11). What a day that will be when nobody listens any longer to Satan's lies and all live by the truth of the One who reigns over all things.

I do not believe in those doomsday scenarios that try to superimpose the events of the Second Coming upon life during this day with nuclear power and computer technology. It would be truly scary if such things were available to the powers of evil over a three-and-one-half-year period where they were given authority over all things. That will not be the case because Jesus returned during the apostolic generation and has now been reigning for nearly two thousand years. Jesus has brought us a long way in His reign over the last twenty centuries. People think we live in terrible days because the media continually directs our attention to all that is wrong in our world. There is no doubt that there remains suffering, persecution, and injustice, however, I will guarantee you that the apostles would have given anything to trade centuries with us. We would do well to get beyond the doomsday scenarios related to the last days mentality and focus on building the Body of Christ, challenging all disciples to find their spiritual gifts and ministries, and to grow to maturity and appropriate the experiential dimension of the Second Coming. Jesus, our Divine Bridegroom, is also the mighty Warrior who stands ready to fight these battles with us enabling us to be victorious.

The Old Testament tells about a time when the Moabites and the Ammonites came in great numbers against Judah during the days of King Jehoshaphat. He led the people in crying out before God in the face of an impossible situation. "For we have no power against this great multitude that is coming against us; nor do we know what to do, but our eyes are upon You" (2 Chron. 20:12). I believe that is the key. Jehoshaphat looked to God in utter dependence. God responded to the king through His prophet.

> Do not be afraid nor dismayed because of this great multitude, for the battle is not yours, but God's. (2 Chron. 20:15)

A strange battle ensued. As King Jehoshaphat led his armies into battle, he appointed singers to praise the Lord. As they began to sing, "Praise the Lord, for His mercy endures forever" (2 Chron. 20:21), the

Bible tells us that God acted to defeat the enemy without involving Jehoshaphat and his army. What a faith-building day that was for the king and his army as they won the battle without actually directly engaging the enemy. How much we have to learn about trusting God in our battles and how to appropriate His mighty power.

If we are to overcome and appropriate the experiential dimension of the Second Coming, we must learn, as did Jehoshaphat, that our battles likewise belong to the Lord. He has gone before and pioneered this way of appropriating the life of heaven while on earth. He is sufficient for every battle we face and able to bring us through victorious. Jesus is that mighty Warrior in whose strength we may win all the battles our spiritual foes will wage against us. They will seek to prevent us from this completed Christlike nature and the life of spiritual union on this earth with the Divine Bridegroom, Jesus Christ. As long as we take care to huddle with the Lord, live in obedience to His plan for our lives, and utterly rely upon Him in dependent trust, we shall emerge in our Promised Land of the Divine Presence.

Our country and the world entered a new day with the terrorist attacks on September 11, 2001. We were awakened to the reality of Satan's activity to deceive and mislead person to think that their hatred and murder of innocent persons is a just cause in a holy war. Satan and his hosts were the first terrorists. The Bible tells us that Satan is a liar and disguises himself as an angel of light (2 Cor. 11:14). He tries to conceal himself and work in what appears to be harmless ways, but whose end result is to do us harm. The terrorists function in the same way. They lie and conceal their identity, wishing to appear as persons of peace. In truth, they are cold-blooded murderers whose hate-filled hearts are looking for ways to destroy innocent people.

What a contrast to how Jesus taught His followers to live in this world. They are to repent of sin, walk in truth, and do their good deeds of loving service out in the open. They are to forgive their enemies and love them. While holy wars existed for God's people during the days of the Old Covenant of law, Jesus made it clear that day ended with His ministry. Under the New Covenant, God's people are not to take the sword. His disciples are to walk in His ways of righteousness and loving service while trusting their lives into His care. God has, however, given authority to nations to preserve law and order and to take whatever measures are necessary in dealing with those who murder innocent people or initiate war (Rom. 13:1-4). Hence, God's people need to pray continually for their political leaders who must make tough decisions.

17

THE LAST FRONTIER

The presence of the Father constitutes the last frontier for human beings on this earth. Only there will we be able to find the victory over sin, death, and the powers of evil and bring about the prophetic dream of peace upon the earth. How we need people fully appropriating all the resources God has made available to us. We have already opened so many frontiers closed for centuries to mankind. I am thinking of the world of microcosm where we have discovered the secrets of the atom, human DNA, and genes. I am thinking of the world of macrocosm as we have begun to explore outer space. The most important frontier for us is the one that was lost back at the beginning. The Divine Presence consisting of God the Father, God the Son, and God the Holy Spirit dwelt in that Garden of Eden along with our first ancestors. The Hebrew word for God in the Genesis creation account is *elohim*. This plural form suggests the trinity. Adam and Eve were banished from the Divine Presence as a result of one sin, which ought to give us a clue regarding the importance of cooperating with the sanctifying work of the Holy Spirit to have the Christlike nature formed within us. It is the only way we shall ever regain the fullness of that holy ground.

The Bible witnesses that the living God, though One, has revealed Himself in three persons. The New Testament tells us that God the Son came as the Jewish Messiah, Jesus Christ. As a result of His life, ministry, Crucifixion, and Resurrection, God made a New Covenant with the peoples of this earth. After returning to heaven to be with God the

Father, God the Holy Spirit came into and upon the disciples of Jesus. He formed a new community called the Body of Christ. He empowered those first followers to reach others and bring them into the fellowship. He prepared hearts for the Return of Jesus when the faithful would be perfected, wed to their Divine Bridegroom, and raised into the Father's presence. Here they would experience the last member of the Trinity. Those first faithful were restored to what our first ancestors lost back at the beginning, except now this is a world enveloped by the powers of darkness and nearly six millennia of their corrupting works passed on from generation to generation. In the Presence of the Godhead lies the key to the future. Here we shall discover all that we need to conquer sin, death, and the powers of darkness and hold our lives together in this world of corruption. Here is the key to bring heaven to this earth, now possible because we live in a world where Jesus has returned.

When through resurrection power we cross this last frontier and enter the Father's presence where Jesus the Pioneer of our faith has gone, we shall make amazing discoveries, first witnessed briefly by the apostolic generation in the New Testament. We shall become partakers of the Christlike nature and learn what it means to reign with Christ. We shall discover the reality and fullness of what was meant by a loud voice in heaven after the mystery is accomplished in Revelation 12:1-6 and Satan is cast from heaven in 12:7-9. "Now salvation and strength, and the kingdom of God, and the power of His Christ have come." (Rev. 12:10). The Body of Christ today has made advances in these directions, but there is more to be discovered when we get beyond the "second-coming hasn't happened" barrier and appropriate the experiential dimension of the Second Coming.

This Divine Presence dwells on the heavenly Mount Zion. This was the scene of triumph during the Second Coming. Some have believed that Jesus would bodily come down at the Second Coming to rule over this earth from the earthly Mount Zion during those significant events. That was not the way it happened. The New Testament makes it clear that the faithful made their way during those last days not to the earthly Mt. Zion, but the heavenly Mt. Zion. It was also the heavenly mountain from which Jesus would reign in the days following His Second Coming.

The earthly Jerusalem and Mt. Zion played an important part for a time in history through God's dealings with the Jewish people during the days of the Old Covenant. The Ark of the Covenant witnessed to the Presence of the living God dwelling among His people at the temple in Jerusalem. During those days when God's kingdom was related to a particular nation on this earth, they did take up weapons and wage warfare. They destroyed entire cities as they took over the land promised to them by God. The Jewish Messiah taught that His kingdom would not come that way with violence or weapons of destruction. It would come through the New Covenant that would release the Holy Spirit to form the Christlike nature within His disciples and demonstrate His love through the ministries of His servants.

After the Second Coming, the heavenly Mt. Zion and the New Jerusalem play an even greater role because they are eternal, and the focal point for God's reign during the days of the New Covenant. Isaiah 8:18 refers to "the Lord of hosts who dwells in Mount Zion." Isaiah 18:7 refers to Mount Zion as "the place of the name of the Lord of hosts." Isaiah 24:23 reports "the Lord of hosts will reign on Mount Zion and in Jerusalem." The first Christians, who learned the higher ways of God through the apostolic ministry, were raised up to the heavenly Mount Zion during the days of the Second Coming.

Paul tells us about this in Hebrews as he discusses the climax of Christian faith for the first followers of Jesus during those last days.

> For you have not come to the mountain that may be touched and that burned with fire, and to blackness and darkness and tempest, and the sound of a trumpet and the voice of words, so that those who heard it begged that the word should not be spoken to them anymore. (For they could not endure what was commanded: "And if so much as a beast touches the mountain, it shall be stoned or

thrust through with an arrow." And so terrifying was the sight that Moses said, "I am exceedingly afraid and trembling.") But you have come to Mount Zion and to the city of the living God, the heavenly Jerusalem, to an innumerable company of angels, to the general assembly and church of the firstborn who are registered in heaven, to God, the Judge of all, to the spirits of just men made perfect, to Jesus the Mediator of the new covenant, and to the blood of sprinkling that speaks better things than that of Abel." (Heb. 12:18-24)

We clearly see in Hebrews that the heavenly Jerusalem and heavenly Mount Zion are the focal point for the faithful remnant during those days after the seventh trumpet. They have not come to an earthly mountain, as did the Israelites before them during the days of the Old Covenant under the leadership of Moses. The earthly Mount Zion was the scene of destruction during the Second Coming as God terminated the Old Covenant and Roman armies destroyed Jerusalem. No joy was found there during the days of Christ's Return. God led His people to flee that doomed city. As a result of revelation, they turned their attention heavenward. "But you have come to Mount Zion and to the city of the living God, the heavenly Jerusalem" (Heb. 12:22) where His people would be rewarded, a scene of great rejoicing.

I believe the light that shone over the altar at the temple in Jerusalem and the opening of the eastern gate in A.D. 66 pointed to this great wonder. That temple on the earthly Mt. Zion would soon be destroyed, as the Old Covenant would come to an end. The faithful were emerging on the heavenly Mt. Zion having been changed into the likeness of Christ and raised into the Father's presence. These unusual events at the temple in Jerusalem witnessed that God had fulfilled His promises made to the people who worshiped at that earthly temple in Jerusalem, even though they broke the covenant and killed the Messiah. The promised remnant had been perfected and raised into the Father's presence receiving the fulfillment of the promises. The rest who rejected God's grace offered through the New Covenant would sustain the judgment and wrath of God.

Though confined by their bodies to this world where they were undergoing persecution, those first Christians soared to heavenly heights as Christ returned to complete His life within His faithful and raise them to heavenly places, on the heavenly Mount Zion. Hidden from the rest of the world and usually bypassed by the church, we only know about this revelation through those amazing writings in the Bible where the New Testament fulfills the promises of the Old Testament as witnessed by the apostolic generation. Its writers tell about the exciting discoveries they made during the days of the Return of their Lord.

Isaiah refers to Mount Zion more than any other book in the Bible. It is important in His theological perspective. He describes the way to this heavenly mountain as the "Highway of Holiness" (Is. 35:8). Anybody can travel to the earthly Jerusalem and walk up the earthly Mount Zion. Any desiring to ascend the heavenly mountain where dwells the Divine Presence must begin by turning from sin to the righteous ways of God. The psalmist asks, "Who may ascend into the hill of the Lord?" (Ps. 24:3). His answer is clear. It is the one "who has clean hands and a pure heart" (Ps. 24:4). Apart from such holiness and righteousness, this highway remains hidden.

The gospel of Jesus calls for such repentance and embracing Jesus as Lord to be obeyed. Jesus opened this way to us on this earth by dying for our sins so that we could be forgiven and cleansed. Jesus said that He was the Way (John 14:6) and Acts 9:2 refers to Jesus' followers as those who belonged to the Way. This Way leads to the heavenly Mount Zion and Jerusalem where faithful disciples will ascend with praise and singing and discover the promised victory. At the same time, they will be building the peace that the reigning King works to spread over this earth. Listen to Isaiah who centuries ago foretold this.

> A highway shall be there, and a road, and it shall be called the Highway of Holiness. The unclean shall not pass over it...No lion shall be there, nor shall any ravenous beast go up on it; it shall not

> be found there. But the redeemed shall walk there, and the ransomed of the Lord shall return, and come to Zion with singing, with everlasting joy on their heads. They shall obtain joy and gladness, and sorrow and sighing shall flee away. (Is. 35:8-10)

Jesus called His people to follow Him in the Way of holiness and righteousness.

Leading to the mountain of the Lord, this Way will be hidden to the unclean and fools. Banned from this mountain will be all beasts, the prophetic way of referring to the powers of darkness, similarly portrayed in the Book of Revelation. They may battle believers in the valleys, but God banished them forever from heavenly places during the days of the Second Coming, opening the way to victory for God's people while still on earth. While God's people journey through the valleys of this world, their inner persons look to this heavenly Mount Zion with singing expressing their worship and praise to the living God. On top of this mountain where dwells the Divine Presence, they shall discover God has provided for eternal salvation and deliverance from all our enemies. Appropriating resurrection power enables them to spiritually live on the mountain and pass through the valleys of this world in victory.

The Holy Spirit is leading members of the Body of Christ to this heavenly mountain as He returns us to the apostolic wisdom in building the Body of Christ culminating in the experiential dimension of the Second Coming. In recent years, there has been such an outpouring of new music as the Spirit inspires such as a vehicle of praise and worship. "Amen! Blessing and glory and wisdom, thanksgiving and honor and power and might, be to our God forever and ever. Amen" (Rev. 7:12). This reigning King of glory is worthy of such adoration and worship. This emerges in the lives of God's people when through enlightened eyes they approach the heavenly Mount Zion where dwells the Divine Presence. "And the ransomed of the Lord shall return, and come to Zion with singing, with everlasting joy on their heads" (Is. 35:10).

The Holy Spirit has also been renewing the call for holiness. Against the backdrop of an "anything goes" culture, people are hungering for right and holy living, precisely what the Holy Spirit works in God's people. The character of sin-controlled human nature has become apparent through self-gratification, breaking laws when they stand in the way of our pleasure, and lying to conceal truth or protect ourselves. It is seen in the greed and corruption often accompanying the pursuit of power and money. We live in a world that has abused the gift of freedom and ignored the accompanying responsibility. This has resulted in the spread of homosexuality, promiscuous sex, unwanted pregnancies, and abortions. The Holy Spirit is renewing the biblical call for righteous living and holy character found in the straight and narrow way into which Jesus called people to walk.

Great things happen on this mountain to which the "Highway of Holiness" leads. Here the presence of the Father dwells. At the Father's right hand is the presence of His Son, Jesus, to whom the Father has given the kingdom and the authority to reign over all things. This king of righteousness orchestrates peace on this earth. He leads His people to this heavenly destination as they journey to maturity preparatory to the spiritual resurrection that will raise them into the Father's presence. Isaiah foretold this conquest of death.

> And He will destroy on this mountain the surface of the covering cast over all people, and the veil that is spread over all nations. He will swallow up death forever, and the Lord God will wipe away tears from all faces; the rebuke of His people He will take away from all the earth; for the Lord has spoken. And it will be said in that day: "Behold, this is our God; we have waited for Him, and He will save us. This is the Lord; we have waited for Him; we will be glad and rejoice in His salvation." (Is. 25:7-9)

During the last days, death was swallowed up on this mountain of the Lord and His salvation revealed to the faithful.

God gives us a picture here to help us understand what happened in the spiritual realm during the second-coming events. He says to imagine a shroud spread out over all the peoples of the earth, like a covering of darkness separating them from the Divine Presence on the heavenly Mount Zion. I believe this portrays what happened on this earth when sin entered the picture. The presence of God withdrew from His creatures and the world came under the curse and the authority of Satan like a blanket of darkness, corruption, and death over all people. This is what Paul means in Romans 8:20 when he says "the creation was subjected to futility." Alienated from the Presence of the living God who is light, life, and glory, the powers of evil formed the spiritual environment encompassing this rebellious planet in darkness and death. Human efforts would be absolutely futile to put this world together without mighty acts by the living God setting human beings free from bondage to sin and the corrupting powers of darkness.

Jesus pierced that shroud from our side when He rose from the dead and ascended into heaven. From there, He poured out the Holy Spirit to create new life in those who responded to the gospel and build Christ's Body on earth. At His Return, the faithful similarly experienced the breaking through of this encompassing and corrupting spiritual blanket of darkness and death by resurrection power. Once the Divine life is completed in the prepared saints, they are raised to heavenly places. Satan and his hosts are then cast to earth and a great voice cries out in heaven: "Now salvation, and strength, and the kingdom of our God, and the power of His Christ have come" (Rev. 12:10). The apostolic ministry built the Body of Christ to appropriate this victory when Jesus returned, forming Christ within faithful disciples, and raising them to heavenly places while still on earth. Jesus was truly the Pioneer of our salvation.

I believe Peter refers to this in his last epistle when he tells about becoming a partaker of the Divine or Christlike nature, escaping the corruption of this world, and entering the kingdom (2 Pet. 1:3-11). The corruption of this world refers to the activity and influence of those powers of darkness enveloping this world, and those who become partakers of the Divine or Christlike nature are raised up on high and enter the kingdom. I believe Paul speaks about this same escape when he says God delivered them from the dominion of darkness and transferred them to the kingdom of His beloved Son (Col. 1:11-13). Resurrection power accomplishes this amazing escape and deliverance for those in whom Christ has been formed, or in Peter's words, those who have become partakers of the Divine or Christlike nature. Jesus likened this kingdom to a pearl of "great price" and "treasure hidden in a field" for which one gives all (Matt. 13:44-46). His first disciples who were faithful to follow their Lord made these discoveries during those last days when Jesus returned to manifest His glory and kingdom in their midst, enabling them to escape the corruption in this world. They learned to give their all, some even suffering martyrdom. They enjoyed this victory on earth briefly before being removed during those last days of the Old Covenant when God poured out His wrath as foretold under the Old Covenant and terminated that agreement with the Jewish people.

The Old Testament tells us about how people sought to build a tower reaching to heaven. God confounded their efforts. In the New Testament, after the Messiah has come and made a New Covenant, God reveals His own plan for us to work with Him and erect a spiritual building called the Body of Christ. It reaches to highest heaven because the Head of the Body is the Lord of heaven reigning from His throne in the New Jerusalem. Through spiritual gifts and ministries, the Holy Spirit erects this building that helps people grow to spiritual maturity, enabling them to be raised with Christ to live in heavenly places while still dwelling on earth.

Let us observe God's strategy to take over this world, bringing the life of heaven to earth and finally peace among all peoples under the rule of Jesus Christ. His kingdom will not come by force. Its king will win the hearts of people and their willing submission to His authority. At the Second Coming, angels cast Satan and his hosts out of heaven to the earth. At long last, God removed all traces of rebellion from heaven leaving only the ones united in worshiping Him and wholeheartedly submitting to His rightful authority. The redeemed from this earth joined the righteous angels to comprise this joyous throng. John reflects this new heaven when he observes that there is no longer any temple there. "But I saw no temple in it, for the Lord God Almighty and the Lamb are its temple" (Rev. 21:22).

God utilizes a temple for His dwelling place when He faces a hostile environment. Satan and his rebellious hosts provided such opposition to God in heaven prior to the Second Coming. While disobedience may be all about, at least in His temple, things go according to His will and agenda. Revelation refers to the temple in heaven during those last days (11:19; 15:5-8; 16:17). When "the dust settles" from all the second-coming events, John sees a new heaven, a new earth, and a New Jerusalem. In this new arrangement, there is no longer any temple in heaven (Rev. 21:22). With Satan and his hosts removed, from that moment on, God was everything to everybody in heaven.

God still needs a temple in this world where the rebellion continues. Anticipating during the second-coming days the destruction of the old temple at Jerusalem related to the Old Covenant, God decided to create a new temple. He accomplished this through the New Covenant by creating the church, the Body of Christ, the new Israel. Paul tells how God created something new through Jesus and the New Covenant by bringing together Jews and Gentiles in one family "in whom the whole building, being joined together, grows into a holy temple in the Lord" (Eph. 2:21).

This temple is vitally linked to heaven because the Head of the Body of Christ is Jesus, at the right hand of the Father, the Lord of heaven and earth, who rules over all things. The Holy Spirit flowing from that throne down into this world through the people comprising this new temple prepares the way for the spiritual union between the Lord of heaven and His people on earth. The Spirit teaches us from the Divine blueprint of the New Testament how to build the Body of

Christ, nurture disciples on God's word, and bring people to maturity. As this temple spreads throughout the world, serving as a conduit for the life and love of heaven, the day will come when there will be no need for a temple on earth any longer.

Paul writes about this day in Philippians when "at the name of Jesus every knee should bow, of those in heaven, and of those on earth, and of those under the earth, and that every tongue should confess that Jesus Christ is Lord, to the glory of God the Father" (Phil. 2:10-11). As the New Testament church spreads, producing Christlike people raised up on the heavenly Mount Zion, the day will come when earth unites under the rule of the living God, as did heaven during the days of the Second Coming. What a glorious day that will be when the peoples of this earth will have crossed the last frontier and heaven will have come to earth when we shall have finally appropriated the victory over sin, death, and the powers of darkness. The disciples of Jesus during their life on earth have a contribution to make to this end as orchestrated by the reigning Christ who rules from the heavenly Mount Zion making "all things new."

When this occurs that the earth has united under the rule of Christ, and every enemy is put under His feet, then Jesus will give back to the Father the kingdom so that "God may be all in all." This will be the fulfillment of the prophecies of the Bible. Paul writes about this in the following passage.

> But now Christ is risen from the dead, and has become the firstfruits of those who have fallen asleep. For since by man came death, by Man also came the resurrection of the dead. For as in Adam all die, even so in Christ all shall be made alive. But each one in his own order: Christ the firstfruits, afterward those who are Christ's at His coming. Then comes the end, when He delivers the kingdom to God the Father, when He puts an end to all rule and all authority and power. For He must reign till He has put all enemies under His feet. The last enemy that will be destroyed is death. (1 Cor. 15:20-26)

Jesus was the first to rise from the dead around A.D. 33. At His coming during Daniel's Seventieth Week from A.D. 63 to A.D. 70, He raised the faithful from the dead and began His reign over all things. When Paul states then "comes the end," I believe he jumps ahead beyond the Second Coming into the future to the climax when after centuries of the reign of Christ, every enemy will have been put under His feet and the earth will have united under His rule. That did not happen during Daniel's Seventieth Week. The world was in no shape to be given back to the Father so that He could be "all in all." Jesus only began to reign during those days. Isaiah 9:7 tells us about how this kingdom will advance in the world once God's chosen One begins to reign: "Of the increase of His government and peace there will be no end." It would begin in this world barely noticeable because of all the tribulation that occurred during those last days. Slowly but surely in those years following the Second Coming, His kingdom and reign would increase, and of that increase, there would be no end according to Isaiah. Paul looks ahead to the grand climax after centuries of the increase of the reign of Christ. Then every enemy, the last being death, will have been placed under the feet of Christ. When that day comes fulfilling God's purposes and uniting the earth under the rule of Christ, then He will give the kingdom back to the Father so that "God may be all in all" on earth as He is right now in heaven. There will no longer be any temple on the earth. It will not be necessary. The enemy will be confined to the lake of fire and under the feet of the people remaining on earth. They will no longer listen to the lies of Satan. What was lost through Satan's schemes will have been reclaimed, and even more. In addition to dwelling in the blessed Presence of the living God in all His fullness as was the case back in the Garden of Eden, we shall possess His very nature and be surrounded by the same kind of people. The long night of sin, evil, and death witnessed to in Scripture will be past, replaced by the eternal day of righteousness, good, and eternal life. Hallelujah! We shall be part of that great company of the redeemed bowing at the name of Jesus and confessing "that Jesus Christ is Lord, to the glory of God the Father."

18

THE VIEW FROM THE MOUNTAIN

You can see things from the top of a mountain not visible down in the surrounding valleys. The Bible gives us the view from the heavenly Mount Zion, established as the highest of all the mountains during the days of the Second Coming when God the Father and His Son took authority over this world, thereby displacing Satan. From this lofty perspective, we see things with eyes of faith that are totally hidden from the secular mind and so foreign to all the news reported through the media. God's word through Scripture reports an amazing climax to human history, the prophetic dream of peace among the peoples of the earth. Scripture also relates the Divine strategy by which God is going to bring it about. We want to look at this view from Mount Zion as recorded by the prophet Isaiah many centuries ago.

What a great vision God gave us on this earth through the Hebrew prophets. It inspires us to submit wholly to Jesus Christ, the reigning King, so we may do our part to advance the cause of His kingdom in this world. Such a dream seems so "out of touch" with reality when we look at the world where sin and evil still abound. Isaiah writes about this amazing dream for peace on our earth. "They shall beat their swords into plowshares, and their spears into pruning hooks; nation shall not lift up sword against nation, neither shall they learn war anymore" (Is. 2:4). Updating these ancient but timely words, the nations will dismantle their nuclear warheads and stop making weapons; they will stop training for war and invading other countries. Movements in that direction by the major powers of the world have been slowed somewhat by the threat of terrorism which may very well be the war to end all major wars. As we become a global community, we are slowly learning that we have to get along, and the major powers are already taking steps in this direction. The day will come according to the Bible when we shall have put behind us the things of war and focus our energies on the things of peace. God is heading up all things through Jesus Christ who will be at the center of this great work along with the New Testament church.

Isaiah tells about what must transpire before these golden days come upon this earth when its people will live in peace with one another.

> Now it shall come to pass in the latter days that the mountain of the Lord's house shall be established on the top of the mountains, and shall be exalted above the hills; and all nations shall flow to it. Many people shall come and say, "Come, and let us go up to the mountain of the Lord, to the house of the God of Jacob; He will teach us His ways, and we shall walk in His paths." For out of Zion shall go forth the law, and the word of the Lord from Jerusalem. He shall judge between the nations, and shall rebuke many people; they shall beat their swords into plowshares, and their spears into pruning hooks; nations shall not lift up sword against nation, neither shall they learn war anymore. O house of Jacob, come and let us walk in the light of the Lord. (Is. 2:2-5)

Come, O peoples of the earth, let us walk in this light first given to Israel under the Old Covenant, but now available to all entering into the New Covenant made through the Jewish Messiah. This marvelous light reveals four things that must happen before peace will come upon our earth. There is no bypassing these steps. Each one is essential and by establishing Jesus Christ as ruler over all things during the Second Coming, God accomplished the first step and at the same time guaranteed that the rest of the blueprint will be followed. Notice the significance of the mountain of the Lord or Mount Zion. He reigns from this mountain and the people of the earth will come here to learn about His ways. This is not the earthly Mt. Zion upon which the earthly Jerusalem was situated. As we saw in the last chapter, this was the heavenly Mt. Zion where you find the heavenly Jerusalem, from which God orchestrates everything during these days since the Second Coming. As we view things from this heavenly mountain by the light of God's word, we see the Divine game plan to bring heaven to earth. Let us look at the four steps of this plan culminating in peace upon our earth.

JESUS MUST REIGN IN RIGHTEOUSNESS

Peace is impossible in a world where Satan rules. He aimed from the first to deceive and destroy. Isaiah says that in the last days, "The mountain of the Lord's house shall be established on the top of the mountains" (Is. 2:2). In other words, God would establish His authority over this world during the last days. As we saw in this book, the Bible says that this begins at the seventh trumpet. The place of His dwelling on the heavenly Mount Zion was established as the highest of all such mountains in regard to this earth when Jesus began His reign over all things at the seventh trumpet, displacing Satan as ruler of this earth. The next words after the seventh trumpet in Revelation tell about this new government: "The kingdoms of this world have become the kingdoms of our Lord and of His Christ, and He shall reign forever and ever" (Rev. 11:15). The mountain of the Lord, the place for His dwelling, was then established on "the top of the mountains."

The seventh trumpet accomplished the first step down this road to peace on earth as the government of this world was established in the hands of the One who would reign over all things in righteousness. The prophet Isaiah foretold the pathway toward peace on this earth when once the government of this world was placed on the shoulders of God's Chosen One: "Of the increase of His government and peace there will be no end" (Is. 9:7). It began back then during those second-coming days and will culminate someday with peace upon the earth. Jesus inherited a world reeling at the brink of destruction after centuries under Satan's rule and the traumatic events of the Second

Coming. Things looked even worse when the Lord removed His faithful from the earth. From such barely perceptible beginnings, His government and peace have been spreading throughout this world. Though hardly noticeable at first, like leaven in the loaf of bread, it has been growing and there will be no end to "the increase of His government and peace." Someday it will fill the earth.

WE MUST COME TO THE MOUNTAIN

"Many people shall come and say, 'Come, and let us go up to the mountain of the Lord.'" (Is. 2:3). The New Covenant calls us to repent of sin and turn to follow Jesus as Lord. All who thus respond to the living God have begun the journey that will come to completion upon the mountain of the Lord. At conversion, we cease wandering in the darkness of the valley of death and look to the Lord of light and life who dwells on Mount Zion. While in a human body, we still live in the valley of darkness and corruption in this world. Through the Body of Christ, the indwelling Holy Spirit flowing from God's throne in the New Jerusalem begins to form within us the heavenly life of the One on the mountain while we live out our days in this world of corruption. New Covenant people represent the next step toward peace on this earth. They have come to the mountain of the One who for a time came down to live on earth. Here He died for our sin, and made possible the spiritual journey up the heavenly mountain. The Body of Christ must continually be concerned about reaching people for Christ because this activity reflects the passion in the heart of the living God. The gospel is spreading throughout the world, and churches employing the principles of the New Testament church are turning out witnessing and serving disciples.

WE MUST LEARN GOD'S HIGHER WAYS

"He will teach us His ways" (Is. 2:3). God's ways are not our ways. After years of groping in sin and darkness, responding to the gospel opens the way for us to the Lord who dwells on Mount Zion. From the word of the living God who dwells there, we learn how our Creator intended us to live from the first. We became mired in sin and blind to God's ways. Isaiah 55:9 reminds us that His ways and thoughts are higher than ours. Jesus revealed these things to His disciples. Now, in the Body of Christ, the Holy Spirit using gifted servants and particular ministries teaches us from the apostolic witness in the New Testament about those higher ways and thoughts, so different from ours. We have made decisive steps in recent years to teach the ways of the Lord. Christian television and radio along with many books, videos, and cassettes enable the pilgrims journeying up the mountain to learn those ways of the Lord. The road to peace on this earth consists of the wisdom and righteousness revealed in the Bible that enables us to do the will of the living God. We got off that road through sin. Jesus and the New Covenant make it possible to walk that highway leading up the holy mountain. People learning the ways of the Lord will lead the way to peace on this earth.

WE MUST WALK IN HIS PATHS

"He will teach us His ways, and we shall walk in His paths" (Is. 2:3). Hearing is good, but not enough. The Bible is a book of life, and we must translate that into our daily lives through a living faith expressed in good works of obedience and service. "Hearken to the voice of the Lord" was the frequent yet usually unheeded cry of the Hebrew prophets. Through the New Covenant, God forms a new heart within us on which His laws are written. No Christian will ever grow to maturity who does not walk the straight and narrow way of God's righteousness. Christian radio, television, videos, books, and cassettes have opened many avenues for learning the ways of the Lord. It is one thing to learn, however, and another thing to do. We have a long journey ahead to do God's will and walk in His ways. During those last days, Paul prayed for the Colossians that they may "be filled with the knowledge of His will in all wisdom and spiritual understanding" (Col. 1:9).

Paul prays in this manner so they may "walk worthy of the Lord" (Col. 1:10) and fully please Him in every way. We shall never have peace on this earth until we learn to please the Lord rather than ourselves, and walk in His ways rather than our own. Jesus taught that the promises are realized in "whoever hears these sayings of Mine, and does them" (Matt. 7:24). Doers of God's word are the kind of people that He will use to finally bring about peace on this earth. Isaiah 32:17 tells us that righteous deeds will finally result in peace.

THE REMAINING TASK

Pope John XXIII issued an encyclical on April 11, 1963 entitled *Pacem in Terris*. It was a vision for peace upon the earth and steps that would lead toward that dream. It inspired many persons. A few years later, the vice-president of the United States at the time commented in the setting of a gathering of world leaders for the cause of peace that it was the duty of their generation to convert this vision of peace into reality. That was a noble challenge and the pope and the leaders are to be commended for keeping alive the biblical vision in a world where such seems totally impossible.

Their generation did not accomplish the task. This points to one very important fact. Neither the United Nation nor any other human organization will accomplish this vision. God alone will bring it about, and He will receive the glory for the realization of this amazing dream. He has revealed to us His strategy, and He is sticking to the plan. He graciously receives sinners, forgiving the past and giving them another chance to turn from their own ways to God's. He gives them the Holy Spirit and spiritual gifts with which to serve in some kind of ministry. He incorporates them into the Body of Christ where they learn to live according to the will of Jesus, the Head of the Body, and not according to their wills or that of the world. God aims to change them into the likeness of Christ. Jesus has begun His reign and fulfilled the promises in those first followers as reported in their witness in the New Testament. He has revealed the plan and the power to accomplish it.

He needs humble servants who will obediently and faithfully accomplish their part of His plan for their lives.

When All Else Fails, Read the Directions was the title of a book written some time ago. I never read the book, but those words express what I believe God is trying to get through to us on earth. The Bible contains the wisdom and direction we need in order to rectify the mess we have made of our lives and this world. God has provided for victory over sin, the powers of evil, and death through the Incarnation and Return of Jesus Christ. Scripture makes clear the response we are to make to Jesus by turning from sin and obeying Him as Lord. The Scripture tells us how to build the Body of Christ that extends to heaven where Jesus, the Head of the Body, dwells at the right hand of His Father. As we go on to maturity, reach others for Christ, and lead them on to maturity, we cooperate with the living God as He builds the Body of Christ and orchestrates history's grand finale of peace someday upon the earth. We do not need to look for any antichrist or other fulfillment of second-coming prophecies in current events. We need to look to Jesus and hear God's word so we may learn how He wants us to live on this earth. We need to learn about the authority we have in Jesus and how to utilize that in dealing with the powers of darkness. We need to read the directions on how to claim this earth for God. He has preserved this for us in Holy Scripture, and He will not complete this great work without our cooperation. Our Promised Land is before us as was Canaan for the Israelites centuries ago. Just as they had to enter the land and drive out the enemy, we must likewise defeat our enemies in spiritual warfare and claim our land. Just as they had to learn to depend upon the Lord for such conquest, we must also learn that the battle belongs to the Lord and that we shall never defeat Satan and his hosts on our strength. God waits for our submission and cooperation and is ready and waiting to help us claim this prize.

Soren Kierkegaard highlights the uniqueness of the Bible, especially the New Testament, as he distinguishes between a genius and an apostle. I am dependent upon a speaker I heard years ago and believe the following paraphrase is accurate, though I have never read the exact reference myself. This distinction highlights the uniqueness of what the apostles gave to the world through the New Testament. Geniuses are creative and innovative persons during their generation. Their ideas are absorbed and built upon and surpassed by future generations. An example that came to my mind was the Wright brothers. They were geniuses pioneering in flight. Succeeding generations absorbed their concepts and surpassed them as we now send vehicles into space. Such are geniuses during their day, but surpassed by future generations.

Apostles differ from this in that what they gave to the world has never been absorbed or surpassed by any succeeding generation. Two thousand years later, we are learning that we must get beyond centuries of tradition in the church where sometimes the original understanding was altered or lost and see afresh the wisdom in the writings of the apostles in order to appropriate their discoveries. They learned from the Lord of heaven, who first made a covenant with their ancestors called the Old Covenant. Then in the fullness of time, the Lord Himself came to earth and those apostles lived with Him during those years of His ministry and witness to the truth they learned in the New Testament. That is why their writings are unique and no other religious writings can compare. Only Jesus has been able to make the claim to be God stand the test of time. If we want to know God's will, Jesus and the Holy Spirit stand ready to teach us if we enter into the New Covenant by responding to Jesus as Savior and Lord. While we may read the writings of other Christians in past centuries or currently, it is basically to see what light they may shed for us in understanding the apostolic witness in the New Testament, as well as the entire Bible. It tells us in direct opposition to church tradition that Jesus returned during the apostolic generation. It reveals God's appointed climax to history on earth, and how we can and must learn to cooperate with the living God whose Son works to make all things new as He reigns right now over all things.

God's word through Scripture tells us that we now live in a new earth surrounded by a new heaven. Let us look at what that means. What is new about this earth? It seems that things are pretty much the same as they have always been with evidence of sin and evil all around. What does John mean when he reports seeing a new earth? Let me share the following illustration that may help in understanding how we may look at the earth about us as new since the Second Coming occurred around two thousand years ago.

Imagine a large slum tenement owned by an evil landlord. He cares nothing for the people except to exploit them and collect his due. Some people want to make improvements, but finally give up, finding no cooperation from the landlord. Others, like the landlord, care nothing about the condition of the tenement while others fight with their neighbors and destroy their surroundings. The state of the tenement remains hopeless as long as it continues in the hands of its evil landlord.

Suppose one day a beneficent person with limitless resources purchases the tenement, bringing it under the authority of a new landlord intending to invest both himself and his resources in the building and the people. He shares his dream about what he plans to do with the apartments and enlists the help of the tenants. He knows lasting results require their cooperation. He also sets guidelines for the behavior he expects from those wishing to occupy his apartments.

Let us note one fact. A new day dawns at the very moment when the beneficent landlord takes control. Nothing seems different, but to those knowledgeable about the change of management and the new manager's plans, it is a new day. Prior to that time, all was hopeless. Individual efforts to make things better were of little consequence. Under the new manager who desires to repair the tenement and possesses the authority and the resources to accomplish the task, a new day has indeed dawned. The new landlord needs only time to share the vision and enlist the cooperation of the tenants.

Our planet was like that slum tenement prior to the Second Coming of Jesus Christ. Under the management of its evil landlord, Satan, properly called in Scripture a "liar" and a "destroyer," God's dream of peace given through the prophets was impossible. The best human efforts accomplished little against the powers of darkness organized for destruction. After the Second Coming in the midst of which God gives to Jesus Christ the authority to govern this world, this became a new earth. The new ruler in His new government works "to make all things new" in contrast to Satan's previous government bent upon evil and destruction.

A new heaven also emerged during those last days. The new Sovereign casts Satan and his rebellious hosts forever out of heaven. Jesus thereby cleared the way for His disciples whom He told He would go and prepare a place for them. Heaven was new not only because of the absence of Satan and his hosts, but because for the first time, the redeemed from this earth now swelled its ranks. The faithful from the Jewish people as well as the faithful from among the nations who responded to the gospel now occupied heaven. The way was now forever open to all those who would follow in their footsteps in the years ahead by responding to the gospel, submitting to Jesus as their Lord, and cooperating with the sanctifying work of the Holy Spirit.

I want to reiterate. There are no shortcuts, no second-coming events ahead to bail us out of the mess we have created through sinful and selfish living, neglecting the ways of the living God. He conquered those enemies of sin, death, and the powers of darkness before which we were powerless. He has done this through the Incarnation and Return of Jesus Christ. He has revealed in Scripture His victory over all of this through the marriage of His Son with His bride, the church. We must go there in order to hear His word and to prepare the Body of Christ to become the bride whom the Spirit fashions after the likeness of Christ. There is no other way. Man's efforts are absolutely futile to accomplish peace on this earth because the real enemies are sin and the powers of darkness. God is fully capable to accomplish the task, and through His people on earth is working to that end right now as He heads up all things in Christ. God will put the powers of darkness under our feet as we learn to be faithful to His word and submit to the sanctifying work of the Holy Spirit. How long it takes is related to how long it takes us to learn and do His ways. One thing is certain. God will cut no corners nor take any shortcuts. He will do it correctly and thoroughly, however long it may take, producing Christlike people on this earth through the Body of Christ.

My hunch is that it is not going to take as long as we are inclined to think! Jesus and the faithful reigned the first thousand years preserving the world that teetered on the brink of destruction. This world was in terrible shape after centuries of Satan's rule, the 1,260-day Period of the Authority of the Beast, and the removal of the faithful at the Return of Christ. The church that continued on earth preserved the apostolic witness in the New Testament for future generations. One thousand years later at the great white throne judgment, heaven's ranks were greatly increased, and the advances in the second millennium have expanded significantly. If we had spiritual eyes to see as God gave the prophet Elisha on one occasion, we would agree with him as he exhorted his servant Gehazi to see beyond the numbers of the enemy coming against them: "Those who are with us are more than those who are with them" (2 Kings 6:16).

The advance of the kingdom has accelerated dramatically in the last 500 years. During the 1,500 years prior to that, the New Testament witness was not translated into the language of the common people, so the masses knew very little about Scripture, the primary source through which we hear God's word. Since the invention of the printing press and the Reformation that awakened the Body of Christ to the authority of Scripture over church tradition, the Bible has been translated into most languages upon the earth. Churches are learning the apostolic wisdom in the New Testament on how to build the Body of Christ. Now the masses have access to Scripture through which they learn about God's word. With all the resources available to understand the Bible, coupled with the Internet that makes worldwide communication instantly possible, it remains to be seen what the advances will be in the next generation.

Peace will someday in the future emerge on the earth as a result of centuries of the reign of Jesus Christ over all things and finally our submission to His authority that opens the way for the kingdom of heaven to come to earth. He rules to this end while continuing to make people and relationships new as they learn to do things His way. As we journey to maturity, you and I are vital parts in what lies ahead according to the plan orchestrated by the reigning King who is right now heading up all things. He will accomplish His purpose through His Body on this earth, the church.

We began this chapter with the prophetic vision of peace among the peoples of the earth in Isaiah 2:2-5. He expands upon this vision in chapter 11 to even include the world of animals as man and beast live in harmony. What a vision God gave us through the prophet regarding what God will bring about on this earth.

> The wolf also shall dwell with the lamb, the leopard shall lie down with the young goat, the calf and the young lion and the fatling together; and a little child shall lead them. The cow and the bear shall graze; their young ones shall lie down together; and the lion shall eat straw like the ox. The nursing child shall play by the cobra's hole, and the weaned child shall put his hand in the viper's den. They shall not hurt nor destroy in all My holy mountain, for the earth shall be full of the knowledge of the Lord as the waters cover the sea. (Is. 11:6-9)

The reason for such peace is because "the earth shall be full of the knowledge of the Lord." What does that mean? What is this knowledge? I believe it was the knowledge of the Lord that Paul and Peter witness to in their writings after the seventh trumpet. Man has pursued the knowledge of truth for centuries. We know that such knowledge in and of itself does not bring peace. The two witnesses tell about a kind of knowledge that can bring peace when they talk about the knowledge of the Lord. A careful study of the word "knowledge" and its use by Paul is very informative. Paul can use *gnosis* in regard to knowing the Lord, or *epignosis* referring to a fuller and complete knowledge of the Lord. He uses the former in his writing before the seventh trumpet as in Philippians 3:8 where he talks about having *gnosis* of Christ. After the trumpet when Jesus has completed His life within the faithful, joined Himself to His bride, and raised her to heavenly places, Paul now uses the word *epignosis* as he writes Ephesians and Colossians indicating that he has come into a full or complete knowledge of Christ.

Paul prays for the Ephesians in 1:17 that God may give them "a spirit of wisdom and revelation in the knowledge (*epignosis*) of Him." In the verses that follow, Paul says that this revelation or appearing or *epiphaneia* and the full knowledge it brings of the Lord will help them to see more clearly and appropriate all that is theirs in Christ. This includes the hope of their calling, the riches of their inheritance of glory, and the greatness of His resurrection power in them. In Ephesians 4:13, Paul tells us that God uses the ministries to build the Body of Christ and prepare its members for "the knowledge (*epignosis*) of the Son of God." Paul writes similarly to the Colossians that they may increase "in the knowledge (*epignosis*) of God" (Col. 1:10) and attain "to all riches of the full assurance of understanding, to the knowledge (*epignosis*) of the mystery of God, both of the Father and of Christ" (Col. 2:2). Peter also does not use this word until after the seventh trumpet as we see in his second letter. Four times he now uses *epignosis* to refer to the knowledge of God and of Jesus, His Lord and Savior (2 Pet. 1:2; 1:3; 1:8; 2:20).

When the earth is finally filled with such people who have come into this full knowledge of their holy, righteous, and loving Lord as a result of appropriating the experiential dimension of the Second Coming, then we shall be able to have a world where its inhabitants can live together in peace. "They shall not hurt nor destroy in all My holy mountain, for the earth shall be full of the knowledge of the Lord as the waters cover the sea" (Is. 11:9). Such people who know the Lord do not hurt or destroy wherever they are but serve as healers and helpers. Evidently as more and more people make the journey up the mountain of the Lord and come into this full knowledge of their Lord while they still live on earth, the effects will even reach out beyond the human realm into the animal world. Who knows what effects this will also have on the natural world in which we live when God is able to bring heaven to this earth through the faithful followers of Jesus appropriating the discoveries made by the apostolic generation.

"What is there to look forward to if Jesus has returned?" I can still see the look of disappointment on the face of the young lady asking that question in a Bible study group about thirty years ago after I shared what I believed. I was not sure how to answer her then. I am now. We have everything to look forward to when we know Jesus has returned. We shall never pass through that 1,260-day period when terror reigned because the powers of darkness were given authority over all things on this earth. Because the trumpet has sounded, we know that our loved ones who have lived faithfully and died in the Lord have been resurrected and gone to heaven. We know that when we leave this earth, we shall join that rejoicing throng rather than a group of disembodied spirits still waiting for the trumpet. To live in a world where Jesus has returned means He reigns right now over all things and we need await no future intervention by God. He has done everything necessary to put this world together.

Now we must fully cooperate with the reigning King by submitting to His authority and obeying Him in all things. Because we are involved in spiritual warfare that is primarily a truth-battle, we must devote ourselves to learning from Scripture the truth about God's promises, His ways, and His power. We shall have to defeat our spiritual enemies to claim our Promised Land as Israel under the Old Covenant had to overcome physical enemies in claiming their Promised Land. Each of us has a vital part in God's overall plan to bring an end to the dark night of sin and its withering blight upon human lives and relationships. We messed things up, and God requires that we work with and in dependence upon Him to finally get it right. We are essential players in God's strategy to bring heaven to this earth. Yes, there is much to look forward to when we see the vision and challenge resulting from living in a world where Jesus has returned.

Let us close with some words from the last chapter in Revelation. "And the Spirit and the bride say, 'Come!'" (Rev. 22:17). Do not wait for prophetic signs pointing to the cosmic dimension of the Second Coming. Begin now to look with resolute perseverance to Jesus. The last book of the Bible reveals Him as the glorified Son of Man (Rev. 1:13), the One who holds the keys of Hades and Death (Rev. 1:18), the First and the Last (Rev. 2:8), the Son of God (Rev. 2:18), the Lion of the tribe of Judah (Rev. 5:5), the Lamb that was slain (Rev. 5:6), the Word of God (Rev. 19:13), the King of kings and Lord of lords (Rev. 19:16), the Alpha and the Omega, the Beginning and the End (Rev. 21:6), the Root and the Offspring of David, and the bright Morning Star (Rev. 22:16). The variety of Names given to Jesus witnesses to His limitless resources to meet all our needs. In addition, the Revelation identifies Him as our Divine Bridegroom waiting to be joined eternally with the bride for whom He died. What an exciting challenge awaits each believer to overcome and claim the high ground on the heavenly Mt. Zion, and serve and witness as opportunities arise about us on the lower ground of earth, working toward that day when heaven and earth shall become one.

> And I saw a new heaven and a new earth, for the first heaven and the first earth had passed away. And there was no more sea. Then I, John, saw the holy city, New Jerusalem, coming down out of heaven from God, prepared as a bride adorned for her husband. And I heard a loud voice from heaven saying, "Behold, the tabernacle of God is with men, and He will dwell with them, and they shall be His people, and God Himself will be with them and be their God. And God will wipe away every tear from their eyes; there shall be no more death, nor sorrow, nor crying; and there shall be no more pain, for the former things have passed away." Then He who sat on the throne said, "Behold, I make all things

new." And He said to me, "Write, for these words are true and faithful." And He said to me, "It is done! I am the Alpha and the Omega, the Beginning and the End. I will give of the fountain of the water of life freely to him who thirsts. He who overcomes shall inherit all things, and I will be his God and he shall be My son." (Rev. 21:1-7)

I want to add one closing note to women reading this. You who overcome are included in those sons, just as men who overcome are included as part of Christ's bride through whom the Lord shall bring heaven to this earth. Paul reminds us in Galatians 3:28-29 that when you belong to Christ, there is neither "male nor female." "And the Spirit and the bride say, 'Come!'" (Rev. 22:17). I say to all reading this, male or female, "Let's go!" "Yes!"

APPENDIX

FIGURING JULIAN DATES FROM JEWISH LUNAR CALENDAR

The Jewish people used a lunar calendar where each new month began with the new moon. *New and Full Moons, 1001 B.C. to A.D. 1651,* by Herman Heine Goldstine[77] enables us to convert Jewish dates provided by Josephus as well as the dates of significant Jewish feasts in particular years to their Julian equivalents. When the Jewish historian tells us that the continual burnt offering ended on *Tammuz* 17, A.D. 70, we can go to Goldstine's tables, identifying the new moon determining the first month of Nisan in the Jewish year. We then find in Goldstine's tables the fourth new moon corresponding to the fourth month of *Tammuz*. In this way, we eventually arrive at July 13, A.D. 70 as the Julian date matching *Tammuz* 17. We may be confident that this is within one day of the accurate date, as we shall see.

His tables enable us to more readily undertake the task of reconstructing the chronological framework of the second-coming events. We know that the Jewish people determined their months by observing the new moon, and Goldstine enables us to know when that occurred. His scientific computations determine the time of the new moons in the past thus helping us to calculate the beginning of the Jewish month and the dates when particular events happened.

In deciding upon the dates for the Jewish lunar calendar, we must first discover which new moon determined the month *Nisan*, the first month of the year. The Bible does not tell us how they determined this during the biblical era, but there is some extra-biblical testimony to help us. Eusebius says the following criterion was "known to the Jews anciently, and before Christ" and then mentions Aristobulus and a few others predating the Christian era who affirmed "that all ought to sacrifice the passover [*Nisan* 14] alike after the vernal equinox."[78] This means *Nisan* would be the first month whose full moon occurred after the vernal equinox around March 21. The church came to accept a similar criterion in determining Easter as the first Sunday, after the first full moon (the Passover moon or *Nisan* 14) after the vernal equinox.

How did the Jewish people determine what day would begin each lunar month? It takes the moon about 29½ days to complete its monthly journey about the earth, so the Jewish month had either 29 or 30 days. We do not know for sure what method the Jewish people used to determine the beginning of the lunar month prior to the fall of Jerusalem in A.D. 70. The *Universal Jewish Encyclopedia* tells us how this was done after A.D. 70. A council would meet on the thirtieth day and see if anybody observed the thin crescent of the new moon on the previous evening at sun-setting. If at least two persons reported such sighting, the thirtieth would become the first day of the new month. If no such sightings were reported, the day after the thirtieth would then become the first day of the new month.[79] It is difficult to conceive of any other method that could have been used during the biblical period with the means they had at hand.

This method placed the beginning of the Jewish month at least one day after the actual new moon. *The Jewish Encyclopedia* tells us that if the actual new moon occurred after noon on a particular day, it would not be visible yet that evening.[80] So it would be possible for the Jewish month to begin on the second day after the actual new moon. If the actual new moon occurred after noon on the twenty-ninth of a month, then no new moon would have been reported on the thirtieth day even though that was the day after the new moon. The new month would begin in this case on the second day after the actual new moon. By simply taking the day after the new moon as reported in Goldstine's tables, we may be confident that this date is probably accurate but at least within a day of both the actual new moon and what the people would have determined. Accuracy to within a day is well sufficient for our purposes in this book to relate Daniel's Seventieth Week to a specific period of time in history.

The key date in translating Daniel's time intervals to historical dates is the day when the continual burnt offering ended. Josephus says this took place on *Tammuz* 17, A.D. 70. *Nisan* was determined by the new moon occurring on March 30, A.D. 70. Its full moon would occur after the vernal equinox. The previous new moon occurred on March 1 with a full moon on March 15 disqualifying it for the month of *Nisan*. The fourth month of *Tammuz* would be determined by the new moon occurring on June 26 at 7:22 P.M.[81] *Tammuz* 1 would then correspond to June 27 and *Tammuz* 17 with July 13. It is interesting to observe that when we move back 1,290 days from July 13, A.D. 70, we come to January 1, A.D. 67. According to Daniel 12:11, this marks the beginning of the Period of the Authority of the Beast and fits with what took place in history. Nero directs Vespasian at this time to begin the campaign against the Jews that will end in A.D. 70 with the destruction of the temple and the city.

This single date of *Tammuz* 17 provided by Josephus regarding the ending of the continual burnt offering is the key to relating the time framework for Daniel's Seventieth Week to history. That framework is determined by the time intervals in the Book of Daniel. When we know the continual burnt offering ended July 13, A.D. 70, we can then assign Julian dates to the other parts of the time framework.

Table 2 presents the information regarding the new moons in A.D. 70 that led to the dating of the continual burnt offering. This table also includes the dates for other key events related to the Second Coming such as John's receiving the Revelation in A.D. 63, the seventh trumpet and mystery of God in A.D. 65, the *Parousia* and the Day of the Lord in A.D. 68, and finally the beginning of Armageddon in A.D. 69. The table will include the dates for the Feast of Trumpets, the Day of Atonement, and the Feast of Booths during these significant years for understanding second-coming chronology. The same criterion is used in determining the first of the Jewish month by taking the day after the actual day of the new moon as determined by Goldstine's tables.

Table 2 Relating Jewish Dates to Julian Equivalents

Jewish Dates from Lunar Calendar	New Moon at Jerusalem Determining the month*	Julian Equivalent to the Jewish Date
Nisan 1, A.D. 70	9:43 P.M. Mar. 30, A.D. 70	Mar. 31, A.D. 70
Tammuz 1, A.D. 70	7:22 P.M. June 26, A.D. 70	June 27, A.D. 70
Tammuz 17, A.D. 70		July 13, A.D. 70
Nisan 1, A.D. 63	10:44 P.M., Mar. 18, A.D. 63	Mar. 19, A.D. 63
Tishri 1, A.D. 63	4:38 A.M., Sept. 11, A.D. 63	Sept. 12, A.D. 63
Tishri 10, A.D. 63		Sept. 21, A.D. 63
Tishri 15, A.D. 63		Sept. 26, A.D. 63
Tishri 22, A.D. 63		Oct. 3, A.D. 63
Nisan 1, A.D. 65	5:40 P.M., Mar. 25, A.D. 65	Mar. 26, A.D. 65
Tishri 1, A.D. 65	10:03 P.M., Sept. 18, A.D. 65	Sept. 19, A.D. 65
Tishri 10, A.D. 65		Sept. 28, A.D. 65
Tishri 15, A.D. 65		Oct. 3, A.D. 65
Tishri 22, A.D. 65		Oct. 10, A.D. 65
Nisan 1, A.D. 68	4:18 A.M. Mar. 22, A.D. 68	Mar. 23, A.D. 68
Tishri 1, A.D. 68	9:19 A.M. Sept. 15, A.D. 68	Sept. 16, A.D. 65
Tishri 10, A.D. 68		Sept. 25, A.D. 65
Tishri 15, A.D. 68		Sept. 30, A.D. 65
Tishri 22, A.D. 68		Oct. 7, A.D. 65
Nisan 1, A.D. 69	8:41 P.M. Mar. 11, A.D. 69	Mar. 12, A.D. 69
Tishri 1, A.D. 69	9:21 A.M. Sept. 4, A.D. 69	Sept. 5, A.D. 69
Tishri 10, A.D. 69		Sept. 14, A.D. 69

*Subtract thirty-seven minutes from Goldstine's numbers to arrive at the time of the new moon at Jerusalem. Times taken from Goldstine's Tables on pages 89-90 are used by permission of the American Philosophical Society, Philadelphia, Pennsylvania.

Notes

Chapter 1: Rethinking the Time of the Second Coming

1. For a summary by William E. Biederwolf of the different interpretations of Matthew 16:27-28, see pp. 320-322 in *The Second Coming Bible* (Grand Rapids: Baker House, 1972). Reprinted from the original, *The Millenium Bible*.

Chapter 2: Seven Sure Signs That Jesus Has Returned

2. Robert H. Charles, *The Revelation of St. John*, The International Critical Commentary (New York: Charles Scribner's Sons, 1920), p. 367.
3. Flavius Josephus, *The Complete Works of Josephus*, trans. by William Whiston with Foreword by William. S. LaSor (1960; reprint, Grand Rapids: Kregel Publications, 1985), p. 574. *Wars*. 6.2.1.

Chapter 3: Tracking Paul's Ministry and God's Plan

4. H. Wayne House, *Chronological and Background Charts of the New Testament*, Foreword by Harold W. Hoehner (Grand Rapids: Academie Books-Zondervan Publishing House, 1981), pp. 28-32.

Chapter 4: Tracking Paul's Thoughts on the Second Coming

5. Eusebius, *Ecclesiastical History*, trans. from original with Introduction by Christian F. Cruse and An Historical View of the Council of Nice by Isaac Boyle (Grand Rapids: Baker Book House, 1990), p. 233.

Chapter 5: Perfecting in the New Testament.

6. John Wesley, *The Works of John Wesley*. 14 vols. (1872; reprint, Grand Rapids: Baker Book House, 1979), 11: 383-384.
7. Wesley, p. 396.

8. *Ibid.*
9. *Ibid.*

Chapter 6: The Real Enemy

10. Carl Friedrich Keil, *Book of Daniel*, Commentary on the Old Testament by C.F. Keil & F. Delitzsch, trans. M. G. Easton, 10 vols. reprint (Grand Rapids: William B. Eerdmans Publishing Company, 1988), 9: 245-262.
11. Suetonius, *The Twelve Caesars*, trans. Robert Graves (London: Penguin Books Ltd., 1957); revised with Introduction by Michael Grant (London: Allen Lane, 1979), p. 277.
12. Tacitus, *Complete Works of Tacitus,* trans. by Alfred John Church & William Jackson Brodribb, ed. by Moses Hadas, The Modern Library ed. (New York: Random House, 1942), p. 375. *Annals,* 15.36.
13. Tacitus, pp. 324-325. *Annals,* 14.8-9.
14. Tacitus, p. 398. *Annals,* 15.74.
15. Tacitus, p. 401. *Annals,* 16.6.
16. Tacitus, p. 376. *Annals,* 15.37.
17. Tacitus, p. 380. *Annals,* 15.44.
18. Tacitus, pp. 380-381. *Annals,* 15.44.

Chapter 7: The Chronology of Daniel's Seventieth Week

19. See the Appendix for the determination of this date.

Chapter 8: The Period of the Seven Trumpets

20. Tacitus, p. 379. *Annals,* 15.41.
21. Tacitus, pp. 380-381. *Annals,* 15.44.
22. Tacitus, pp. 404-405. *Annals,* 16.13.
23. Suetonius, p. 202.
24. Josephus, p. 582. *Wars,* 6.5.3.
25. Tacitus, p. 334. *Annals,* 14.24.
26. Tacitus, p. 338. *Annals,* 14.32.

Chapter 10: Daniel's Seventieth Week As It Happened

27. See the Appendix for converting lunar dates to our calendar.
28. Tacitus, p. 374. *Annals*, 15.33.
29. Tacitus, p. 375. *Annals*, 15.36.
30. Tacitus, pp. 376-379. *Annals*, 15.37-41.
31. Tacitus, p. 380. *Annals*, 15.44.
32. Tacitus, pp. 380-381. *Annals*, 15.44.
33. Tacitus, pp. 382-390. *Annals*, 15.48-59.
34. Tacitus, pp. 390-392. *Annals*, 15.60-64.
35. Josephus, p. 582. *Wars*, 6.5.3.
36. *Ibid.*
37. *Ibid.*, see footnote at bottom of p.582.
38. *Ibid.*
39. *Ibid.*
40. Eusebius, p. 105.
41. Josephus, p. 582. *Wars*, 6.5.3.
42. Josephus, p. 490. *Wars*, 2.17.2.
43. Josephus, pp. 490-492. *Wars*, 2.17.3-9.
44. Josephus, p. 492. *Wars*, 2.17.10.
45. Josephus, p. 492. *Wars*, 2.18.1.
46. Josephus, p. 495. *Wars*, 2.19.1.
47. Josephus, pp. 496-497. *Wars*, 2.19.2-9.
48. Josephus, p. 497. *Wars*, 2.20.1.
49. Eusebius, p. 86.
50. Jerome, *Lives of Illustrious Men*, A Select Library of Nicene & Post-Nicene Fathers of the Christian Church, 2d Ser., ed. by Philip Schaff & Henry Wace. 14 vols. (Grand Rapids: Wm. B. Eerdmans Publishing Co., 1961), 3: 365.
51. Josephus, p. 502. *Wars*, 3.1.1-3.
52. Josephus, p. 507. *Wars*, 3.7.1.
53. Josephus, pp. 507-514. *Wars*, 3.7.3-36.
54. Josephus, pp. 518-521. *Wars*, 3.10.1-10.
55. Josephus, pp. 522-525. *Wars*, 4.1.1-10.

56. Josephus, pp. 527-528. *Wars*, 4.3.8.
57. Josephus, p. 527. *Wars*, 4.3.7.
58. Josephus, p. 528. *Wars*, 4.3.8.
59. Josephus, p. 528. *Wars*, 4.3.10.
60. Josephus, p. 529. *Wars*, 4.3.10.
61. Josephus, p. 531. *Wars*, 4.4.3.
62. Josephus, p. 534. *Wars*, 4.5.1.
63. Josephus, p. 534. *Wars*, 4.5.2.
64. Josephus, p. 536. *Wars*, 4.6.3.
65. Josephus, p. 540. *Wars*, 4.9.2.
66. Tacitus, p. 420. *History*, 1.2.
67. Tacitus, pp. 420-421. *History*, 1.3.
68. Josephus, p. 546. *Wars*, 4.11.5.
69. Josephus, p. 581. *Wars*, 6.5.1.
70. Einar Johnson, *The Great German Pilgrimage of 1064-65*, The Crusades and Other Historical Essays, ed. Louis J. Paetow (New York: F. S. Crofts & Co., 1928), p. 12.
71. Johnson, pp. 20-42.
72. Johnson, p. 43.
73. Johnson, p. 44.

Chapter 12: Discovering God's Eternal Jubilee

74. *Yobel* and *shophar*, two words for trumpet in the Old Testament, appear to be used interchangeably. This is the case in each of the three ways that *yobel* is used in the Old Testament. It first appears in Exodus 19:13 as the trumpet that announces the coming of the Lord to meet Moses and the people at Mount Sinai. *Shophar* is also used in Exodus 19:16,19 in regard to the same trumpet. *Yobel* is used repeatedly in Leviticus 25, and *shophar* is likewise referred to twice in Leviticus 25: 9. Then both words are used to refer to the trumpets employed by Joshua at the battle of Jericho.

75. *A Concordance to the Septuagint*, Edwin Hatch & Henry A. Redpath, 3 vols. (1897; reprint, Grand Rapids: Baker Book House, 1983). See 1:182 for *aphesis* and 2:1263 for *semasia*.

Chapter 15: Grace and Accountability

76. James Dobson, *Straight Talk to Men* (Nashville: Word Publishing, 1995), pp. 235-36. Used by permission of Dr. James Dobson.

Appendix: Figuring Julian Dates from Jewish Lunar Calendar

77. Heine Goldstine, *New and Full Moons, 1001 B.C. to A.D. 1651* (Philadelphia: American Philosophical Society, 1973), pp. 89-90.

78. Eusebius, p. 313.

79. Simon Cohen, *Calendar*, The Universal Jewish Encyclopedia, ed. Isaac Landman. 10 vols. (New York: The Universal Jewish Encyclopedia Inc., 1940), 2.632.

80. Michael Friedlander, *Calendar*, The Jewish Encyclopedia, prepared under the direction of Cyrus Adler [and others], ed. Isidore Singer. 12 vols. (New York: Funk & Wagnalls Company, 1903), 3:503.

81. Goldstine's tables are computed with respect to ancient Babylon, equivalent to present-day Baghdad. To determine the correct time for the new moon at Jerusalem, we subtract 37 minutes. The longitude at Baghdad is 44° 30' minutes and at Jerusalem 35° 15'. The difference is 9° 15'. Since each degree of longitude is equivalent to four minutes of time, 37 minutes is the necessary adjustment.

Bibliography

Biederwolf, William E. *The Second Coming Bible.* Grand Rapids: Baker House, 1972. Reprinted from the original *The Millenium Bible.*

Charles, Robert H. *The Revelation of St. John.* The International Critical Commentary. New York: Charles Scribner's Sons, 1920.

Cohen, Simon. *Calendar.* The Universal Jewish Encyclopedia. Edited by Isaac Landman. 10 vols. New York: The Universal Jewish Encyclopedia Inc., 1940. 2:632.

Dobson, James. *Straight Talk to Men.* Nashville: Word Publishing, 1995.

Eusebius. *Ecclesiastical History.* Translated from original with Introduction by Christian F. Cruse and An Historical View of the Council of Nice by Isaac Boyle. Grand Rapids: Baker Book House, 1990.

Friedlander, Michael. *Calendar.* The Jewish Encyclopedia. Prepared under the direction of Cyrus Adler [and others], Edited by Isidore Singer. 12 vols. New York: Funk & Wagnalls Company, 1903. 3:503.

Goldstine, Herman Heine. *New and Full Moons, 1001 B.C. to A.D. 1651.* Philadelphia: American Philosophical Society, 1973.

Hatch, Edwin & Redpath, Henry A. *A Concordance to the Septuagint.* 3 vols. 1897. Reprint, Grand Rapids: Baker Book House, 1983. 1:182, 2:1263.

House, H. Wayne. *Chronological and Background Charts of the New Testament*. Foreward by Harold W. Hoehner. Grand Rapids: Academie Books-Zondervan Publishing House, 1981.

Jerome. *Lives of Illustrious Men*. A Select Library of Nicene & Post-Nicene Fathers of the Christian Church. 2d Ser. Edited by Philip Schaff & Henry Wace. 14 vols. Grand Rapids: Wm. B. Eerdmans Publishing Co., 1961. 3:365.

Johnson, Einar. *The Great German Pilgrimmage of 1064-65*. The Crusades and Other Historical E*ssays*. Edited by Louis J. Paetow. New York: F.S. Crofts & Co., 1928.

Josephus, Flavius. *The Complete Works of Josephus*. Translated by William Whiston with Foreword by Wm. S. LaSor. 1960. Reprint, Grand Rapids: Kregel Publications, 1985.

Keil, Carl Friedrich. *Book of Daniel*. Commentary on the Old Testament by C.F. Keil & F. Delitzsch. Translated by M. G. Easton. 10 vols. Reprint, Grand Rapids: William B. Eerdmans Publishing Company, 1988. 9:245-262.

Suetonius, *The Twelve Caesars*. Translated by Robert Graves. London: Penguin Books Ltd., 1957. Revised with Introduction by Michael Grant. London: Allen Lane, 1979.

Tacitus. *Complete Works of Tacitus*. Translated by Alfred John Church and William Jackson Brodribb. Edited by Moses Hadas. The Modern Library ed. New York: Random House, 1942.

Wesley, John. *The Works of John Wesley*. 14 vols. 1872. Reprint, Grand Rapids: Baker Book House, 1979. 11:383-384,396.

About the Author

The author was raised in the home of a minister's family in Ohio in the former Evangelical Church that became the Evangelical United Brethren Church. Upon graduation from high school, he pursued a career in mathematics at Ohio State University with a B.S. in 1957 and M.S. in 1959. Following a call to enter the ministry, he attended United Seminary in Dayton, Ohio where he graduated with a M.Div. in 1962 and was ordained the same year in the Evangelical United Brethren Church. He served as a minister in that denomination until 1968 and then in the United Methodist Church after that as the result of a merger. Sometime after retirement, he and his wife moved to Lincoln, Nebraska. It was during his first pastorate that he was led to those verses in the New Testament indicating the Second Coming happened during the apostolic generation. This book represents the culmination of the research and spiritual journey through the years since then.

0-595-24829-2